145

THE LANGUAGE OF LITERAT
General Editor: N. F. Blake
Professor of English Language and
University of Sheffield

THE LANGUAGE OF LITERATURE
General Editor: N. F. Blake

Further titles are in preparation.

The Language of Jane Austen

A Study of Some Aspects of her Vocabulary

MYRA STOKES

MACMILLAN

First published 1991

Published by
MACMILLAN EDUCATION LTD
Houndmills, Basingstoke, Hampshire RG21 2XS
and London
Companies and representatives
throughout the world

Typeset by Footnote Graphics,
Warminster, Wiltshire

Printed in Hong Kong

British Library Cataloguing in Publication Data
Stokes, Myra
The language of Jane Austen: a study of some aspects of
her vocabulary — (The language of literature)
1. Fiction in English. Austen, Jane, 1775–1817
I. Title   II. Series
823.7
ISBN 0–333–48304–9
ISBN 0–333–48305–7 pbk

Contents

Abbreviations

1 The Social Context: Time, Place and Manner

TIME

Literature of the past requires some re-orientation from the reader, for the meaning attributed to words changes, radically or subtly, from period to period. Semantic re-orientation of the least figurative kind – in time and place – may in fact be necessary, for even here the co-ordinates may have shifted. Consider the following, for instance:

> There could hardly be an happier creature in the world, than Mrs. John Knightley, in this short visit to Hartfield, going about every morning among her old acquaintance with her five children, and talking over what she had done every evening with her father and sister . . . In general their evenings were less engaged with friends than their mornings. (*E* 108)

> "While I can have my mornings to myself," said she, "it is enough. – I think it no sacrifice to join occasionally in evening engagements." (*PP* 87)[1]

> I pass my mornings at the Armenian convent studying Armenian. My evenings here & there. (*BLJ* 5.146)

Those who have read such statements, and who have noticed the illustrations for 'morning dress' and 'evening dress' in Dr Chapman's edition of the novels, may well have wondered what happened to the *afternoons* at this period, and whether people spent them in bed, since they appear to have engaged in no activities during them, or even to have had any clothes to wear for them. In fact, as Chapman points out (in a useful appendix, entitled 'The Manners of the Age', to his edition of *Emma* 499–516), the word *morning* was used to refer to the whole of that period of the day before *dinner* (which occurred any time after about 4 p.m.), and the *evening* to what remained of it thereafter. *Luncheon*, though it was often eaten, was a cold meal, as with "the nicest cold luncheon in the world" at the George Inn Lydia claims to have "treated" Jane and Elizabeth to (*PP* 222; in fact, her elder sisters had paid: 220)[2]; and as with the 'cold meat, cake', etc, Elizabeth enjoys at Pemberley (268) when she makes a *morning* visit (it is actually after noon: 266) to Darcy and his sister[3]. It was therefore a moveable and informal feast, not felt to constitute such a fixed and major meal as to create a division in the mind as to time before it and time after it – as *dinner* did.

That it was dinner that marked the termination of the morning is evident in such remarks as the following, which occurs in one of the letters from Jane Austen to her sister Cassandra:

> We breakfasted before 9 & do not dine till ½ past 6 on the occasion, so I hope we three shall have a long Morning enough. (*JAL* 359)

When the *morning* is mentioned, then, it must be remembered that it refers to the whole of this period of the day. This will explain why, in *Emma*, the outing to Donwell Abbey is called "a morning scheme" (355), and why the one to Box Hill seems to Emma 'a morning . . . completely misspent' (377), when it is quite clear that both extend well into the afternoon. The point is that they are daytime as opposed to evening schemes; the former is arranged precisely to accommodate Mr Woodhouse's distaste for "dinner-visiting" and "late hours" (209). Apparent contradictions – such as Anne's promise to the Musgroves 'to be with them the whole of the following morning' and the statement shortly afterwards that 'She had promised to be with the Musgroves from breakfast to dinner' (*P* 227, 229) – will also be resolved by a proper understanding of what is meant by the *morning*.

In fact the social activities referred to as 'morning engagements' or 'morning visits' rarely took place before noon. The 'morning's engagements' in London that occupy Elinor, Marianne and Mrs Jennings in *Sense and Sensibility* (230) apparently take place in what we call the afternoon, for Marianne writes to Willoughby that "we are generally out by one" (187). Twelve noon is referred ✗ to in *Emma* as about the earliest at which one might expect a *morning* visitor (190). Only persons so specially circumstanced as a grandmother going to visit her daughter and new grandchild, as Mrs Jennings regularly does 'as soon as she was dressed' (*SS* 246), or a fiancé such as Bingley calling on his new fiancée, would feel themselves free to arrive at an hour in which it was otherwise still 'too early in the morning for visitors' (*PP* 351); though a high-handed Lady ✗ Catherine de Bourgh with a piece of her mind to give will autocratically and unapologetically disregard such niceties (*ibid*).

On the rare occasions on which it was felt necessary to distinguish between the a.m. and p.m. parts of the *morning*, the word used for what *we* call the 'morning' was *forenoon*. Two lengthy journeys in *Sense and Sensibility* have recorded or projected arrival times 'in the forenoon of the third' day and 'the following forenoon' (302, 308). *Afternoon*, however, was used less logically, and with more reference to *dinner* than to the position of the sun overhead. In order to determine what period of the day is generally indicated by the word, therefore, it is first necessary to ascertain some facts about *dinner* hours and about the ceremonies that followed *dinner*.

Dinner was preceded by a half-hour devoted to dressing for it:

> The silvery bell rung, not for 'dinner ready',
> But for that hour, called 'half-hour', given to dress,
> Though ladies' robes seem scant enough for less.
> (*DJ* XV.61)

Catherine Morland can thus feel sure at 4 p.m., when she undertakes her exploration of the room in which Mrs Tilney had died, that her absence will not be remarked, for 'it would be only her retiring to dress half an hour earlier than usual' (*NA* 193). The Tilney household dines *very* punctually at 5 p.m. (183).

Dinner hours varied considerably. London hours were later than those in the provinces. The letter from Jane Austen herself quoted above indicates that 6.30 was rather after the usual dining hour at Godmersham Park, Kent, the house of her brother Edward, with whom she was staying at the time of writing – which would put the usual hour not much out of line with that of Northanger Abbey. But even out of London dinner hours differed widely. The elderly or infirm would dine earlier; and the rich and fashionable considerably later. Mr Woodhouse, predictably, keeps earlier hours than General Tilney: Harriet and Emma separate 'in preparation for the regular four o'clock dinner' (*E* 81). Another valetudinarian, Mr Watson of *The Watsons*, also dines early. Visitors arrive just as the maid 'at five minutes before three, was beginning to bustle into the parlour with the Tray & the Knife-case'; she interrupts the conversation shortly afterwards to say, "Please Ma'am, Master wants to know why he be'nt to have his dinner" (*MW* 344, 346). Elizabeth Watson explains apologetically about the "early hours" of the household to her visitors, who are the wealthy Lord Osborne and his fashionable friend, Tom Musgrave, who 'had hitherto disregarded every symptom, however positive, of the nearness of that Meal' (346), as if defying their humbler hosts to admit to such an unfashionably early dinner. Their own hours are considerably later. Mr Edwardes, when his wife reproaches him for the late hours kept by his whist club, retorts: "We are always at home before Midnight. They would laugh at Osborne Castle to hear you call *that* late; they are but just rising from dinner at midnight" (325). That, of course, is an exaggeration, but it is a measure of the later hours associated with the rich and fashionable. Nor is the incident referred to above the only occasion on which the social distance between Tom Musgrove's Osborne circle and the much humbler Watson home is measured by the discrepancy in their dining hours. The point is made even more forcibly when Tom, returning from London, visits them specifically to boast to them 'that he was going home to an 8 o'clock dinner' (355). He stays an hour, after which he is forced to leave, as he would have otherwise to join the family in their nine o'clock *supper*, 'which to a Man whose heart had been long fixed on calling his next meal a Dinner, was quite insupportable' (359); and the point about the later hours of his own circle is further emphasized when he accepts only provisionally the dinner invitation offered him for the next day: "With the greatest pleasure . . .. That is, if I can possibly get here in time – but I shoot with Ld Osborne, & therefore must not engage – You will not think of me unless you see me" (360).

After dinner (from which the ladies retired before the gentlemen), there followed, after an interval, *tea* (coffee might also be available: *PP* 37; *MP* 104). There ensued cards, music, etc, if one had visitors. It is within the context of such normal and general social patterns that the particular situations within the novels develop, as with the following brief description of an evening at the Bennet household toward the end of *Pride and Prejudice*:

> Bingley of course returned with [Mr. Bennet] to dinner; and in the evening Mrs. Bennet's invention was again at work to get every body away from him and her daughter. Elizabeth, who had a letter to write, went into the breakfast room for that purpose soon after tea; for as the others were all going to sit down to cards, she could not be wanted to counteract her mother's schemes. (346)

When such things as *tea* visits, invitations to *tea*, taking *tea* with someone, etc, are mentioned, the reference is to this *after* dinner ceremony, not to the light afternoon refreshment taken *before* the evening meal which the word now indicates. For instance, in the following account of Mrs Goddard, the headmistress of the High-bury boarding-school in *Emma*, the *tea-visits* and card games she allows herself at times are in effect occasional 'evenings out':

> She was a plain, motherly kind of woman, who had worked hard in her youth, and now thought herself entitled to the occasional holiday of a tea-visit; and having formerly owed much to Mr. Woodhouse's kindness, felt his particular claim on her to leave her neat parlour hung round with fancy work whenever she could, and win or lose a few sixpences by his fireside. (22)

Dinner and *tea* were distinct social occasions, and might be passed in different company (cf. *SCG* IV.302). *Tea* thus formed a usefully separate social slot from *dinner* for 'second class' invitations. That is, persons not invited to dinner might be invited to the evening tea after it – much as we today might invite someone to 'come round for a drink' as a second-best to inviting them to a meal. So *dinner* and *tea* can on occasion serve to stratify the guests invited. The dinner party given by the Coles in *Emma*, a highly socially conscious novel, may serve as an illustration. The Coles give it to signal their intention of moving into the social 'first division' of Highbury – and Emma is at first determined to snub the attempt (207). To this dinner they invite all the 'great houses' of the neighbourhood (*ibid*): Donwell Abbey (Mr Knightley), Randalls (the Westons) and Hartfield (the Woodhouses). The only other guests at the *dinner* are 'a proper unobjectionable country family' and 'the male part of Mr. Cox's family, the lawyer of Highbury' (214). Harriet, Emma knows, is to be there 'in the evening', as well as Jane Fairfax and Miss Bates (208; cf. 214): that is, for *tea*. They arrive, in fact, *after* the dinner, to join in the post-dinner ceremonies of *tea* and music (219, 227). These persons of much humbler status are thus not excluded, but are included in such a way as to preserve distinctions of rank; so the Coles have been careful not to offend Emma by committing what we are told she had perceived as an incipient fault in Frank Churchill: an 'indifference to a confusion of rank, [which] bordered too much on inelegance of mind' (198).

A more rudely pointed relegation from the first division of *dinner* to the second division of *tea* occurs in *Pride and Prejudice*, in the intercourse between Rosings and Hunsford Parsonage. The Collinses and Lucases and Elizabeth at first receive invitations to dine at Rosings about twice a week (169). But after her nephews arrive, Lady Catherine brings her graciousness down a notch, and invites them to come over only 'in the evening' (172: that is, for tea, not dinner – the dinner is over when they arrive), and again later "to drink tea" (187). The rather pointed alteration is part of a general change in behaviour which makes it offensively plain 'that their company was by no means so acceptable as when she could get nobody else' (172).

The close of the evening was heralded by *supper*, the last meal of the day. Balls included a sit-down supper, as do those at Netherfield and the Crown (*PP* 98; *E* 254, 328); and kind, punctilious Mr Woodhouse, though himself convinced of 'suppers being very unwholesome', provides one for his evening guests (*E* 24).

Afternoon refers to the period immediately following dinner, and is terminated by the close of *tea*, with which it is often associated. Since people are often referred to as taking exercise or shortish walks during it, it in effect constitutes what is left of daylight after dinner is over. In *Pride and Prejudice*, for instance, on the return of Jane and Elizabeth from London to Longbourn, after the girls have had both *luncheon* and *dinner* (222), the close of the latter leads into the statement that,

In the *afternoon* Lydia was urgent with the rest of the girls to *walk* to Meryton and see how every body went on; but Elizabeth steadily opposed the scheme.   (223: my italics)

Another *dinner* later on is immediately succeeded by the comment that, after it, 'In the afternoon, the two elder Miss Bennets were able to be for half an hour by themselves' (289). When Mr Bennet returns from London, he is as uncommunicative as ever, and his daughters do not like to question him on 'the business that had taken him away':

It was not till the *afternoon*, when he joined them at *tea*, that Elizabeth ventured to introduce the subject.   (299: my italics)

When Henry Crawford arrives for *dinner* at Mansfield Park, the note he brings from his sister to Fanny urges the latter to "smile upon him with your sweetest smiles this afternoon" (303). Later, at Portsmouth, Fanny's father 'came back in the afternoon with the daily newspaper as usual'; this he reads 'while the tea was in preparation' (438–9). When Mr Woodhouse voices his regret that the Coles have gone in for giving *dinners* (for he is not fond of "dinner-visiting"), he adds:

"I think it would be much better if they would come in one *afternoon* next summer, and take their *tea* with us – take us in their *afternoon walk*."   (*E* 209: my italics)

In *The Watsons*, when Emma dines at the Edwardes household prior to accompanying them to a ball for which they set out at 8 p.m., the report of the conversation at dinner is followed by the comment that, 'With nothing to do but to expect the hour of setting off, the afternoon was long to the two young Ladies . . .. The entrance of the Tea things at 7 o'clock was some relief' (*MW* 326). *Northanger Abbey* refers to 'the whole time between morning and afternoon service' on a Sunday (190) – the latter being what we call 'evening service' (cf. *SCG* VI.84), and indicating a time of day for *afternoon* quite consistent with that suggested by the other passages quoted: that is, late afternoon, early evening.

The term is similarly used elsewhere in eighteenth and nineteenth-century writing to refer to the period between dinner and the close of tea.[4]

Jane Austen's most memorably atmospheric use of the *after-noon* occurs in *Emma*. On the day on which she and Mr Knightley finally come to make clear their feelings for each other, the contrast between her gloom before the event (caused by her conviction that he will marry Harriet) and her relief after it has its prelude in an equivalent transition in the weather:

> The weather continued much the same all the following morning . . . but in the afternoon it cleared; the wind changed into a softer quarter; the clouds were carried off; the sun appeared; it was summer again. With all the eagerness which such a transition gives, Emma resolved to be out of doors as soon as possible. Never had the exquisite sight, smell, sensation of nature, tranquil, warm, and brilliant after a storm, been more attractive to her. She longed for the serenity they might gradually introduce; and on Mr. Perry's coming in soon after dinner, with a disengaged hour to give her father, she lost no time in hurrying into the shrubbery. (424)

It is here that Mr Knightley joins her, to effect a metaphorical clearing of the air equally grateful and liberating to her feelings. Once we realize that *morning* means all of the day before the 4 p.m. dinner, and *afternoon* the period after dinner (which cannot be over much before 5 p.m.), the scene-setting gains an extra aptness and expressiveness. It is a whole *day* of real and figurative gloom that a beautiful early evening and Mr Knightley arrive together to dispel. The glow and fragrance mentioned are that produced by the late afternoon sun. Nor would it be appropriate to think of the weather clearing after the lunch hour (as would be suggested by 'in the afternoon' today), but Emma chaffing to get out into it until gone 5 p.m. For the point is that all her problems are solved with magically opportune immediacy. A beautiful evening comes from nowhere out of a foul day; no sooner has the weather cleared than Mr Perry most opportunely appears to release her to the shrubbery; there, most opportunely alone, she is at once joined by Mr Knightley, and in 'one half hour' (432) all is as right as the rain was not.

Whereas *afternoon* for us begins after lunch, then, for Jane Austen it begins after dinner. *Dinner* and *noon* had not always been so out of synch, for the latter had once been the conventional hour of the former.[5] Fielding shows himself conscious of the illogical slippage the terms *morning* and *afternoon* had undergone as a consequence of later dining hours: '. . . and then they parted to dress, it being now past three in the morning, or, to reckon by the old style, in the afternoon' (*Tom Jones*, 674). Our own *lunch* occurs nearer noon than did Jane Austen's *dinner*, but even our use of the term *afternoon* to some degree subordinates the clock to our food. If we say we will do something 'first thing this afternoon', we are more likely to mean 'immediately after lunch' than 12.01 p.m. Jane Austen's usage is but a more marked symptom of the influence of meals on people's conception of the divisions of the day.

PLACE

With regard to place, as well as time, there are words which have altered in meaning and usage. We today use the term *country* either of a nation state, or – in opposition to *town* – of a rural area rather than an urban one. Jane Austen does not often use the word in either of these ways. When it is used alone, and not in explicit or implicit contrast with *town*, it has, not its modern sense of 'kingdom', but its older one of **district, neighbourhood**. For instance, Jane Austen comments shrewdly on the fact that Maria and Julia Bertram suffered no jealousy of the pretty Mary Crawford that this was a piece of magnanimity that cost them nothing, as they were themselves too good-looking to feel threatened by her beauty, which was in any case of a type very different from theirs:

> Had she been tall, full formed, and fair, it might have been more of a trial; but as it was, there could be no comparison, and she was most allowably a sweet pretty girl, while they were the finest young women in the country.   (*MP* 44)

In this context, the modern implications of *country* would probably not much overstate the self-satisfaction of the Misses Bertram, but the term here in fact means 'district' – the 'local area' which forms the chief spatial context and consciousness of all her *personae*.

When *town* is opposed to *country*, the reference is not to urban versus rural environment, but to **London** versus the **provinces**. When Jane Bennet of *Pride and Prejudice* is ill, the sophisticated and fashionable Bingley sisters, 'convinced that no country advice could be of any service, recommended an express to town for one of the most eminent physicians' (40), showing a faith in London prices and a scorn for provincial competence typical of their pampered arrogance. Lady Catherine, on hearing from Elizabeth that none of her sisters draws, similarly declares, "Your mother should have taken you to town every spring for the benefit of masters"; to which Elizabeth, who has a nice line in needling remarks that are not outright rude, replies, "My mother would have had no objection, but my father hates London" (164) – thus implying that there are tastes fashionable London is beneath rather than beyond. In *Sense and Sensibility*, Mrs Dashwood opposes Elinor's suggestion that Marianne should return from London to Barton Cottage, in Devonshire, on the grounds that London is more likely to distract Marianne from her disappointment over Willoughby, and that, since 'his acquaintance must now be dropped by all who called themselves her friends', she would be 'equally safe in town as in the country' from any painful chance meeting with him (213). The environs of Barton Cottage *are* in fact pretty rural, but by *country* Mrs Dashwood means Devonshire as opposed to the metropolis.

The term *country* in this sense gains a certain evaluative charge at the end of *Mansfield Park*, a novel in which there is a tendency to associate the virtues of Fanny, Edmund and Sir Thomas with a *country* honesty, and the vices of Henry and Mary Crawford with their sophisticated London background. Both the latter undergo some degree of rehabilitation under the influence of Mansfield Park and two of its denizens, but relapse into rather worse than their old ways on returning to London, which is also, of course, the scene of the disgrace of Maria and the elopement of Julia. It is not surprising that 'Fanny was disposed to think the influence of London very much at war with all respectable attachments' (433), since the novel has organized things so as to make such an impression inescapable. When at the end we read of Fanny and Edmund that, 'Equally formed for domestic life, and attached to country pleasures, their home was the home of affection and comfort' (473), *country pleasures* does not refer to any ambition on the part of the principals to be budding little homesteaders, but to tastes that do not expose them to the lure of the bright lights of sinful London, with its more hectic social life and the ambition, vanity and worldliness of its ways. It is a novel in which the barricading of *country* against *town* in fact reaches such a pitch of xenophobia as to sanction a virtually incestuous marriage.

Sense of place, then, was more London-oriented than it is now. One was either in it, in *town*, or out of it, in the *country*. Life was divided between the two in a very literal way for many people, for the aspired-to norm of the fashionable was the possession of both a *town* house (in London) and a *country* house to which one could retreat when the London 'season' was over – that is, in summer, when London was felt to be too hot and dusty to be inhabited comfortably[6]. None of Jane Austen's heroines, interestingly, participates in this fashionable custom of dual residence in *town* and *country*. The Dashwoods (who, thanks to the meanness of John Dashwood, have scarcely enough to keep up one decent home in the *country*), the Bennets, the Morlands and the Elliots have not, evidently, the means to maintain a *town* and a *country* house. The Woodhouses probably have the means, but it is obvious that Mr Woodhouse's nerves – for which even the pace of things in the *country* is sometimes over-hectic – could not withstand London. It is presumably a combination of the rather puritanical ways of Sir Thomas and the very indolent ones of his spouse which prevents annual transmigration to London in the case of the Bertrams. The custom is nevertheless often mentioned, and can serve as an important marker of social and economic divisions within the novels. In *Sense and Sensibility* it emphasizes how the means of Mrs Dashwood and her daughters – due in large part to John Dashwood's very narrow interpretation of his promise to his dying father to provide for them – have been reduced below that of those who in other ways are their social peers. Mrs Jennings – socially rather inferior to them in status – 'resided every winter in a house in one of the streets near Portman-square' (153). The Middletons and Palmers have *town* houses where they spend the winter (cf. *SCG* II.311). Both Charlotte Palmer and Lucy Steele assume that the Dashwood girls will be in London at that season – assumptions Elinor is forced to correct (110, 150). Lucy's further assumption – when Elinor tells her they will *not* "be in town this winter" – that "your brother and sister will ask you to come to them" (151) is equally telling: for John Dashwood has, of course, no intention of putting himself even to that expense on their behalf. Elinor and Marianne *do*, in the event, winter in London – as the guests of Mrs Jennings, however, not of their brother, a situation which at one point justly causes him some embarrassment (248). For John and Fanny themselves, of course, spend the winter there; and John even has the nerve, when he meets Elinor, to complain of the "great expense" he is put to in London; to which Elinor pointedly replies, "Your expenses both in town and country must certainly be considerable, but your income is a large one" (225).

The Bennets in *Pride and Prejudice* are not amongst those wealthy enough to rent a house for the London season or to keep one of their own there (it is as guests of the Gardiners that Jane and Elizabeth spend their time in London), although others in the neighbourhood are. After the departure of Lydia and Wickham, the gloom of the household gradually lifts, partly because 'The families who had been in town for the winter came back again, and summer finery and summer engagements arose' (238). It may be that Mr Bennet's tastes are also a factor here (he "hates London": 164). Darcy and the Bingley sisters have little trouble in keeping Charles Bingley in *town* for the winter, where many of their acquaintance are at that season (117). Sir William Lucas takes it for granted that the wealthy Darcy has a *town* house as well as his inherited estate in the *country* (Pemberley, in Derbyshire); Darcy himself takes it so much for granted that he treats the question as not worth making even a minor conversation point out of – at which Sir William tries, somewhat pathetically, to imply that he, too, *could* be as casual about the expensiveness of the place if he chose:

"You have a house in town, I conclude?"
Mr. Darcy bowed.
"I had once some thoughts of fixing in town myself – for I am fond of superior society; but I did not feel quite certain that the air of London would agree with Lady Lucas."   (26)

Darcy's residence in *town* for the London season is also alluded to indirectly in his letter of explanation to Elizabeth, when he states that all communication between himself and Wickham ceased after his payment of £3,000 to the latter:

"I thought too ill of him, to invite him to Pemberley, or admit his society in town. In town I believe he chiefly lived, but his studying the law was a mere pretence, and being now free from all restraint, his was a life of idleness and dissipation."   (201)

The passage furthers, in different ways, the characterization of both Wickham and Darcy. Wickham prefers London, because he is a profligate young man who likes to 'live it up'. At the same time, the reader is reminded that Darcy, as a member of the wealthy *haut ton*, instinctively thinks of two places of residence of his own – Pemberley and *town*, where he habitually spends the winter.

This house in town is one of the first things to come to Mrs Bennet's tongue as articulation returns to her after the comically (and very unusually) speechless state to which she is reduced by Elizabeth's announcement of her engagement to Darcy:

"Oh, my dear Lizzy! pray apologise for my having disliked him so much before. I hope he will overlook it. Dear, dear Lizzy. A house in town! Every thing that is charming."   (378)

It will be apparent that *town* thus refers, not to the nearest town, as it might well today, but to London. If you meant a different town, you would have to name it. For instance, in *Sense and Sensibility*, when Colonel Brandon departs hurriedly and suddenly from Barton Park on receipt of a letter he claims requires his "immediate attendance in town", it is London that is meant; hence Mrs Jennings's surprise – for it is summer, and London life virtually ceased in summer:

"In town!" cried Mrs Jennings. "What can you have to do in town at this time of year?"   (64)

The same device of a summer trip to London to suggest extremely urgent business is used even more pointedly and wittily in *Pride and Prejudice*. After Lydia and Wickham have returned to Longbourn, there occurs an exchange between the latter and Elizabeth, who delivers herself of some beautifully controlled ironies, including the following:

> (Wickham) "I was surprised to see Darcy in town last month. We passed each other several times. I wonder what he can be doing there."
> "Perhaps preparing for his marriage with Miss de Bourgh," said Elizabeth. "It must be something particular, to take him there at this time of year."   (328)

When Julia Bertram, having accompanied her sister on her honeymoon to Brighton, writes home for permission 'to go to town with Maria' (*MP* 284), the reference is again, of course, to London – for she is 'as eager for novelty and pleasure' (204) as her sister. The sentence unobtrusively prepares for the off-stage London scenes and Julia's part in them – and the different kinds of disgracefulness which occur in connection with the Crawford and Bertram siblings in what the novel presents as that sophisticated and fashionable den of iniquity.

For, in these novels, unpleasant and often scandalous developments occur in London, though only *Sense and Sensibility* has substantial and significant scenes actually staged there (in *Pride and Prejudice* and *Mansfield Park* the drama is relayed largely through letters). But even when the action is elsewhere, London toings and froings and the influence of the place upon social and commercial life and the conduct of practical affairs are evident. Fanny can reminisce on the evenings at Mansfield before Sir Thomas went away, when Edmund remarks on a prevailing want of "animation" after his return from Antigua: "I cannot recollect that our evenings formerly were ever merry, except when my uncle was in town" (197) – visits to London on business by the worthy Sir Thomas – whose presence is, sadly, always felt as oppressive by the younger generation – obviously provided the odd liberating oasis even before the arrival of the fascinating and lively Crawfords. Even in *Emma*, there are references to the "new ribbons from town" arrived at Mrs Ford's haberdashery (237), to possible visits by the wealthy Churchills "to town this spring" (259), which may provide Frank with the opportunity to revisit Highbury, and to their later intention of "coming up to town directly, on Mrs Churchill's account – she has not been well the whole winter, and thinks Enscombe too cold for her" (305). Enscombe is in Yorkshire, and the centrality of London in the geographical consciousness of the period is reflected in the idiom that represented a move toward London as a coming or going *up*, even if the journey was, as here, southward and downwards on the map; conversely, a movement from or further from London was a movement *down*, even where it was in fact northwards and, therefore, in our own idiom, 'up'; so Lydia can issue that non-chalantly magnificent invitation to her mother:

> "You and papa, and my sisters, must come down and see us. We shall be at Newcastle all the winter, and I dare say there will be some balls, and I will take care to get good partners for them all." *(PP* 317)

Not only *town*, but even the *world*, was verbally arrogated to themselves by high society. For the latter term often refers in the idiom of the time to the fashionable world. Lady Audley, in the novel *Marriage* by Susan Ferrier, 'lived quite in the world; and gave balls and assemblies . . .'; while Lady Matilda Sufton believes the only true knowledge to be "the knowledge of the world, by which she means a knowledge of the most courtly etiquette – the manners and habits of the great, and the newest fashions in dress" (73, 308; cf. *Evel.* 17, 295). A 'man of the world' was an urbane man, one accustomed to moving in polite circles: 'M de Narbonne is . . . a man of the world, and joins the most courtly refinement and elegance to the quickest repartee and readiness of wit' *(FBD* 313). When Byron stated that the only literary men he could get on with were such of them as were 'men of the world' (8.133; cf. 9.22, 30), he was referring, not to those who knew life in the raw, but to those who moved in genteel circles and had some polish to their manners, and were not mere literary 'tradesmen'. Men of the world with knowledge of the world have come sadly down in the world since then, for both phrases now connote experience and awareness especially of the less insulated – rather than the most civilized – aspects of life.

Elizabeth Bennet replies obliquely to Darcy's not very apologetic reference to his being "ill-qualified to recommend [himself] to strangers" by addressing herself thus to Colonel Fitzwilliam:

"Shall we ask him why a man of sense and education, and who
has lived in the world, is ill-qualified to recommend himself to
strangers?"   (*PP* 175)

Elizabeth does not mean that Darcy has knocked about a bit
(which he has not), as she might be taken to mean today; but that
his status and fortune have privileged him to mix with the 'quality',
and that he should therefore be as *well* qualified by circumstance
(education and environment) as by nature (intelligence) to perform the common social duty of making himself agreeable, and to
acquire the conversational and social skills that Fanny Burney also
saw as the mark of the 'man of the world'. Elizabeth, who has seen
far less of the *world* (in this sense) than he has, but who is naturally
easy and graceful in company, is predictably disinclined to allow
the plea her more privileged social superior has advanced.[7]

MANNER

From standard conceptions of time and place one may pass to
accepted standards of speech – and to what would have been
heard as 'substandard' or inelegant in some way. For both serve, in
different ways, to relate events and persons to an assumed social
context. There is a distinct body of verbal mannerisms in the Jane
Austen canon which does not occur as a rule in the mouths of her
heroes and heroines. These are not used primarily to signal less
genteel social status, though some certainly are characteristic of
the speech of, for instance, Mrs Jennings (the widow of a man who
made his money through trade) and the Steele sisters in *Sense and
Sensibility*. More often, they constitute a coarseness of expression
symptomatic of something more innate, since members of the
same family may be distinguished in their speech habits by their
adoption or avoidance of them. For example, the exclamation
Lord! is uttered by Mrs Bennet and (frequently) by Lydia, but
never by Mr Bennet or by Jane and Elizabeth. The person who
uses it most often (along with *Lord bless you/me*) is Mrs Jennings.
The distinction between elegant and inelegant expressions was as
arbitrary then as it is in most periods. Those whose speech is
meant to impress as rational and restrained are allowed '(Good)
Heavens!', but they do not say 'Lord' – though they may be

permitted a '(Good) God!' under severe stress – and only then. The following instances, for example, all mark an emotional crisis that is indeed critical in the respective novels:

(Darcy) "Good God! what is the matter?" cried he.
(Emma, of Harriet) "Oh God! that I had never seen her!"
(Marianne) "Good God! Willoughby, what is the meaning of this?"   (*PP* 276; *E* 411; *SS* 176)

Lydia and her mother are also pretty free with 'Good gracious', 'Gracious me', etc – feeble exclamatories which are also used by Maria Lucas and by the Steele sisters in *Sense and Sensibility*, but which the more sophisticated characters do not affect.

Flat adverbs (adjective form used where an adverb in -*ly* would be expected) and ungrammatical *don't* (for he/she/it 'does not') or *was* ('you was') are also markers of vulgarity of mind or background; so is *an't*. So is addiction to the common cant intensifiers of the day – *shocking, monstrous, prodigious, vastly, excessively*, and so on – the equivalents of such modern emphatics as *terribly, horribly, extremely*, etc, which are often used as mindlessly today as Jane Austen's less intelligent or less polished characters use the above-listed ones. *Charming* and *sweet* were the gush equivalents of modern *super, lovely, wonderful*, etc.

The silly and the vulgar tend to use other vacuous emphatics as well as those in the *prodigious* and *excessive* category – such as '--*est in the world*' – and they are also prone to an overuse of those phrase-fillers *to be sure, I declare* and *I dare say*[8] that were often used as pleonastically as are, for instance, *actually, really, you know* or *I think* today. *Aye* is much more likely to be heard from a Mrs Jennings or a Mrs Bennet than from those who are represented as being both genteel and intelligent.[9]

Different types of solecism are associated (with much overlap) with different kinds of character. *Marriage* and *Evelina* provide convenient illustrations. With the affected and fashionable Lady Juliana in the former and Lady Julia in the latter, the emphasis is on exclamations and intensifiers: "Lord!", "monstrous", "charming", "charmed", "doat upon", "shocking", "shocked" (' "Dear! I hope you did not wait for me – I shall be quite shocked!" drawled out her Ladyship'), "vastly attentive", "that frightful thing" (of a carriage cover), "the kindest manner imaginable"; pleonasm and

slack grammar also figure: "I dare say ... he don't ...".[10]
Evelina's downright vulgar grandmother, Madame Duval (an
ex-barmaid: 13), also uses such expressions as "a shocking thing",
"a monstrous vulgar look", "vastly too polite" and "I dare say"
(59); but in her case there is more emphasis on grammatical
solecisms: "... don't ask me no more about it ... Was you ever in
Paris?" "... you knowed where we was ... he shouldn't have fell
... if the horses had runn'd over me" (60, 74). In *Marriage*, Aunt
Grizzy, garrulous and not very bright, but neither fashionably
affected nor ungenteel, also uses a lot of feebly emphatic super-
latives, but it is pleonasms that are most typical of her: "I declare
it's the most distressing thing", "I'm sure I wish to goodness ...",
"To be sure ...", "I'm sure, I'm thankful you're come .... It's a
thousand pities, I declare ... to be sure, I must always think ... I
daresay he'll come to know you yet. But I'm sure, I hope to
goodness ..." (26, 408, 459–60).

Certain items of vocabulary are also evidently regarded in the
novels as fashionable affectations or vulgarisms. Anne Steele's use
of the word *beau* in the sense of an 'admirer' (though the term was
in regular use as a semi-facetious reference to any male escort or
attendant: cf. *FBD* 148, 150; *WS* 122) Elinor affects not to
understand (*SS* 124). When Caroline Bingley uses it in her letter to
Jane, it is evidently with a touch of tactical facetiousness – a lightly
jesting vulgarism meant to imply that Jane's amorous interests are
not really seriously affected:

> "I sincerely hope ... your beaux will be so numerous as to
> prevent your feeling the loss of the three, of whom we shall
> deprive you."   (*PP* 117)

Fun was also a vulgarism, and was used only by the ungenteel or
the silly genteel. Dr Johnson's Dictionary labels it 'A low cant
word'. Harriet Byron uses it when she is mimicking the foolish and
would-be fashionable Mr Singleton: "We had rare *fun*, at dinner,
and after dinner" (*SCG* I.72). In *Evelina*, the word is used very frequently by the heroine's horribly vulgar cousin, young Branghton:
"Lord, you can't think, Miss, what fun it is!" (175; cf. 232); *fun,
good fun* and *funny* are all included among those of his vulgarisms
to which Evelina gives emphasis marks when writing to her

guardian in order to make it clear that they are his, not her own, expressions (169, 213, 220). In this novel, the word is otherwise used only by the equally ungenteel Mr Smith and by the rather coarse Captain Mirvan, who shares with Jane Austen's Admiral Croft the somewhat broad idiom of the old sailor (187, 400). The term more normally selected in unmarked speech is *sport* or (for *funny*) *diverting* or *ridiculous*. In Jane Austen's novels, the only persons who talk of *fun* are, significantly, John Thorpe and Lydia Bennet (*NA* 49; *PP* 112, 316 and (six times in two speeches) 221–2). Similarly, 'I have no notion of' had a colloquial sense of 'I think very poorly of', but is used in this way only by Isabella Thorpe ("I have no notion of treating men with such respect": *NA* 43; cf. 40) and Mrs Jennings ("I have no notion of men's going on in this way": *SS* 192; cf. 259); the expression is likewise used by Evelina's awful grandmother (*Evel.* 220).

Gender distinctions can to some extent be observed to operate within the body of fashionable cant. Such intensifiers as *frightful* and *horrid* Dr Johnson specifically designated as 'women's cant'.[11] Both words were in regular use in their strict sense ('such as to inspire fear or horror': see, for example, the discussion of *horrid* books (i.e. thrillers) by Catherine and Isabella at *NA* 40); but in their looser role as mere emphatics they are distinctly more common amongst the female contingent of Jane Austen's fashionable silly or ungenteel. *Frightful* in its looser sense is confined to women (Isabella Thorpe and Mrs Allen: *NA* 216, 238). *Horrid* (used by, for example, Isabella Thorpe, Mrs Bennet and Lydia; and once (*MP* 361) by Mary Crawford) is used only twice by men. The exclamation *La!* is used *only* by affected/vulgar/ignorant and usually young women (to wit, Anne Steele, Maria Lucas, Kitty and Lydia Bennet). *Charming* used of persons is not at all uncommon, but as a vague hyperbole is mostly feminine (the Thorpe women in *NA*, for instance, are very prone to it). *Sweet*, similarly, was not so empty a word as it is now, and is frequently used of persons; but in loosely emphatic praise of things (e.g. "a sweet room", "sweet concerts", "sweet flower-beds") it is used exclusively by women: e.g. Harriet Smith, Mrs Bennet, Charlotte Palmer, Mrs Elton, Mrs Clay, Isabella Thorpe); in vocatives ("My sweetest Lizzy", "My sweet Catherine") it is also a feminine affectation – used by, for instance, Mrs Bennet and (very frequently) by the gushy hypocrite, Isabella Thorpe. *Shocking* was in more common use than it is today, but in virtually meaningless hyperbole (with virtually no residual semantic reference to what might shock or outrage the sensibilities) is more or less confined to the women: used, for instance, by Mrs Allen, Isabella Thorpe, Mrs Norris, Miss Bates, Mrs Elton, Lucy Steele, Mrs Bennet and the Bingley sisters (who declared 'how shocking it was to have a bad cold': *PP* 35). Mr Woodhouse's comment that Mr Knightley must have had "a shocking walk" (*E* 10) is probably not, for him, a loosely hyperbolic usage: Mr Woodhouse is very easily shocked. *Excessive* used loosely as a mere intensifier (that is, not counting its strict sense) is a colloquialism that can on occasion be heard from almost any character, but those who use it frequently are women (e.g. Isabella Thorpe, Miss Bates, Charlotte Palmer).[12]

The idiom of the arch male vulgarian, John Thorpe, on the other hand, includes two usages only found elsewhere in Jane Austen in the mouths of men. His mild oaths invoking the devil, the adjective *devilish* ("the devil take the rest", "a devilish long fortnight": *NA* 124, 123; cf. 61, 65) and his *confounded* usages ("a confounded hurry": 61; cf. 123) are confined to him, Mr Price of *Mansfield Park*, Mr Weston of *Emma*, Willoughby and Mr Palmer in *Sense and Sensibility* and Robert in *The Watsons*. *Famous(ly)* (a fashionable colloquialism for 'fine') he uses extremely frequently ("a famous ball", "they will quiz[13] me famously": 61, 76, cf. 63, 64, 66, 96, 122), but it is otherwise used only by Charles Musgrove (*P* 219) and Tom Musgrave in *The Watsons* (*MW* 327, 335, 340, 358).[14] It was a word Jane Austen obviously associated particularly with young-buck-speak. John's slang thus studiously preserves an aggressively male stamp, just as that of many of his female counterparts maintains an affectedly exaggerated and gushy femininity. *Knowing* – fashionable slang for 'Showing knowledge of 'what is what' in fashion, dress, and the like' (*OED sv knowing ppl adj* 4) – falls into the same category as *famous*. John is ushered into *Northanger Abbey* by a 'most knowing-looking coachman' (44) driving rather recklessly – a fact and an idiom that do much to pre-announce the would-be fashionable bravado characteristic of this imperceptive show-off. There are similar implicit inverted commas round the word when it figures, again in the context of the macho and narcissistic concern with their equipages typical of the sort who would use it (or of whom it would, sincerely or in ironical imitation, be used), in Edward Ferrars's depreciative description of the objections raised to his wish to enter the Church by his family, who would prefer him to cut a more fashionable figure as one of those men who "drove about town in very knowing gigs" (*SS* 103).[15]

Many of the expressions discussed above would, in fact, have been not at all abnormal in the speech of perfectly genteel and well-educated speakers, if their letters are anything to go by – even ungrammatical *don't* and *was*[16] – though perhaps not in such concentration or with such consistency as they are used by Jane Austen to mark certain people's speech habits. That they are avoided more strictly by her 'superior' characters than they would probably have been in real life need cause no surprise. Most of us permit ourselves in speech what we might well guard against as a solecism in writing, and nearly all of us allow ourselves many more *super*s, *lovely*s and *terribly*s than we would give to fictional characters whose speech we wished to come across as intelligent and decorous. Art does not necessarily deal with the truths of life by imitating them exactly (if it did, it could reveal few that were not already obvious without it).

'Vulgarity' is a rather tendentious over-generalization for what some of the above speech-habits convey about a character, though it often enters into the matter. Some of them simply signal a loosish, colloquial idiom: Mr Weston, for instance, uses *Aye* (*E* 305), and Admiral Croft *Aye* and *Lord* (*P* 126, 128). These two men are not sophisticated, but they are not precisely vulgar. Mr Weston is a friendly, chatty, not very thinking man, apt to use common idioms instinctively; Admiral Croft a blunt, downright one, whose speech is never, however, really coarse.

The speech of the horribly common Steele sisters in *Sense and Sensibility* is perhaps the best, though not the subtlest, example of the verbal mannerisms which impress as vacuous, affected or vulgar. Their voices find a prelude in that of Sir John, himself rather a coarse man with little polish of manner; his own speech seems to have so much instinctive sympathy with theirs that his enthusiastic account of them verbally heralds many of their own distinctive idioms. The following passages are selected from the overture provided by him and from what prove to be the theme tunes of the sisters; the words and phrases that mark their gushy, vulgar style are italicized, together with the other vacuous phrase-fillers, hyperboles and intensifiers especially characteristic of this register:

"Do come now," said he – "pray come – you must come – *I declare* you shall come – You can't think how you will like them. Lucy is *monstrous* pretty, and so good humoured and agreeable! . . . And they both long to see you *of all things*, for they have heard at Exeter that you are the most beautiful creatures *in the world* . . . You will be delighted with them *I am sure* . . ."

"And here is my *sweet* little Annamaria," she added, tenderly caressing a little girl of three years old, who had not made a noise for the last two minutes; ". . . Never was there such a quiet little thing!" . . .

"What a *sweet* woman Lady Middleton is!" said Lucy Steele . . .

"And Sir John too," cried the elder sister, "what a *charming* man he is!" . . .

"And what a *charming* little family they have! I never saw such fine children *in my life*. – I declare I quite *doat* upon them already, and indeed I am always *distractedly* fond of children . . . and *for my part*, I love to see children full of life and spirits . . ."

"Norland is a *prodigious* beautiful place, is not it?" added Miss Steele.

"We have heard Sir John admire it *excessively*," said Lucy, who seemed to think some apology necessary for the freedom of her sister . . .

"And had you a great many *smart beaux* there? I suppose you have not so many in this part of the world; *for my part*, I think they are a *vast* addition always."

"But why should you think," said Lucy, looking ashamed of her sister, "that there are not as many genteel young men in Devonshire as Sussex?"

"Nay, my dear, *I'm sure* I don't pretend to say that there *an't*. *I'm sure* there's a *vast* many agreeable *smart beaux* in Exeter . . . *For my part*, I think they are *vastly* agreeable, provided they dress *smart* and behave *civil* . . . Now there's Mr. Rose at Exeter, a *prodigious smart* young man, quite a *beau* . . ."   (119–23)

Anne Steele is much worse than Lucy, and when Jane Austen later wishes to epitomize her style, she describes how it was her custom, after bestowing a presumptuously inquisitive stare on Marianne's dress, to remark to the latter that "*upon her word* she looked *vastly smart*, and she *dared to say* would make a great many *conquests*" (249: my italics).

Lucy is shrewder than her sister and her own speech reads less like a parody of the tittering vulgarity of a shallow and ill-educated mind. It is noticeable how, in the above passage, she hastily rephrases her sister's *smart beaux* into "genteel young men", and tries to cover the total want of manners evident in Anne's impertinent nosiness. When, therefore, a few pages later, there occurs the first of those very disingenuous conversations between her and Elinor on the subject of Edward, Lucy's speech is more subtly observed. Since she is here trying very hard to represent herself as a decent girl, she is careful about how she puts things, and certainly does not commit the more ghastly gaffes of Anne. She gives herself away, however, by the odd error in grammar;[17] but even more well-observed is the way her reliance on empty tags, intensifiers and line-fillers becomes even more marked under the effort to impart an appearance of ingenuousness and honesty to her artful and calculated strategies:

> "You will think my question an add one, *I dare say* . . . I cannot bear to have you think me impertinently curious. *I am sure* I would rather do anything *in the world* than be thought so by a person whose good opinion is so well worth having as yours. And *I am sure* I should not have the smallest fear of trusting *you* . . ."
>
> "*I dare say* you are, and *I am sure* I do not wonder at it . . . . You may well be surprised . . . for *to be sure* you could have had no idea of it before; for *I dare say* he never dropped the smallest hint of it to you or any of your family; because it was always meant to be a great secret, and *I am sure* has been faithfully kept so by me to this hour . . . I never should have mentioned it to you, if I had not felt the greatest dependance *in the world* upon your secrecy . . . he has the highest opinion *in the world* of all your family. . ."   (128–30)

Slips in grammar serve to strike a beautifully telling false note in the ambitious construction she attempts as the dénouement of her revelations:

> ". . . you must allow that *I* am not likely to be deceived, as to the name of the man on who all my happiness depends. . ."   (131)

When she comes to her fears about Anne's discretion – a subject on which she *is* probably sincere – she falls into a mode closer to that of her sister's own, but she soon reverts to her more guarded manner, with only the odd error in grammar and the persistent tags to suggest it does not come quite naturally to her:

> "She does not know how to hold her tongue, as you must perceive, and I am sure I was in the greatest fright in the world t'other day, when Edward's name was mentioned by Sir John, lest she should out with it all . . . I am sure I wonder my heart is not quite broke." (133)

The characteristic marks of her idiom become particularly evident at the close of the conversation, when she shows Elinor a letter written to her by Edward. This is proof positive of an engagement in Jane Austen's world,[18] and this is the point Lucy wishes Elinor to take. She attempts to conceal her stratagem by an over-affectation of carelessness and casualness, relying heavily on common line-fillers and intensifiers:

> "You know his hand, I dare say, a charming one it is; but that is not written so well as usual. – He was tired, I dare say, for he had just filled the sheet to me as full as possible." (134)

A vacuous head and an utterly imperturbable good temper combine to make Charlotte Palmer, in the same novel, extremely prone to the cant expressions of delight, *charming* and *sweet*. She is apparently perfectly genuinely and totally indiscriminately delighted with everything. Her voice is first heard in raptures over the parlour in Barton Cottage and the drawings by Elinor that adorn its walls, which are all alike pronounced *delightful, charming, sweet* (107–8). Even the public rudeness with which she is treated by her husband fails to elicit any other response than a delighted laugh at how *ridiculous* and *droll* he is (107, 112). Her silly and inept use of fashionable intensifiers draws direct comment from him at one point:

> "How charming it will be," said Charlotte, "when he is in Parliament! – won't it? How I shall laugh! It will be so ridiculous to see all his letters directed to him with an M.P. . . . ."
> Mr. Palmer took no notice of her.

"He cannot bear writing, you know," she continued – "he says it is quite shocking."

"No," said he, "I never said anything so irrational. Don't palm all your abuses of language upon me."   (113)

For Charlotte is, of course, equally given to truly *monstrous, shocking* and *excessive* idle emphatics: "I am monstrous glad of it" (114), "I think you both excessively pretty" (116). Parodying the mindless use of the fashionable hyperboles of any period is not difficult, however, and what Jane Austen more wittily reveals in Charlotte is a type of social silliness not uncommon, though not commonly as comically exaggerated as it is in Charlotte's case. For her addiction to overstatement is more fundamental than a mere reliance on empty approbative adjectives and intensifiers, which are simply the surface structure of her deep structure:

"We do not live a great way from [Willoughby] in the country, you know. Not above ten miles, I dare say."

"Much nearer thirty," said her husband.

"Ah! well! there is not much difference. I never was at his home; but they say it is a sweet pretty place."

"As vile a spot as I ever saw in my life," said Mr. Palmer . . .

"Is it very ugly?" continued Mrs. Palmer – "then it must be some other place that is so pretty I suppose." (111)

[Elinor] began by inquiring if they saw much of Mr. Willoughby at Cleveland, and whether they were intimately acquainted with him.

"Oh! dear, yes; I know him extremely well," replied Mrs. Palmer – "Not that I ever spoke to him indeed; but I have seen him for ever in town" . . .

"[Colonel Brandon] is such a charming man, that it is quite a pity that he should be so grave and so dull . . ."

"Is Mr. Willoughby much known in your part of Somersetshire?" said Elinor.

"Oh! yes, extremely well; that is, I do not believe many people are acquainted with him, because Combe Magna is so far off; but they all think him extremely agreeable I assure you." (114–16)

Of the heroines, it is only Catherine Morland whose speech betrays any consistent or characteristic addiction to the conventional hyperboles and pleonasms of conversation mentioned above. Henry Tilney actually mocks her expressed assumption that "young men despised novels *amazingly*" and her description of Udolpho as "the *nicest* book in the world" (*NA* 107: my italics).[19] *I declare, I'm sure, to be sure, I dare say, sweet, -st in the world* are also expressions that can regularly be heard from her ("it is the prettiest room in the world . . . what a sweet little cottage . . .": 214). For, though in many ways the most endearing of the heroines, she is the least clever, and is not meant, as the others are, to seem a cut above the average in intelligence; she therefore talks as thoughtlessly as most girls of seventeen do.

The occasions on which the other heroes and heroines may slip into some of these trite verbal mannerisms are often of interest. For instance, unlike Mrs Bennet, Mr Bennet and Elizabeth use *prodigious(ly)* only in rather ironic contexts:

> "Oh! yes," said Elizabeth drily – "Mr. Darcy is uncommonly kind to Mr. Bingley, and takes a prodigious deal of care of him."

> (Mr. Bennet of his son-in-law, Wickham) "I am prodigiously proud of him."   (*PP* 184, 330)

And only once does Elizabeth fall into the *excessive* mode: in response to her father's reference to a forthcoming marriage between herself and Darcy, which he treats as a joke, she replies somewhat over-emphatically: "Oh! . . . I am excessively diverted" (364).

In these obvious and demonstrable ways, then, words 'mean' by placing within mental categories (in these cases, perceived divisions in the day, the environment and modes of speaking) or ways of dividing up the world. These models may or may not correspond with the models inherited by a later reader, for whom the same words (such as *morning* and *tea*) may have been slotted into different mental and/or social arrangements. Even a model or division more or less shared with the earlier writer (a distinction between decorous and sloppy or substandard speech) may no longer realize itself in the same linguistic items. We do not hear the difference Jane Austen heard between *God!* and *Lord!*, though we might well hear a similar one between *Christ!* and

Crikey! or *Cripes!* Similar considerations apply when one turns to more abstract phenomena such as 'character', which is the subject of the remaining chapters. Here too a significant part of the 'meaning' of the words used in connection with this concept lies in their reference to and place in a mental organization of the subject. This needs to be recovered if the part played by such words in these novels is to be fully understood.

2 Character: The Conceptual Context

To define and type a person discursively (by descriptive analysis) as opposed to dramatically (through his/her words and actions) requires a vocabulary capable of dealing with more than just physical attributes. That vocabulary in turn requires a conceptual scheme or grid: that is, some general theory or notion of what the range and nature of these non-physical aspects of person are. The terminology generated by such a notional scheme usually takes the form of antithetical doublets (extrovert/introvert, silly/intelligent, etc), selection from which can then map individual instances onto this grid. That grid, the pre-existent notion of what, in this instance, we call *character*, governs the way we both see and describe people, and may be likened to the *schema* posited by the art historian, E. H. Gombrich, for the visual arts.[1] Artists, he argued, do not simply paint 'what they see'; they see individual objects in terms of 'schemes' or conventional visual representations of them, and they reproduce them by adapting or manipulating that scheme. Similarly, our notions of what constitutes 'character' are to a large extent culturally determined. The accuracy or otherwise of that cultural scheme itself is probably unverifiable, and is not as important as the use made of it in particular contexts to conduct interesting appraisals or make significant discriminations.

The *schema* for character has varied from period to period, and the conceptual territory it organizes has not always been called *character*. In the Middle Ages, it consisted in the theory of the four 'humours' (the bodily fluids which were believed to determine the physiological and psychological constitution of persons); and it allowed for four broad types, resulting from the predominance of one of the four humours over the others in any one person's make-up: sanguine (blood), choleric (red bile), melancholic (black bile) and phlegmatic (water). These were the categories of what was called, not *character*, but *complexion* ('commixture'). Jane Austen inherited a scheme of which the chief parameters were the head and heart, which appear in her writings in a number of related doublets figuring sometimes together, sometimes singly: head and heart; *temper* (which she uses in its earlier sense of 'temperament') and *understanding*; *disposition* and *abilities* or *talents* (by which she nearly always means mental abilities generally, not, as today, abilities in particular directions); *sense* and *sensibility*.

The same scheme can be detected in other literature of the period. In Thackeray's *Vanity Fair*, Jos's father, Mr Sedley, declares: "Let Jos marry whom he likes . . . it's no affair of mine. This girl has no fortune; no more had Mrs. Sedley. She seems good-humoured and clever, and will keep him in order, perhaps" (89). He thus counterbalances Becky's lack of fortune against what he defines as her perfectly acceptable personal character; the scheme is here evoked in a straightforward and even perfunctory way (in keeping with the deliberately affected tone of cool indifference) – rather over-perfunctory, in fact, since this favourable verdict on Becky's heart, though it testifies to her powers to please where she chooses, is scarcely one that the novel allows. In fact, another character has already appealed to the same categories only to arrive at a significantly different judgement of the heroine. Miss Pinkerton, the principal of the Academy for young ladies where Becky is first an inmate and later a teacher, writes her a reference and 'reconciled the recommendation to her conscience' by phrasing it thus: ". . . her talents and accomplishments are of a high order. As far as the head goes, at least, she does credit to the educational system pursued at my establishment" (52). She is thus significantly silent on the question of Becky's heart or disposition, leaving it to be deduced by no very great ingenuity that Becky's *temper* leaves much to be desired. The scheme allowed pointed innuendo of this kind.

The categories of head and heart, in various different guises, were used to describe, analyse, commend or discommend as much in real life as in fiction. Of his sister, Augusta, Byron wrote to Lady Melbourne:

she surely is very clever – and not only so – but in some things of good judgement . . . I know her to be in point of temper – & goodness of heart almost unequalled. (*BLJ* 4.111)

and of this confidante herself to her niece, Annabella (his own future wife):

she is doubtless in talent a superior – a *supreme* woman – & her heart I know to be of the kindest. (*BLJ* 4.56)

and, rather more wittily, of that most notorious of the women in his life, Lady Caroline Lamb (to Lady Melbourne, again):

I am sorry to hear that she is still fermenting her weak head and cold heart to an *ice-cream* which will only sicken every one about her. (*BLJ* 4.116)

He can also exploit these well-known categories to turn the neat and memorable phrases at which he is an adept:

A chymic treasure
Is glittering youth, which I have spent betimes,
My heart in passion and my head on rhymes. (*DJ* I.217)

He occasionally calls in aid two other factors regularly consulted by Jane Austen and her contemporaries: spirits and manners. Two further mistresses of his will serve as examples: Lady Frances Wedderburn Webster, 'not very animated – but good tempered'; and a Venetian opera-singer (an ex whom he is recommending to a friend) – 'Her temper very good – (as you know it had need to be) and lively' (*BLJ* 3.133; 5.145). All four categories were regularly appealed to when the intention was to provide a complete assessment of a character. So Sir Charles Grandison describes a surgeon friend of his thus: 'Mr. Lowther is a man of spirit, tho' a modest man . . . and has a heart tender as manly . . .. He is a man of sense and learning *out* of his profession, and happy in his address' (*SCG* IV.451). As regards *manners*, though it was frequently dealt with in terms of felicitous address, as here, it is important to remember that the word was broader than it is today. It embraced not only the observance of polite punctilios ('good manners'), but also what we would today call, using the singular, one's manner generally.

Good manners, that is, might mean ease and friendliness rather than courtesy, and unhappy ones might as readily imply stiffness or reserve as rudeness. Even this was a fairly recent specialization of a word that had been used even more broadly to refer to one's whole conduct and pattern of behaviour. The proverb 'manners maketh man' preserves this former and more moral sense, which had not yet been forgotten. It figures, for instance, in a novel that preceded her own by some half a century, but which Jane Austen much admired, Richardson's *Sir Charles Grandison*, in the pious wish that "in all nurseries of learning, the manners of youth were proposed as the principal end", and in the collocation '. . . integrity of heart, and innocence of life and manners' (I.55, VI.188). Hence in the novel *Marriage* (which came out in the same year – 1818 – as *Persuasion*), the prim, dour, old-fashioned Highlander, Miss Jacky, a woman of little intelligence and no polish, defends the formidable Lady Maclaughlan thus:

"... a woman of family – of fortune – of *talents* – of *accomplishments*! – a woman of unblemished reputation! of the strictest *morals*! sweetest *temper*! charming *heart*! delightful *spirits*! so charitable! every year gives fifty flannel petticoats to the old people of the parish . . ."   (*Mar.* 31: my italics)

Aunt Jacky is appealing to the conventional categories to emphasize the personal perfections of this (in fact extremely eccentric) character. But she is using them in her own way – and her own way forms part of the pervasive half-serious, half-comic contrast between the Scottish and the English worlds of this novel. In her churchy rusticity, she fills the slot of *manners* by reference to Christian probity of conduct rather than grace and polish of address. Lady Maclaughlan's manners are actually downright in the extreme (and sometimes downright rude) and could not score high on any interpretation of what should fall under this head except Miss Jacky's narrow and primly old-fashioned one.

This sense of *manners* – (**moral**) **conduct** – remained especially prone to activation in contexts of Christian morality and the ministry. Thus Sir Walter Scott could describe a 'venerable priest' as one

Whose life and manners well could paint
Alike the student and the saint.
(*Marmion*: Introduction to Canto III, 221–2)

In Jane Austen, therefore, it is in that novel in which 'ordination' is a serious issue, *Mansfield Park*, that *manners* of this more serious kind are alluded to – in Edmund's claim that the clergy have "the guardianship of religion and morals, and consequently of the manners that result from their influence" (92). But Edmund plainly feels that even the context may fail to alert Mary to the fact that he is drawing into play an older and more serious sense of *manners* than the one she (with her background and priorities) would herself more naturally associate with the word, and is therefore careful to discriminate between the two usages (the contrast between which epitomizes the opposing values of the entire exchange):

> "And with regard to their influencing public manners, Miss Crawford must not misunderstand me, or suppose I mean to call them the arbiters of good breeding, the regulators of refinement and courtesy, the masters of the ceremonies of life. The *manners* I speak of, might rather be called *conduct*, perhaps, the result of good principles." (93)[2]

There was, then, a twofold (expandable to a fourfold) *schema* available for description or assessment of character. Jane Austen frequently uses the head and heart categories, but as frequently supplements them with those of *spirits* and *manners* or *address* – with good reason. Though most of us will doubtless fit into one of the four categories the narrower scheme allows for (clever and nice; clever but not nice; silly but good-hearted; silly and ill-natured), there is a lot it would fail to tell us about people. It will not tell us, for instance, if they are good company; many intelligent and well-disposed people are not. And that, in an age when persons of the class Jane Austen belonged to and wrote about had (especially the ladies) more leisure and fewer means of filling it than we have today, was an important consideration. Conversation and society were a major source of interest and amusement. In *Pride and Prejudice* it is conceded that the Bingley sisters, unlikeable as they are, can be good company when they choose: 'Their powers of conversation were considerable. They could describe an entertainment with accuracy, relate an anecdote with humour, and laugh at their acquaintance with spirit' (54).[3] Conversely, Byron could point to 'a good man . . . an honourable man, a most inoffensive man, a well informed man, and a *dull* man, & this last damned epithet undoes all the rest' (*BLJ* 2.102). Besides intelligence and good nature, therefore, Jane Austen regularly refers to those two further factors influencing the impression of and response to a character: whether or not they have *spirit(s)* (animation and cheerfulness); and whether they have *address* or good *manners*. This last can refer to either or both of two things: courtesy and polish; or (what is not quite the same thing) the command of a social manner (relaxed, friendly, etc) calculated to please – one or both of these types of good manners will render the happy possessor *civil* and/or *agreeable*.

In *Sense and Sensibility* there occurs a singularly unenjoyable evening party hosted by the arrogant Mrs Ferrars; its awfulness is explained as being chiefly due to the fact that

> almost all laboured under one or other of these disqualifications for being agreeable – Want of sense, either natural or improved – want of elegance – want of spirits – or want of temper.   (233)

Of those present, Anne Steele and Lady Middleton have a *natural* or innate lack of intelligence; Lucy does have intelligence, but the novel emphasizes repeatedly that the deficiency in her upbringing had left it improperly developed and directed, un*improved*. Lady Middleton, John and Fanny Dashwood, Lucy and Mrs Ferrars are all, in their different ways, ill-natured, and so rendered unagreeable by faults of *temper* – a term which refers to temporary or characteristic 'state of mind'; it is often equivalent to **(good) nature** or **(good) humour**, and may sometimes refer to the retention of same under trying circumstances, in which case it can virtually be rendered 'self-control';[4] this last may well be what is at issue in the above passage – there are those present who have succumbed to a bad mood. *Elegance* refers to the social graces,[5] and here Sir John Middleton and Mrs Jennings, both very vulgar, and Anne Steele achieve negative scores: their lack of any social tact or manner makes them grating and embarrassing company. Want of spirits is what Colonel Brandon and Marianne are suffering from; and gloomy people, no matter how well-endowed with intelligence and feeling, cannot be agreeable company.

This supplemented version of the basic scheme of head and heart is one peculiarly suited to a major concern of Jane Austen's –

character as manifested in social and personal relationships; for it is one capable of identifying and distinguishing personal and social strengths and weaknesses, intrinsic worth (head and heart) and social charm (*address* and *spirits*). These four categories form the basic reference points by which characters in all her novels are drawn and evaluated and their interactions and contrasts with one another developed. In *Persuasion* Anne is a girl whose spirits were never high (15, 152), but who is, as Mr Elliot perceives, 'in her temper, manners, mind, a model of female excellence' (159). She knows her sister Elizabeth has 'well-bred, elegant manners', but has some doubts as to how 'her temper and understanding might bear the investigation' of this discerning gentleman (140). 'Though better endowed than the elder sister, Mary had not Anne's understanding or temper'; when things went well for her, 'she had great good humour and excellent spirits' – but both are rather uncertain qualities, easily overset by trifling annoyances (37). Anne judges that her husband, Charles Musgrove, constitutes good material wasted by an idleness he might have been weened from had he married a woman of 'real understanding', for he has no obvious defects in any department: '. . . civil and agreeable; in sense and temper he was undoubtedly superior to his wife . . . He had very good spirits, which never seemed much affected by his wife's occasional lowness' (43). Louisa Musgrove has 'higher spirits' (74) than her sister, and is, on these grounds, at first preferred by Frank Wentworth, who feels that *spirit* is what Anne had lacked in allowing herself to be persuaded out of her engagement with him. The man Louisa eventually marries, Captain Benwick, has, ironically, very depressed spirits on his entry into the novel, the result of a bereavement acting on a 'disposition . . . uniting very strong feelings with quiet, serious, and retiring manners, and a decided taste for reading, and sedentary pursuits' (97). Though Mary tells Lady Russell that he is not "a well-bred young man", as he is too silent to be entertaining company, Anne is confident "she would be so much pleased with his mind, that she would very soon see no deficiency in his manner" (132). Frank and Anne agree that Benwick and Louisa form a surprising pair, for, though there is congruency in "good temper", there is not much in "mind": Louisa is a "sweet-tempered girl, and not deficient in understanding; but Benwick is something more. He is a clever man, a reading man" (182). *Sweet* is an adjective often used to commend the temper.

Less patronizing and more serious in tone and wider in reference than today, it indicated a disposition ready of good will and responsive in sympathies. It collocates with 'obliging' and 'gracious', is the opposite of 'ill-natured', is slow to take offence, is associated with *complacency* (desire to please), and opposes such words as 'severity' and 'austerity'.[6] The *sweetness* mentioned in *Mansfield Park* as the quality Fanny has, but which a man will always believe the woman he loves to possess whether she does or no (294), is not 'cuteness', but good nature, a *temper* slow to hurt or disoblige. The word could be applied to men as readily and as seriously as to women (e.g. *SCG* IV.359, V.564, VII.281).

Mrs Smith had 'the good sense and agreeable manners' to make her a very acceptable companion to Anne, and, above all, a resilience of *spirits* at which Anne (whose own are not her strongest point) marvels (153–4). Head is the only department in which the scheming Mrs Clay shines, and, though she uncharacteristically allows her heart to rule it at one point (under Mr Elliot's influence), we are reminded at the close of the novel that 'She has abilities, however, as well as affections; and it is now a doubtful point whether his cunning, or hers, may finally carry the day' (250). Lady Russell, 'a woman rather of sound than of quick abilities' (11), is eventually forced to acknowledge that she had been influenced by what did and did not please her in the *manners* of Frank Wentworth and Mr Elliot to form quite erroneous conclusions as to their respective characters (249).

In Mr Elliot's case, the categories are exploited according to a more dramatic principle to produce a more gradual and sequential development of his character. The deployment of them is calculated to bring about a growing suspicion in the mind of the reader quite as much as in Anne's own. He makes a very favourable impression on all when he enters the novel, and Anne's reflections on him thereafter take their starting point from matters in which he cannot be faulted: his head and his *manners* or *address*. Even in the brief encounter on the steps at Lyme, he can impress himself at once as 'completely a gentleman in manner' (104). We next learn his name and are invited to surmise with Anne that he is an intelligent man as well as a well-bred one: he 'was undoubtedly a gentleman, and had an air of good sense' (106). When she re-meets him, the excellence of his *manners* – 'so exactly what they ought to be, so polished, so easy, so particularly agreeable' – is again the first thing to impress her; and her surmises as to his being not a foolish man are quickly confirmed: 'There could be no doubt of his being a sensible man. Ten minutes were enough to certify that' (143). The silence in all this resounding tribute to his head and address on the question of what was variously referred to as *heart*, *feelings*, *temper*, *disposition* (the most definitive aspect of character) is marked. Only in a description mediated through the impressions of Lady Russell is he credited with a corresponding excellence in this area:

> His manners were an immediate recommendation . . . . Everything united in him; good understanding, correct opinions, knowledge of the world, and a warm heart. He had strong feelings of family-attachment and family-honour . . . never run away with by spirits or by selfishness, which fancied itself strong feeling; and yet, with a sensibility to what was amiable and lovely, and a value for all the felicities of domestic life, which characters of fancied enthusiasm and violent agitation seldom really possess. (146–7)

The order in which his virtues impress themselves is significant. His manners are an 'immediate recommendation', and the intelligence and decorum of his conversation reinforce the favourable impression. Lady Russell is then ready to perceive signs of an equally sterling heart and *temper* – aided by two characteristics of his especially likely to recommend him to *her*. His sense of the dignity of the family to which he belongs provides, to a woman of her aristocratic notions, strong evidence of proper feeling; and the temperate self-collectedness of his demeanour is bound to appeal to one whom the ardour and enthusiasm of the young Wentworth had simply made nervous, and who had been led by it to write him down as a bit wild and headstrong (27). For in the last sentence quoted above Lady Russell is obviously comparing the more sedate ways of Mr Elliot with the greater warmth and energy of Frank's – and is only too happy to conclude that the former provide more reliable evidence of real sensibility than what she somewhat tendentiously terms '*fancied* enthusiasm' and '*violent* agitation' can do.

Anne, in love with Frank where Lady Russell is not, naturally sees things rather differently. Her analysis of Mr Elliot starts off from the same place as Lady Russell's – 'he was a sensible man, an agreeable man . . .' (160) – but it does not carry him beyond that, as her friend's does:

> Mr. Elliot was rational, discreet, polished, – but he was not open. There was never any burst of feeling . . . .   (161)

Anne, in fact, finds cause for mistrust in precisely that guarded dissimilarity from Frank's 'warmth and enthusiasm' (*ibid*) that Lady Russell found reassurance in.

The question of the *heart* and "real character" (199) beneath all this intelligence and address is, of course, finally resolved (in rather over-melodramatic style) by the revelations of Mrs Smith: "Mr. Elliot is a man without heart or conscience; a designing, wary, cold-blooded being, who thinks only of himself . . . . He is totally beyond the reach of any sentiment of justice or compassion. Oh! he is black at heart, hollow and black!" (199). This "Bloody, bawdy villain!" stuff is not exactly what Jane Austen is best at, but the point that one can be misled by manners that do or do not suit one into erroneous estimations (as Lady Russell had been by those of Frank and Mr Elliot: 249) is one the authoress makes in other works.

Pride and Prejudice raises the same issue with regard to the prejudice for Wickham and against Darcy created in Elizabeth by the respective manners of the two. For Darcy's *address* is flat terrible. This is noticed immediately, and creates as immediate a dislike. Within half an evening, 'his manners gave a disgust' which turns all Meryton against him (10; cf. 207) – naturally enough, since most people do not like the suggestion, irresistibly conveyed by his haughty demeanour, that he considers them inferior to himself (which they generally are; but that, of course, is in such cases no palliative). These manners as inevitably give Elizabeth the most decided conviction that he is an "ill-tempered man", 'not a good-tempered man' (78, 248), as his "softened" manners (255) later give Mrs Gardiner an equal predisposition to believe the contrary: "He has not an ill-natured look . . . . And there is something of dignity in his countenance, that would not give one an unfavourable idea of his heart" (258). This is not illogical. Darcy himself later attributes his earlier behaviour to an upbringing that had encouraged him to be "selfish and overbearing": "I was not taught to correct my temper" (369), he declares – meaning, not that he was allowed to get into tantrums, but that faults of **temperament** – "pride and conceit" – were indulged. There *is* a connection between the *temper* and the *manners*; but it is often far from a straightforward one. Elizabeth implies as much to Wickham, when he contrasts Darcy's manners with those of Colonel Fitzwilliam, which are much more engaging. Elizabeth replies that Darcy "improves on acquaintance", and explains herself thus:

> "When I said that he improved on acquaintance, I did not mean that either his mind or manners were in a state of improvement, but that from knowing him better, his disposition was better understood."   (234)

With Wickham himself, Elizabeth makes the reverse mistake. He has all the *address* Darcy lacks. This 'very pleasing address' (72) is the only one of the four categories to be mentioned at his entrance into the novel, and the same "happy manners", "engaging manners", 'smiles and . . . easy address' (92, 200, 284, 316) continue to be stressed. Even before his history has been revealed to her by Darcy, Elizabeth, instinctively thinking in terms of the traditional categories, realizes to which of them his virtues pre-eminently belong – and that he may not score so high under the other heads. The courteous friendliness of Colonel Fitzwilliam reminds her of Wickham, 'and though, in comparing them, she saw there was less captivating softness in Colonel Fitzwilliam's manners, she believed he might have the best-informed mind' (180). When Darcy's letter informs her of his 'real character', she sees that his manner had prompted unexamined assumptions about his disposition, that 'His countenance, voice, and manner, had established him at once in the possession of every virtue'; she conjures up his image 'in every charm of air and address', and tries in vain to recall some 'more substantial good' of him to validate her instinctive disinclination to believe what Darcy has revealed of his *temper* (206).

Darcy's manners are also contrasted with those of Bingley, which are as calculated to endear as Darcy's are to alienate. Bingley's *temper, manners* and *spirits* are all excellent: a "sweet tempered, amiable, charming man" (82) with 'easy, unaffected manners' (10), his good-humoured cheerfulness and relaxed ways (261, 345) make him as instantly (though more deservedly) popular as Wickham. Jane expresses her pleased approbation of him by passing him with honours through all four of the tests of human worth:

> "He is just what a young man ought to be," said she, "sensible, good-humoured, lively; and I never saw such happy manners! – so much ease, with such perfect good breeding!"   (14)

The two young men are drawn so as to contrast with each other on all four counts. Where Darcy's manners are stiff and off-putting, Bingley's are relaxed and engaging; where Bingley is lively and cheerful, Darcy lacks animation and liveliness (180, 325); and where the one excels in *sweetness* of *temper*, the other has the better *understanding*:

> Bingley was endeared to Darcy by the easiness, openness, ductility of his temper, though no disposition could offer a greater contrast to his own .... On the strength of Darcy's regard Bingley had the firmest reliance, and of his judgment the highest opinion. In understanding Darcy was the superior. Bingley was by no means deficient, but Darcy was clever. He was at the same time haughty, reserved, and fastidious, and his manners, though well bred, were not inviting. In that respect his friend had greatly the advantage. Bingley was sure of being liked wherever he appeared, Darcy was continually giving offence.   (16)

There are other passages designed to emphasize this contrast between Bingley's sweetness of *disposition* with Darcy's more rigorous and critical *understanding* (39, 49–50, 82). Darcy himself, as suits his superior *abilities*, is well aware of their relative strengths: "I have faults enough ... But they are not, I hope, of understanding. My temper I dare not vouch for. – It is I believe too little yielding – certainly too little for the convenience of the world" (58).

Elizabeth and Jane are contrasted in a similar way. Both are, as heroines, credited with the conventional perfection of a good *heart* and *temper* united with a good head. Darcy writes to Elizabeth that the contrast between them and the rest of the Bennet family "is honourable to the sense and disposition of both" (198). Jane's *temper* is as generous and compliant as that of Bingley (348), and her 'steady sense and sweetness of temper' (239), her 'excellent understanding and super-excellent disposition' (348), are commended. That last phrase implies what the novel well illustrates: that Jane's especial strength lies in her *temper*, in what Elizabeth calls her "sweetness . . . really angelical" (134). The contrast with Elizabeth presents a muted version of that between Darcy and Bingley, for Elizabeth is revealed in their discussion of the Bingley sisters (in whom she sees more to criticize than does Jane) to have 'more quickness of observation and less pliancy of temper than her sister' (15) – which is not to say that either girl is foolish or ill-natured (any more than either Darcy or Bingley is). Jane Austen is using the traditional categories with more finesse than does, for instance, Thackeray in *Vanity Fair* in the more broadly-drawn contrast between the good heart and weak head of Amelia and the hard heart and shrewd head of Becky.

Distinctions in *sense* are, in fact, as marked as those in manners. The contrasts within the Bennet family are emphatically drawn. Mr Bennet is a man of *abilities* and *talents* (236–7) married to a woman whose heart and head, *temper* and *talents*, do little to recommend her: 'she was a woman of mean understanding, little information, and uncertain [easily soured] temper. When she was discontented she fancied herself nervous'[7] (5; cf. 236). Elizabeth and Jane are much more intelligent than their "three very silly sisters" (232; cf. 5). Mr Bennet includes Mary – who furnishes a good example of the art of providing entertaining variety *within* a category, here that of sense, or rather the want of it. Mary's pompous would-be intellectualism furnishes a superb foil in folly to the empty-headed giddiness of Kitty and Lydia. Her moralizing response to Lydia's elopement is as unlike Lydia's as it well can be, but hardly more perceptive than the latter's brazen unembarrassment; and the response of Elizabeth and her father is the same in each case: to 'lift up [their] eyes in amazement' (289, 316). Kitty and Lydia resemble their mother in their 'Want of sense, either natural or improved', being, like her, both *ignorant* (231) and foolish.

Lydia herself is not conceived of as an ill-*natured* girl, but as a rather dangerous combination of a *temper* certainly not sour and a surplus of *spirits*, on the one hand, with a total want of sense and

manners (230–31), on the other. Of 'good-humoured countenance' and 'high animal spirits' (45), she is drawn to Mrs Forster
by a 'resemblance in good humour and good spirits' to herself
(230), and Elizabeth fears the worst from her "exuberant spirits",
which, coupled with her folly, have given her "the wild volatility,
the assurance and disdain of all restraint" characteristic of her
(231). Again, the novel is contrasting differences in kind and effect
within a category. The *spirits* so engaging in Elizabeth herself[8]
have produced in her youngest sister a parent's nightmare.

Head, heart, manners and spirits also underlie the characterization (in the narrative or by other characters) of more minor
personae. Sir William Lucas's daughter, Maria, is 'a good
humoured girl, but as empty-headed as himself' (152). Miss
Bingley's praise of Georgiana Darcy to her brother shows a rather
snobbishly selective reference to the categories that takes into
account only those aspects of them which had some social kudos:
"Such a countenance, such manners! and so extremely accomplished for her age!" (38–9). The narrative provides less shallow
commendation: 'there was sense and good humour in her face, and
her manners were perfectly unassuming and gentle' (261).

The above comments on these two narratives are not, of course,
meant as explanations of those narratives themselves – which are
much less schematic and more nuanced and mobile in their total
effect – but as illustrations of a conceptual model which influences
their organization and construction, and of the vocabulary associated with that model. Reference to the categories can even be
made with a touch of self-conscious humour, so regular a pro-
cedure was it with regard to character depiction. Of her heroine in
Northanger Abbey, Jane Austen early declares that, lest the
ensuing plot should fail to give 'any idea of what her character is
meant to be', she will briefly give some 'certain information' on
that point. She proceeds to run briskly through the categories,
awarding good marks for heart and spirits and indifferent ones for
manners and head:

> . . . her heart was affectionate, her temper cheerful and open,
> without conceit or affectation of any kind – her manners just
> removed from the awkwardness and shyness of a girl . . . and her
> mind about as ignorant and uninformed as the female mind at
> seventeen usually is.   (18)

It will be observed that Jane Austen is particularly interested in exploring the relative importance of the four different aspects of character, and that such evaluation of character is often a central principle of the narrative itself. For the very storyline may centrally concern the gradual revision (by reader and/or character(s) within the novel) of judgements of and comparisons between different persons. It will also be apparent that she is only too aware of how insidiously our judgement of people can be influenced by those qualities it is their felicity rather than their merit to possess: social *address* and/or spirits. Such people have a dangerous power of recommending themselves to the good opinion and affections before they have really deserved either. This is demonstrated most clearly (though rather over-emphatically for my own tastes) in *Sense and Sensibility* and *Mansfield Park*, in the rejection of Willoughby and the Crawfords in favour of Edward Ferrars, Colonel Brandon, Edmund Bertram and Fanny Price, whose manners are less animated and winning. But if the three former remain the more attractive characters, that may be a fault of life rather than of art. Jane Austen is herself fully aware that charm does not cease to charm the disabused. Willoughby's explanation of himself to Elinor is not accepted by her or by the novel as acquitting him, though it is allowed to mitigate his guilt somewhat; but even Elinor, with her exceptionally clear judgement, and fresh as she is from the bedside of a sister whose death has so nearly been the indirect result of his behaviour, is not exempt from the powerful spell cast by his personal presence:

> She felt that his influence over her mind was heightened by circumstances which ought not in reason to have weight; by that person of uncommon attraction, that open, affectionate, and lively manner which it was no merit to possess . . . But she felt that it was so, long, long before she could feel his influence less.   (*SS* 333)

Manners with the power to exert such an influence can be referred to precisely as *powers*, which are, in effect, powers to please.[9] Fanny, a young lady whose moral judgement is as incorruptible as Elinor's, finds, like Elinor, that she cannot be unaffected by the exercise of such *powers* in someone of whom that same judgement deeply disapproves; she cannot remain totally unresponsive to the felicity of Henry's address, once he has determined to make himself agreeable to her: 'she felt his powers; he was entertaining, and his manners were so improved . . .' (*MP* 232). Edmund, too, though observing Fanny's resistance to Henry's advances, reflects that, 'with such powers as his', he must succeed eventually (*MP* 335). The reference is to manner(s) calculated to please, the power of *address* possessed by a type presented to us in the varying guises of Willoughby, Wickham, Bingley, Henry Crawford, Frank Churchill, Frank Wentworth and William Elliot. Very worthless people can possess such powers. Lady Susan, the utterly unprincipled heroine of a comic story in the epistolary mode, has arts to please in abundance; and a prospective acquaintance of hers looks forward with mixed feelings to a display of those 'attractive Powers' of hers (*MW* 247) – *attractive* here having a sense closer to its etymology (Latin *ad-trahere* = draw towards) than it often has today. These powers the novels demonstrate to be often dangerously influential in assessment of and reaction to persons whose proper false is so easily impressed on waxen hearts – especially, though not exclusively, female hearts. Catherine, in the unfinished novel of that name, having met Edward Stanley, finds it 'impossible' to deduce anything but a very nice person from 'Manners at once so animated & insinuating' (*MW* 234). *Insinuating* has here the once common meaning of 'winding into one's good graces': Johnson's dictionary defines *insinuation* as 'the power of pleasing or stealing upon the affections [=feelings]'. The narrator then elaborates upon the many blessings of such winning ways that accrue to their possessor:

> He knew the powers of them himself; to them he had often been endebted for his father's forgiveness of faults which had he been awkward & inelegant would have appeared very serious; to them, even more than to his person or his fortune, he owed the regard which almost every one was disposed to feel for him, and which Young Women in particular were inclined to entertain.
>
> (235)

But on this matter the waters are deep, and errors of judgement of a reverse kind can also occur. There are two occasions on which a character excuses imperfect *powers* of this kind by referring his or her interlocutor to the good *heart* or disposition of the person under discussion. Emma, who has good taste in such matters, does not actually much like the rather studied and flowery gallantry with which Mr Elton attempts to recommend himself (*E* 49). Neither does Mr Knightley; but when he says as much, she replies:

> "Mr. Elton's manners are not perfect . . . but where there is a wish to please . . .. Where a man does his best with only moderate powers, he will have the advantage over negligent superiority. There is such perfect good temper and good will in Mr. Elton as one cannot but value." (111–12)

In *Sense and Sensibility*, Robert condescendingly qualifies his scorn at Edward's awkwardness in company with praise of his good heart and excellent disposition:

> ". . . a very good-hearted creature; as well-meaning a fellow perhaps, as any in the world . . . Poor Edward! – His manners are certainly not the happiest in nature. But we are not all born, you know, with the same powers – the same address. – Poor fellow! – to see him in a circle of strangers! – to be sure it was pitiable enough! – but, upon my soul, I believe he has as good a heart as any in the kingdom." (299)

In both cases there is obvious irony at work at the expense of the speakers, who (using the established categories) are voicing a piece of easy wisdom everyone can attain to but few can apply correctly or objectively. Emma's judgement is clouded by her plans for Mr Elton, who is simply a fortune-hunting hypocrite. Robert Ferrars, a shallow and affected fool, has no right at all to patronize his elder brother's temperament or manners, which are both much superior to his own. Furthermore, the distrust of personal charm can itself become pathological – as in the case of Lady Russell and Frank Wentworth, who (possessed of charm and spirit unbelied by any deficiencies in sensitivity and judgement) is more or less Willoughby rehabilitated. Anne's early attachment to him could well have formed matter for the plot of a cautionary novel such as the earlier *Sense and Sensibility*. But in *Persuasion*, interestingly, such suspicions, such a potential plot, are firmly set in the past and revealed by time to have been nearly tragically overcautious and inhibited.

The vocabulary generated by, and implicitly referring to, this mental model of 'character' is discussed in the following chapters, which, with respect to each in turn of the four major components of that model, attempt (a) to demonstrate how it figures in general terms in the novels, and in which of them it is more particularly at issue; and (b) to explain what words are used to place where within its particular lexical field. Occasional illustrative comparison will be drawn with other contemporary or near-contemporary writings to establish what kind of accepted usages Jane Austen was writing with, or against, or between. I have generally concentrated on actual usages rather than on codifications of usage (which are bound to some extent to simplify the material they rationalize). But, besides the *OED*, two further already-cited works of reference compiled nearer to Jane Austen's day have also been fairly frequently consulted: Dr Johnson's dictionary (published in 1755) and George Crabb's *English Synonymes* (1816) – which in some ways has a purpose quite opposite to that of the thesaurus its title suggests, concerned as it is to distinguish *from* each other words that occur in the same general category of meaning (thereby demonstrating the extent to which they are *not* synonymous).

3 Spirits

To be *in (good) spirits* implies cheerfulness and animation – qualities which make an important contribution both to personal happiness and to social intercourse. When Catherine Morland returns home from Northanger Abbey, her parents notice her most atypical 'loss of spirits': in her increased restlessness, 'she might only be a caricature of herself; but in her silence and sadness she was the very reverse of all that she had been before' (*NA* 240). Here, the loss both of cheerfulness and of the related ability to respond with animation to the environment occur simultaneously, and mark the twin results of subdued spirits: to be 'silent' and 'sad' is to be poor company both for oneself and for everyone else. This is abnormal for Catherine, who shares with Elizabeth Bennet the blessing of naturally buoyant and resilient spirits; Elizabeth cannot be dejected (even with good reason) for long (*PP* 90); and Catherine is naturally cheerful (18), talkative and active. Lack of *spirits* renders someone both miserable in himself/herself and boring or depressing company for others. Charles Musgrove's 'very good spirits' both make him agreeable company and enable him to put up with his fretful wife with rather more forbearance than another might be able to (*P* 43). Conversely, even that same querulous and selfish wife can be good company when she happens to be 'in excellent spirits' (219). So if one has them not, one had better be able to feign or command them – as Elinor Dashwood can (*SS* 141). Consistent *cheerfulness* thus regularly figures in depictions of male or female excellence, as it does in those of the (to modern tastes) repellantly perfect hero and heroine of Richardson's *Sir Charles Grandison* (e.g. II.441; cf. III.96).

Social occasions which have *spirit*, or where the conversation has 'spirit and flow' (*PP* 172), are, of course, remembered with pleasure. When Emma reflects on her feelings about Frank Churchill, with whom she has been toying with the idea of falling in love, she finds that her state of mind during his absence rather indicates that she has indeed done so; though it sounds to the reader as if the mild flirtation with him has simply given a certain agreeable *frisson* to a life in which Highbury, Mr Woodhouse and Harriet Smith offer little scope for the play of a lively intelligence:

> Certainly his being at Randalls had given great spirit to the last two weeks – indescribable spirit; the idea, the expectation of seeing him which every morning had brought, the assurance of his attentions, his liveliness, his manners! (*E* 262)

In a rather different context, Henry Crawford reflects with not dissimilar regret on the Mansfield theatricals: "There was such an interest, such an animation, such a spirit diffused! . . . We were all alive" (*MP* 225). Possessed, like Emma, of a lively mind, he can, like her, be bored into mischief and flirtation. *Spirit(s)*, then, can be associated with activities "more pleasant than prudent" (226); so it is perhaps apt that the theatricals had been aborted by the timely or untimely return of Sir Thomas, whose presence has in general, for good or ill, a rather repressive effect on the exercise of *spirit(s)* (463), and who speedily restores Mansfield life to its wonted blameless tranquillity and its 'sameness and gloom . . . rarely enlivened' (196).

Mansfield Park is one of the three novels in which the heroine is contrasted with, and to some extent even overshadowed by, the brighter *spirits* of an alternative heroine (someone, that is, who might well be the heroine in a different novel) to whom she is ultimately proved superior. For Mary Crawford is *lively* where Fanny is *gentle* – two epithets which regularly figure as antonyms in the literature of the period.

Liveliness connoted gaiety, zest and a sense of fun: the high spirits to which we would today apply the term **vivacity** (which, deriving from the Latin verb *vivere* (=to live), is itself the equivalent of *liveliness*). For instance, Elizabeth Bennet, simply for fun and out of 'high spirits', asks the solemn Mr Collins if he will think it proper to dance at Mr Bingley's ball; but the joke backfires when he replies by soliciting her hand for the first two dances – her consequent dilemma being attributed to an ill-timed 'liveliness' (*PP* 87) on her part, a quality obviously related to what in the same passage is referred to as her 'wit and vivacity' (88). Elsewhere the word is associated with *merry* and opposed to *serious* (*MP* 197, 348) and *sad* (*JAL* 478). Maria Bertram, having rather jealously observed the 'laughing' between Julia and Henry during the journey to Sotherton, anxiously and resentfully remarks to Henry that he finds her sister "more light-hearted" (fearing she may be outscored by Julia in the matter of *spirits*), and takes care to assure him that she is not, by nature, less "lively" than Julia (99). In other writers of the period, the word similarly refers to jesting, merriment and wit:

> . . . my uncle and cousin James laughed out at several places in your lively Letter. Lucy, Nancy, smiled. (*SCG* V.554; cf. I.107, 210; III.100; V.495)

And, though *lively* can be used in other contexts with its broader meaning of 'animated', it regularly has this narrower sense when used to characterize personality, speech or behaviour; as Crabb puts it in his *English Synonymes*, 'mirth and *jocundity* are the forms of *liveliness* which display themselves in social life'.[1] Jane Austen's gallery of very or slightly untrustworthy charmers, all well-endowed with address and spirits, regularly number *liveliness* among their personal assets: Willoughby (*SS* 333, 338), Bingley (*PP* 10, 14, 136), Crawford (*MP* 350) and Frank Churchill – to whom Emma, on first being introduced to him, at once mentally awards high scores in three of the four components of character: noting with approval his intelligence, his 'unexceptionable' address and the 'spirit and liveliness' in his countenance (*E* 190; cf. 262). But the *lively* aspect of *spirit(s)* figures especially in *Pride and Prejudice* and *Mansfield Park*.

Lively is a word much used of Elizabeth Bennet and Mary Crawford, often in association with such words as 'playful' and 'sportive', and it refers especially to their witty and often teasing manner of speech, their facility in turning an amusing jest, their flair for the comic. Elizabeth has a 'lively, playful disposition, which delighted in any thing ridiculous' (12); and uses 'a lively tone' when she turns a potentially serious moment with Colonel Fitzwilliam into a sprightly jest ("And pray what is the usual price of an Earl's younger son?", etc: 183). Mrs Gardiner in her letter to Elizabeth opines with arch pointedness that the one deficiency in

the solemn Darcy, his want of *liveliness*, may be rectified if he
marries judiciously (325); and Georgiana regards with admiring
horror Elizabeth's 'lively, sportive' manner of addressing that
same august personage (388).

Jane Austen delights unreservedly in the *liveliness* of Elizabeth,
but looks more critically at the same attribute in *Mansfield Park* –
the novel in which she is particularly concerned with that dangerous
charm of address and spirits which can so suborn the judgement
into a favourable verdict on the essential worth and disposition of
their fortunate possessor. Early in the novel she comments significantly of Tom Bertram that 'his agreeableness was of the kind to be
oftener found agreeable than some endowments of a higher stamp,
for he had easy manners, excellent spirits, a large acquaintance,
and a great deal to say' (47). The Crawfords are at once found to
possess 'manners . . . lively and pleasant, and Mrs. Grant immediately gave them credit for every thing else' (42). Mary Crawford's
spirits are her chief charm, and these are of the same *lively*
character as Elizabeth's: laughing, teasing, witty, merry. Her
'smiles and liveliness' (57) are always with her, and others repeatedly use the word *lively* to characterize her (65, 186, 199). The
term refers particularly to a manner of speaking – or writing (376)
– that is playful, witty, diverting, jesting. She does not, like Fanny,
respond to 'inanimate nature', for 'her attention was all for men
and women, her talents for the light and lively' (81). There seems
pretty certainly to be a pun intended here: Mary prefers **living**
people to inanimate nature and is not susceptible to the less
light-hearted reflections the latter evokes in Fanny.

Mary's *talents*, then, are for the light and merry rather than the
serious – and herein the novel seems to locate her limitations as
well as her charm. She is incapable of being serious on what the
narrative requires us to see as serious matters. Fanny finds the
sentiments expressed in her witty jests often offensive – especially
her comments on her boorish uncle and on short letters from
brothers. Fanny is perhaps too serious, too little *lively*, here; but it
is plain that Edmund too is uneasy, though he determines to see in
Mary's witty irreverence and cynicism only "a lively mind . . .
seizing whatever may contribute to its own amusement or that of
others" (64). Her "amusing sketch" of a very reluctant household
at divine service forces even him to hint at ill-timed levity,
however: "Your lively mind can hardly be serious even on serious

subjects", he comments (87).[2] When he later tells Fanny how
Mary made them "laugh" by her comic comments on Fanny's
reception of Henry's suit, Fanny is very pained by that particular
sample of 'Miss Crawford's liveliness' (354): and it must occur to
the reader that Fanny's evident extreme reluctance is worth
Mary's more serious concern. Towards the end of the novel,
Edmund meets Mary on her own home ground (in London)
instead of his, and writes to Fanny of his concern, associating
Mary's "high spirits", "lively mind" and "playful manner" (her
tendency to treat lightly and jestingly rather than seriously) with
"the weak side of her character" (421) which makes her vulnerable
to the potentially corrupting influence of fashionable society and
its worldly focus. The chain of events leading to Maria's elopement
with Henry begins in the home of 'a family of lively, agreeable
manners, and probably of morals and discretion to suit' (450).

Liveliness is one fairly typical form taken by *spirits* – an invaluable
instinct (constitutional or occasional) to find life fun. *Spirit*, in the
singular, can today imply pride, courage, independence, resolution –'poor-spirited' creatures are those with no fight in them,
quick to yield to pressure, whereas to have some *spirit* is to have a
tenacious sense of self and one's own desires, views or dignity. A
similar usage obtained in Jane Austen's day, when the singular
spirit was used with especial frequency of resentment or resistance
to insult or injustice:

> I thought I should have some difficulty to manage my own spirit,
> if I were to find myself insulted, especially by the General. (*SCG*
> III.229; cf. I.206; IV.366; *BLJ* 3.29)

> . . . her spirit was naturally high and would have revolted from
> the tyranny and injustice with which she was treated . . . . (*Mar.*
> 246; cf. 78–9)

Revulsion at any humiliating position, fancied or real, similarly
belongs to *spirit*. When Mary, the heroine of *Marriage*, realizes
that it must appear to Colonel Lennox that she has been "laying
snares for him", she weeps from the shame and anger born 'of a
naturally high spirit and acute feelings' (336; cf. 462; *SCG* VI.32).
Modern usage prefers the term 'pride' in these contexts –

especially in such as the last, for Mary is a quiet, serious, obedient girl, with whom we would not today associate 'a naturally high spirit'.

This sometimes rather painful kind of spirit the Bertram girls do not lack. Julia, we are told, has 'a warm temper and a high spirit' that inevitably make her resent keenly Henry's preference for her sister (162). Maria, 'who wanted neither pride nor resolution', can maintain an outward composure when Henry makes it quite clear that, despite the tenderness he has shown her, he has no intention of proposing to her: 'Her spirit supported her, but the agony of her mind was severe' (193). In a rather interesting passage, Henry is said, at the game of Speculation, to 'inspirit [Fanny's] play, sharpen her avarice, and harden her heart', he himself being 'in high spirits' and possessed of all the 'playful impudence that could do honour to the game' (240). So the kind of *spirit* that keeps one aware of and determined in one's own interests can manifest itself in resentment, pride, ruthlessness, shamelessness. But a total lack of any of those dubious qualities is not actually desirable; at the very least, it would probably render one incapable of giving anyone a good game of cards; but it would probably also result in a want of what we might today call 'strength of character'.

The connection through some of its connotations between *spirit* and 'strength of character' is one the Bertram girls are quick to make. Being themselves not without spirit, and being themselves good horsewomen, it suits them to praise Mary for the boldness that makes her quick to ride well. She rides as well as her brother, says Julia, and Maria adds that "her spirits are as good, and she has the same energy of character. I cannot but think that good horsemanship has a great deal to do with the mind". The complacency of this remark is, however, undercut by a comment from the narrator in which it is suggested that the girls are making an unwarranted deduction from the energy and gameness natural to *spirit(s)*:[3] '[Mary's] merit in being gifted by nature with strength and courage was fully appreciated by the Miss Bertrams' (69).

Fanny certainly lacks the *spirits* of Mary, and others have 'higher spirits' than she (234, 348). One of the chief and real benefits of her marriage with Henry Crawford would, Edmund points out (in an interesting counterpart to Mrs Gardiner's hint: see p. 48–9 *supra*), be the possibility of improvement in this regard:

"He is lively, you are serious . . . his spirits will support yours. It is your disposition to be easily dejected . . . His cheerfulness will counteract this . . . and his pleasantness and gaiety will be a constant support to you."   (348)

The reader is not, I think, intended to dismiss Edmund's arguments, though he has his own reasons for desiring the match. It could be what Jane Austen calls an 'eligible' marriage for Fanny on all sorts of grounds other than the social and economic advantages it would bring her; and that there are ultimately more important considerations making against her acceptance of Henry does not make that less true.

Fanny, then, is conceded by even her best friend to want *spirits*. But that she lacks *spirit* in one of its larger and more serious senses (the unspoken converse of Maria's deduction from Mary's *spirits*) is not true – though Maria, who rather despises Fanny, would doubtless be quite happy for that inference to be drawn. Fanny's resistance to the match pressed on her from all sides with all the arts its advocates can muster is not that of a spineless or poor-spirited girl. Fanny may not be *lively* or animated; but she is not weak. The novel touches on a discrimination within the category of *spirit(s)* which is to figure more pointedly in *Persuasion*. It is a word that much exercised Jane Austen's powers of discrimination. Because the word in the singular and/or plural could connote so many different attributes it was one likely to confuse the judgement. It could be all too easy to assume, because the accidents of semantic history had given one word the power to suggest a variety of things, that someone possessed of or lacking in one of its referents probably had or had not the others.

Such a discrimination certainly occurs in *Sense and Sensibility*, which also features a female character more immediately attractive than the heroine because possessed in a high measure of one form of *spirit*. Marianne has *spirit* of a different kind from that of Mary Crawford, and the attribute in question tends to be denoted by the singular rather than the plural form of the word. There is about her 'a life, a spirit, an eagerness' that immediately endears her (46). This is not the merry, playful, witty sense of fun that constitutes Mary Crawford's charm. Marianne's is *spirit* as it denoted ardour, passion, intensity of response. She is a vibrant girl, much more appealing than her more self-possessed sister. The words particularly associated with her are *animation* and *eagerness*.[4] Jane Austen is careful to emphasize, through Elinor, that one should not be misled into assuming one manifestation of *spirit(s)* presupposes the other qualities the word could also denote. When Edward rather wistfully distinguishes himself from Marianne by commenting that "gaiety never was a part of *my* character" (93), Elinor interposes with some decision:

> "Nor do I think it a part of Marianne's . . . I should hardly call her a lively girl – she is very earnest, very eager in all she does – sometimes talks a great deal and always with animation – but she is not often really merry."

Edward concedes the point, reflecting with some surprise: "and yet I have always set her down as a lively girl". The passage confirms that *lively* implied a sense of fun (it is here associated with *gaiety* and *merry*) – the subdivision of *spirits* in which Mary Crawford especially shines. More importantly, it shows the authoress characteristically careful to discriminate within one of her major categories of character assessment: it should not too hastily be assumed that all kinds of *spirit(s)* will be either co-present or co-absent in any one personality. We might still (especially if, like Edward, we were at the time not only unhappy, but also suffering from a sort of gloomy listlessness) assume that those from whom life called forth a response less lethargic and more animated were also blessed with a disposition naturally less melancholic and more sanguine. The above passage might well, nevertheless, puzzle a modern reader, who is inclined to feel he had not really needed to have it pointed out to him in so underlined a way that the obviously rather intense and solemn Marianne is not especially given to hilarity. That is because the conceptual category of *spirits*, with all its potentially misleading diversity of reference, no longer structures our perception of persons in so regular and major a way as it did at this period. That Edward could confuse *gaiety* with *earnestness*, and that Jane Austen plainly assumed it was an error some of her readers might share, is one example of the insidious influence of language over thought. The terminology we inherit divides and compartmentalizes experience in certain ways: the divisions are useful, but should not be used without question and caution.

Marianne tends to look for animation and spirit that matches her own. She is endearingly somewhat concerned about Edward as a prospective husband for the sister to whom she is truly and deeply devoted, confiding to her mother that "His eyes want all that spirit, that fire, which at once announce virtue and intelligence"; and that a man who reads aloud in such a *spiritless* manner must fall grievously short of what she would look for in anyone "who could seriously attach my sister" (17). One has some sympathy with her own passionate rebellion against genteel concealment of feelings she is not ashamed of having (her refusal to be "reserved, spiritless, dull" (48) with Willoughby); but she does tend to confuse the *spirit* and éclat with which emotions are registered and expressed with the feelings themselves. She therefore tends to deduce from composure (especially Elinor's) a *languid* absence of emotion (39), forgetting that it can equally proceed from control or restraint. Because Colonel Brandon does not show 'extatic delight' in music (35), or Edward 'rapturous delight' (19) in drawing, she suspects their feelings have little depth or reality. Willoughby has all the 'lively spirits' (48) calculated to attract her, and reads aloud 'with all the sensibility and spirit which Edward had unfortunately wanted' (48). As to Colonel Brandon, the two of them are 'prejudiced against him for being neither lively nor young' (50). For Marianne, it is chiefly his want of *spirit* that, for her, devalues any virtues of head or heart he may possess: "he has neither genius, taste, nor spirit . . . his understanding has no brilliancy, his feelings no ardour, and his voice no expression" (51). Against such a charge, Elinor replies that she can oppose only relatively "cold" praise, and she continues:

> "I can only pronounce him to be a sensible man, well-bred, well-informed, of gentle address, and I believe possessing an amiable heart."

By thus ticking off Colonel Brandon's high score in the other three categories of character, she implies an irrational injustice in Marianne's aversion to him on the very superficial grounds of want of spirit. Willoughby certainly takes the full force of Elinor's logic, and replies:

"Miss Dashwood . . . you are now using me unkindly. You are
endeavouring to disarm me by reason, and to convince me
against my will . . .."   (51)

The whole exchange nicely summarizes the merits on both sides of
the argument: Elinor's reason is acknowledged, but the *liveliness*
of this part and the remainder of Willoughby's reply exactly
exemplifies the sort of playful grace which the less vivacious spirits
of Colonel Brandon could never have found.

Though the novel is certainly making a point about the mis-
valuations prompted by the presence or absence of *spirit(s)*, it
mercifully refrains from pressing that point home by consigning
the two heroines to two such spiritless mates as we are earlier
required to visualize Edward and Colonel Brandon to be. That the
two should be sacrificed for life to moping miseries simply to point
a moral is more than human nature can bear. So the two lucky
suitors are restored to some measure of *spirits* before the novel
closes, and care is taken to suggest that at least part of their lack of
same was due to sorrow and anxiety rather than to innate phlegm
or melancholy. Elinor had earlier divined that Colonel Brandon's
marked gravity was the product of some 'oppression of spirits'
produced by circumstances rather than a constitutional 'gloomi-
ness of temper' (50); and we are assured that marriage with
Marianne 'restored his mind to animation, and his spirits to
cheerfulness' (379); and that marriage with Elinor produced
'regular cheerfulness of . . . spirits' in Edward (377).

Mansfield Park and *Sense and Sensibility*, then, are partly concerned with revealing the rather siren-like charm of different kinds
of *spirit(s)*, and with distinguishing between different aspects of
the phenomenon. The third novel in which this occurs is *Persuasion*. Anne is a heroine not unlike Fanny, in that she, too, is
gentle rather than *lively*, and lacks the attractive sparkle of *spirits*.
Her disposition and her history have combined to produce rather
subdued spirits in Anne. Lady Russell reflects that change of
residence might benefit both her 'health and spirits'; for her 'spirits
were not high' (15). She had been unhappy at school, 'grieving for
the loss of a mother whom she had dearly loved, feeling her
separation from home, and suffering as a girl of fourteen, of strong

sensibility and not high spirits, must suffer at such a time' (152). She is conscious of her own lack of spirits. Wondering whether Frank will prefer the prettier of the two Musgrove sisters or the one with the 'higher spirits', she reflects that 'she knew not *now*, whether the more gentle or the more lively character were most likely to attract him' (74). The italicized *now* makes it plain that, since Wentworth had once preferred *her*, Anne would, if she could be confident that his disappointment had not radically altered his tastes, know which of the two dispositions he found most congenial; and which of the two she identifies herself with is self-evident. Anne, in short, is rather sensitive on the subject of want of *spirit(s)* – and predictably becomes more so after she has overheard Wentworth implicitly accuse her of want of *spirit* as it betokens *firmness* in her earlier conduct toward him. Anne (and what he understandably feels to have been her weakness in yielding to Lady Russell's persuasion) is clearly in his mind in his remarks to Louisa, while they are in the hedgerow together, in praise of "fortitude and strength of mind . . . resolution enough to resist idle interference", and the evils of "too yielding and in-decisive a character", though the ostensible occasion for his comments is the relationship of Henrietta and Charles Hayter. Anne, who overhears the conversation, certainly applies his strictures to herself (89). He says to Louisa:

> "Your sister is an amiable creature; but *yours* is the character of decision and firmness, I see. If you value her conduct or happiness, infuse as much of your own spirit into her, as you can."   (88)

Louisa's main exercise of this kind of *spirit* occurs in her jump down the steps of the Cobb at Lyme; she does so against his advice – "I am determined I will" (109) – with near fatal results. Anne draws the appropriate moral for us, reflecting that this ought to make Wentworth reconsider his opinions on the value of 'firmness'; show him that, like other virtues, 'it should have its proportions and limits'; and that 'a persuadable temper' might not be so unquestionably inferior to 'a very resolute character' (116).

The incident is perhaps rather too contrivedly and clumsily designed to occasion precisely these moralizations, but it certainly does make its intended point about *spirit*. The *firmness* it can connote may or may not be a virtue, depending on how and when such *resolution* is exercised.

And there are, of course, other circumstances in which *gentle* rather than *lively* manners are likely to be found more congenial. Persons of raw sensibility will prefer an address that soothes rather than stimulates – persons such as Captain Benwick. A shy and retiring man, grieving under a recent bereavement, he responds positively to the 'mildness' and 'gentleness' of Anne's manner (100), which succeeds in drawing him out and gaining his confidence. And it is on the subject of his own *gentle* rather than *lively* disposition, as previously on Henrietta's, that Anne shows herself somewhat defensive and sensitive about want of *spirit(s)*. Admiral Croft tells her that he is an "active, zealous officer", though one might not predict it from his "soft sort of manner" (171). Anne replies quickly: "Indeed you are mistaken sir. I should never augur want of spirit from Captain Benwick's manners" (171–2). The amused sympathy of the authoress is registered in the minor comic embarrassment that ensues. Admiral Croft, having perfunctorily deferred to "ladies" as the "best judges" in such matters, still finds that Benwick is rather "too piano" for him, and he prefers Frank. Anne, of course, does not want to argue with *that* preference, having only meant, we are told, 'to oppose the too common idea of spirit and gentleness being incompatible with each other' (172). This is interesting, since Anne had herself, in private reflection, used *gentle* as the antonym of the *lively* disposition produced by the 'higher spirits' of Louisa (74). But the apparent contradiction only emphasizes the polysemy of the word, related to, though not exactly congruent with, the distinctions in meaning between the singular and plural form. In the first instance, she had been referring to *spirits* as it implied the *liveliness* of which *gentleness* really did connote one kind of opposite.[5] In the second, what is at issue is the sort of *spirit* that would make a good officer: *firmness* and *resolution*. Anne, being herself of the *gentle* disposition that marks the absence of the 'high spirits' possessed by the *lively*, and having heard herself accused of want of *spirit* in an apparent lack of *firmness* and *resolution*, is naturally anxious that the two meanings of the word should not be confounded: to establish, that is, that those whose *spirits* are not high may nevertheless not be deficient in that *spirit* that is firmness of character. Jane Austen has thus found it necessary to point out that the *eager* are not

necessarily *lively* (Marianne), and the shy and mild do not
necessarily want *firmness* and *resolution*, despite the potentially
confusing fact that *spirit(s)* could refer to any or all of these
qualities.

Persuasion may warn against overestimation of *liveliness*, and
even suggest some reservations on the value of *resolution*; but it
also sings a paeon the most heartfelt to the blessings of those *spirits*
that connoted **resilience**. Anne is struck by the fact that Mrs Smith,
despite her many misfortunes, appears to suffer very few bouts of
'langor or depression'. She is not, however, sustained by the
patience and endurance which philosophy or piety can sometimes
bring to a sufferer. Here, Anne feels, was something more than
that:

> ... here was that elasticity of mind, that disposition to be
> comforted, that power of turning readily from evil to good, and
> of finding employment which carried her out of herself, which
> was from Nature alone. It was the choicest gift of heaven.

In short, Mrs Smith's *spirits* had not failed her (154), had sustained
her through the thousand natural shocks the flesh is heir to. Even
at the close of the novel, as the authoress consigns her *gentle*
heroine of 'not high spirits' to the happiness she deserves, she does
not forget that *good spirits* are their own unfailing source of
happiness to such as Mrs Smith, whose contentment (her 'cheerfulness and mental alacrity') she considers in the same concluding
passage as, and compares with, that of Anne. The two women
have found equal happiness under two different aspects of character: Mrs Smith's was 'in the glow of her spirits, as her friend
Anne's was in the warmth of her heart' (252).

Spirit(s), then, denoted a wide variety of interrelated yet distinct
qualities: cheerfulness, sense of humour, animation, pride,
ardour, independence, resolution, resilience. It is perhaps worth
remembering that *spirits* had been used in medieval physiology as
a scientific term of biology (as it was then understood), denoting
'certain subtle, highly-refined substances or fluids (distinguished as
natural, animal and *vital*) formerly supposed to permeate the
blood and chief organs of the body' (*OED sv spirit sb* IV.16),
which provided the essential power or energy for the normal

operation of the vital functions.[6] The word is not used in this strict sense by Jane Austen, but it has left traces of its earlier reference to some literally animating or vitalizing principle in its association in her writings with (metaphorical) *life* and *liveliness* and in her view of *spirits* (or lack of them) as part of one's genetic make-up: they are not a virtue, but a blessing from 'Nature' (*MP* 69; *P* 154); one deserves no credit for them, but they are an incalculable felicity. In that respect, they are not unlike health; and, like health, they are also subject to environmental influences; that is, individuals can be 'in spirits' or 'not in spirits' according to their circumstances and moods, quite independent of the general health of spirits they constitutionally possess.

The verbal markers of a spirited or spiritless substratum are many and varied. *Lively* could also have a social sense – 'attended by much and varied company'. Mary Musgrove, piqued at Captain Benwick's change of mind about staying with them at Uppercross, declares they are "lively enough" (*P* 130) to provide entertainment for him – suspecting that he had been put off by supposing that there was nothing doing there, that its social life was rather restricted. Elizabeth Bennet realizes the deeper wisdom behind what seems at first Charlotte's strange choice of a room looking 'backwards' as her own sitting-room: Mr Collins's own room 'fronted the road', and he spends much of his time noting the carriages that pass; had the ladies sat in one 'equally lively' (*PP* 168), he would have been more with them. His room is *lively* in the sense that it commands a better view of the social traffic of the neighbourhood.

Gay is the opposite of *grave* (*MP* 349; WS 107), but it also had other senses. In medieval English, it was often used to mean **finely dressed**, and it could still occur in that sense: 'gayly, but not foppishly, dressed', 'She dresses very gaily' (*Evel.* 29, 53; cf. *FBD* 351; WS 297). By extension, it could mean visually **splendid**:

> Murray should *print* very cheap editions to undersell the pirates – and keep his gay Octavos of 7 shillings for the purchasers of higher priced former editions.   (*BLJ* 9.211; cf. WS 318)

Thus *gay* is linked in Crabb's *Synonymes* with *showy* and *gaudy*, from which it is distinguished by being an 'epithet of praise'.

This word, too, is also applied to social activities and events that both enliven and are enlivened by spirits. The plural *gaieties* was conventionally used of such occasions as dinners, balls, parties (*E* 312). Places and times and scenes that are *gay* are those that offer opportunities for socializing: Lydia Bennet and Maria Bertram feel the allure of Brighton, that 'gay bathing place', 'almost as gay in winter as in summer' (*PP* 232, *MP* 203). Persons too could be *gay* in the sense of **addicted to social pleasures** (*OED adj* 2):

> "Marry not a gay creature, who will be fluttering about in public, while you are groaning in your chamber. . ." (*SCG* III.58; cf. WS 284)

'Indulgence in pleasures' (Crabb) is what *gayness* of this kind refers to. Young rakes and officers (e.g. *Mar.* 204, 298) are often characterized as *gay* in this sense of 'compaignable and revelous', as Chaucer put it[7] – and their *gaieties* may be a euphemism for something worse (*SCG* II.322). A *gay* life, or a life of *gaiety*, denoted a life, not primarily of merriment, but one full of junketings (*MW* 116). Hence, in *Catherine*, Mrs Peterson sees with astonishment the entry into the ballroom of a niece she had supposed in bed with toothache, 'or amusing herself as the height of gaity with a book' (*MW* 220) – a rather witty extension of the social sense of the word (which would apply more properly to the ball Catherine arrives at). The word in this sense serves in *Mansfield Park* to mark off the suspect Crawford world from the more retired one into which they intrude. They bring with them occasion for social *gaiety* (70), and the theatrical venture is imported in imitation of the diversions devised by 'a large party assembled for gaiety' (121) by Mr Yates, a friend of the 'gay, agreeable, and gallant' Tom (114). This is the world Maria sells her soul for in marrying Rushworth, and Mary looks forward to owing her "a great many gay, brilliant, happy hours" (210) as a result. Fanny is in fact surprised that Henry returns to Mansfield, since "he is used to much gayer places" (116) – that is, **socially eventful** ones.

Arch meant something like **knowing**, and was an adjective used especially of expressions, facial or verbal, intended to carry implication or innuendo. This is still a basic part of the meaning of the word, which, however, today tends to keep rather more vulgar and silly company than it does in these novels – where it connotes less of affectation and denotes more specifically some knowledge that the speaker has, which he or she wishes it to be known that they possess, but which they often allow it to be understood they are unwilling to refer to more directly (*P* 176, 180, 196). Henry Tilney finds a classic opportunity for *archness* when he expresses the 'hope of [Catherine's] having been undisturbed by the tempest, with an arch reference to the character of the building they inhabited' (*NA* 174).

As Henry's piece of *archness* illustrates, such knowing looks or comments can often be affected for **teasing**, playful purposes. It tends therefore to be especially associated with the wit and fun that marks the *lively* disposition (cf. *SCG* I. 179, IV. 316). It will probably surprise no-one to learn that the most *arch* of Jane Austen's characters are Mary Crawford, Elizabeth Bennet and Emma Woodhouse. Emma is responsible for all such *archness* as occurs in the novel to which she gives her name (171, 287, 478). Mary Crawford accounts for all the instances in *Mansfield Park* (93, 145, 212, 259, 357) and Elizabeth all instances in *Pride and Prejudice* – which occur in conversations with Darcy (26, 91, 174), the mixture of 'sweetness and archness' (52) in her manner being largely responsible for her capturing the heart of that august personage. When the ever-gallant host of a party assembled at the home of Sir William Lucas presents her as a dancing partner to Darcy, asking if anyone could "object to such a partner", Elizabeth 'looked archly and turned away' (26). The knowledge that occasions this look is Elizabeth's awareness that Darcy *had* found her not handsome enough to tempt him at the Meryton ball. The other instances of her *archness* with Darcy also take the form of comments by which she indicates, in a winningly witty and playfully teasing manner, that she is very well aware of his feelings and motives.

Mary, Elizabeth and Emma are arch mistresses of the *arch*. The least competent in the art is the wonderfully naive Catherine Morland, who appears not even quite to understand the word. Isabella prefaces her declaration of being in love with James by an assertion that Catherine must already have guessed this; herself guilty of the coyest kind of *archness* in the modern sense, she declares that "that arch eye" of Catherine's "sees through everything" (117). Catherine, who has seen nothing of the tender feelings Isabella claims to have been aroused in her, and is not nearly *arch* enough to see through Isabella, feels only ashamed that she was not as full of 'arch penetration . . . as Isabella chose to consider her' (119). She later determines to make amends for her deficiency in this respect, and, noticing Isabella's restlessness at the Pump Rooms, decides to be *arch* (143), and says: "Do not be uneasy, Isabella, James will soon be here". Poor Catherine's attempt at *archness* is a miserable and double failure. In the first place, as the word connotes **shrewd, discerning** (the sense in which Isabella had used it: cf. *MW* 399), she has not been *arch* enough even to perceive the very patent change in the object of Isabella's affections; and in the second her comment is in any case rather too naive and explicit to be *arch*, which often connoted more of artful implication than of direct statement (cf. *MW* 350).

The most endearing piece of *archness* comes from a rather unlikely source: the shy and awkward Edward Ferrars, who is not at all of a *lively* disposition. The most engaging of the relationships portrayed in *Sense and Sensibility* is perhaps that between him and Marianne. After he has, with some surprise, heard her number hunting horses among the indispensable requirements of a "proper establishment", and observing later her consciousness at the name Willoughby, he whispers to her that he has been doing some guessing, and "I guess that Mr. Willoughby hunts"; and Marianne, 'surprised and confused', cannot help smiling 'at the quiet archness of his manner' (100).

Brilliant is another word that can have both a personal and a social reference. The word derives ultimately from the Latin word for the beryl, and passed into English via the French verb *briller* (to shine), of which *brilliant* is the present participle. Etymologically, therefore, it means 'glittering or sparkling like a jewel'. The metaphorical use of the term to indicate an abstract quality occurs most strikingly in the characterization of Frank Wentworth, in close association with words denoting the warmth and energy of spirit that constitute his peculiar charm: a man of 'intelligence, spirit and brilliancy . . . full of life and ardour' (*P* 26–7). This does not mean Frank is some kind of genius – which, though *intelligent*, he is not; but that there is an agility and play of imagination and wit in his speech, which makes it such as to 'strike the imagination'

(*OED adj* 2a). For the word is often used of intelligence and skills, especially verbal skills: **scintillating** (another metaphor from sparkling light) is probably the modern equivalent:

> He condescended ... to return wit for her wit ... and was exceedingly brilliant.   (*SCG* VII.266)[8]

The word was used to describe *Pride and Prejudice* by Jane Austen's sister Cassandra (*MW* 432) and by the Austen-Leighs in their *Jane Austen's Life and Letters* (264). The musical sense of *brilliant* (used of pieces that are fast, trillful and dazzling) is probably the most helpful here. *Brilliance* is among the qualities Marianne finds Colonel Brandon deficient in: "he has neither genius, taste, nor spirit ... his understanding has no brilliancy, his feelings no ardour, and his voice no expression" (*SS* 51). There is no wit or sparkle to his conversation; his intelligence is not of the kind to 'strike the imagination'.

As applied in this way to verbal dexterity, the word can shade off from the commendatory into the derogatory. Jane Austen's niece, Anna Lefroy, described Henry, the authoress's favourite brother, as 'the most talented' of the family, though

> There were others who formed a different estimate, and considered his abilities greater in show than in reality ... Brilliant in conversation he was, and ... blessed with a hopefulness of temper which ... seemed to create a perpetual sunshine.[9]

Henry seems not unlike Frank Wentworth, whose *brilliance* likewise raises in Lady Russell suspicions of 'abilities greater in show than in reality'. The word's ambidexterity between a right-handed cheer and a left-handed sniff at the merely flashy does much to explain her far from enthusiastic reaction when Frank's *brilliance* is seen a second time, a page later, through her eyes. Though he has neither money nor secure prospects, Frank, as sanguine by temperament as Henry Austen, speaks of his own hopes and plans with an ardour and confidence that, of course, succeed in 'bewitching' his adoring Anne. Lady Russell listens more sceptically:

> He was brilliant, he was headstrong. – Lady Russell had little taste for wit; and for anything approaching to imprudence a horror. She deprecated the connexion in every light.   (*P* 27)

Lady Russell is old enough to have conceived all the distrust of charming young men blessed with spirit and address that *Sense and Sensibility* counsels – and falls into the opposite error from that of the romantic Marianne by putting too *little* faith in fire and sparkle and *brilliance*.

Brilliant can also be used as an epithet for the eyes and complexion (*PP* 33, 271; *E* 39). Power to strike the eye and the imagination by a possibly unreliable lustre emanating from inner animation are all united in the account given by the Austen-Leighs of Anna Lefroy herself: 'brilliant both in looks and in intelligence, but . . . mercurial and excitable' (241). It is therefore noteworthy that, in Jane Austen's novels, the girl most blessed with that envied radiance or *brilliance* of complexion is Marianne, whose 'complexion was uncommonly brilliant' (*SS* 46) – an obvious analogue to that 'life . . . spirit . . . eagerness' which emanates from her eyes (*ibid*). Interestingly, when beauty is indicated in a girl by nature and circumstances of rather subdued spirits, the term *brilliant* is explicitly rejected. Emma, whose good taste and honesty generally outweigh her prejudices with regard to Jane Fairfax, has always admired Jane's skin; but, when defending that admiration, is forced to acknowledge that its beauty is rather of the fine and delicate stamp, and "was certainly never brilliant" (199).

The word is also regularly found applied to social events of the finer and grander sort, especially balls. Such phrases as 'a brilliant assembly', 'the brilliancy of the ball' are common (*Mar.* 450; *MW* 323, 336; *P* 185). The usage often associates itself with a literal brilliance characteristic of such occasions, on which jewels were worn[10] and on which no expense on lighting and candles was spared: 'The room was very magnificent, the lights and decorations were brilliant, and the company gay and splendid', writes Evelina (39; cf. 37, 193). When Miss Bates arrives at the ball at the Crown Inn, with her usual spate of eager, appreciative comments, her praise of the *brilliance* of the occasion includes particular mention of the lavish provision of lighting: "Well! This is brilliant indeed! – This is admirable! – Excellently contrived upon my word. Nothing wanted. Could not have imagined it. – So well lighted up" (*E* 322; cf. *MW* 327). She uses the same word to describe the supper room: "Well, this is brilliant! I am all amazement! could not have supposed any thing! – such elegance and profusion!" (330). Here the stylishness and lavishness gloss *brilliant*, by which Miss Bates clearly means **splendid** in its modern vaguely superlative sense. The metaphorical and literal senses are played off one against the other in *Marriage*, when the heroine refers to a ball as a "brilliant scene", and is answered by her jaundiced interlocutor that it was "brilliant enough – if you mean, that there was a glare of light, enough to blind the devil" (301). The glamour and splendour of a ball again elicit the adjective when Fanny rather disconsolately compares the excitement of the ball at Mansfield Park with the quiet dullness that prevails the morning after:

> Last night it had been hopes and smiles, bustle and motion, noise and brilliancy in the drawing-room, and out of the drawing-room, and every where. Now it was languor, and all but solitude. (283)

The contrast with one of the antonyms of *spirit – languor –* agrees with the association of *brilliance* with *spirit* at a ball elsewhere (*MW* 336). A similar contrast is apparent in the brief history given of the Crown Inn in *Emma*; it had once been the scene of many a ball, 'but such brilliant days had long passed away, and now the highest purpose for which it was ever wanted was to accommodate a whist-club' (197). Again, *brilliant* characterizes splendid and animating social occasions and contrasts with flatter and duller proceedings. Mary Crawford hopes Maria after her marriage will provide "a great many gay, brilliant, happy hours" (*MP* 210): that is, **splendid** and exciting social occasions.

The word could also be applied to the people whose presence guaranteed the *brilliance* of the occasion. For instance, Jane Austen's cousin Eliza, who made a very prestigious marriage with a French aristocrat, lists among its advantages "a numerous and brilliant acquaintance" (*Life and Letters*, 38), by which she means what we would today term **illustrious**.[11] *Brilliant* people in this sense are celebrities. The disgrace of Maria Rushworth (which in the event deprives society of the "gay, brilliant hours" she might have furnished as a fashionable hostess) is announced with disingenuous "concern" by one newspaper as the loss of one "who had promised to become so brilliant a leader in the fashionable world" (*MP* 440): that is, one who would become illustrious in it, whose presence at and invitations to social events would be sought after.

It is significant that the vocabulary of *spirit(s)* often has a social dimension – for it is in the context of social intercourse that *spirit* is at a premium. Those who possess it may or may not be the most feeling or the wisest of humanity, but they are likely to provide *amusing* company. The human need for *amusement* inflates their value somewhat. It is chiefly company – then and now – that we turn to as our major resource in this respect. Even the rather retiring Fanny can, in the aftermath of that *brilliant* ball, equate 'solitude' with *languor*.

Amusement tends today to imply the comic, and is most often used of what occasions mirth. Jane Austen used the word in its broader sense of whatever provides **interest**, **entertainment** or **occupation**. To *amuse* is 'to occupy the mind . . . by engaging [it] on some present occupation' that 'serves to kill time, to lull the faculties, and banish reflection' (Crabb). It may sometimes happen that such diversion is also 'amusing' in the modern sense, but the term can also be used where there can be no question of a smiling or laughing response. When, for instance, in Scott's *The Highland Widow*, Mrs Bethune Baliol approaches the grim figure of Elspeth Mactavish, the latter guesses that it is 'curiosity, arising out of her uncommon story' which brings her, and 'she could not be pleased that a fate like hers had been the theme of a traveller's amusement' (WS 137) – though Elspeth's terrible history could never *amuse* anyone in the modern sense of the word.

The term is particularly associated with places of social resort, whether this be on a large scale, as with fashionable towns like London, Bath, Lyme – all assumed to be productive of *amusement* to those who frequent them (*SS* 156; *NA* 139, 207; *P* 95); or on a smaller, as with the houses of friends and neighbours and the **entertainment** received there (*SS* 54, 99, 143; *NA* 212, 220; *P* 134). The word can also be used of pastimes and interests generally (*SS* 47), or of anything which serves to occupy the mind and stave off boredom: news and chat (*SS* 193), music (*P* 50), knitting (one of the curtailed range of *amusements* left Mrs Smith: *P* 155) – or books[12] – though here the word tends to be found ironically in connection with those too stupid or self-engrossed to find reading at all **interesting**. John Thorpe declares Mrs Radcliffe's novels "amusing enough" (*NA* 49), but plainly either has not read them or has so imperfect a memory of all books as to muddle them all up with one another. Sir Walter Elliot was a man 'who, for his own amusement, never took up any book but the Baronetage' (*P* 3) – in order to study complacently his own name in it. And then there is that memorable attempt by Caroline Bingley to feign an interest in books in order to impress Darcy – the only recourse left her, since he evidently finds the book he is reading more interesting than conversation with her:

> At length, quite exhausted by the attempt to be amused with her own book, which she had only chosen because it was the second volume of his, she gave a great yawn and said, "How pleasant it is to spend an evening in this way! I declare after all there is no enjoyment like reading! How much sooner one tires of anything than of a book! When I have a house of my own, I shall be miserable if I have not an excellent library."   (*PP* 55)

Unless they are Gothic horror stories, books do not generally succeed in providing much effectual *amusement* to the younger generation in these novels. Indeed there is a strong presumption that *amusement* implies and entails society, and that it is to be found *abroad* as opposed to at home. When Henry Tilney, with a mock sententiousness characteristic of him, remarks that Catherine's time must be spent so much more "rationally" in the *country*, because in town she is "in pursuit only of amusement", Catherine, with the refreshing naiveté and honesty equally characteristic of her, replies that she has no higher aim at home:

> "And so I am at home – only I do not find so much of it. I walk about here, and so I do there; – but here I see a variety of people in every street, and there I can only go and call on Mrs. Allen."   (*NA* 79)

When she eventually returns home, moping and listless, after a long absence, her mother remarks rather severely: "You have had a long run of amusement, and now you must try to be useful" (240). At home the young tend to be bored and/or useful; one goes *out* to be *amused*. That presumption is so strong that *amusement* can even stand in antithesis to 'home', as implying engagements abroad: Jane Fairfax had enjoyed with the Campbells 'all the rational pleasures of an elegant society, and a judicious mixture of home and amusement' (*E* 164).

The world can provide *amusement* of a more informal sort even when it has no express intention of the kind. Charles Bingley finds Elizabeth to be "a studier of character", and observes, "It must be an amusing study"; Elizabeth assents: "Yes; but intricate characters are the *most* amusing. They have at least that advantage" (*PP* 42). Society need not even put itself to the trouble and expense of a ball or a dinner to provide **interest** or *amusement* of this sort to the observer. It is characteristic of Jane Austen's more sophisticated and intelligent heroines to gain *amusement* through their own private observations; and it is in this context that the word most frequently coincides with the modern meaning 'mirth-provoking', for they are often entertained in such a way as to smile. Emma and Elinor can occasionally be *amused* in this way (*E* 27; *SS* 232, 301). This type of *amusement* calls for a certain amount of sophistication and capacity for detachment, and is not therefore open to the naive or the intense: Catherine, Marianne and Fanny must find themselves other *amusements*. It also generally requires an unconsciousness on the part of those furnishing it, for it is essentially private. These two factors taken together perhaps account for the extremely high frequency of this species of *amusement* in *Persuasion*. Anne has the maturity and humility to smile at herself: she 'could not but be amused at the idea of her coming to Lyme, to preach patience and resignation' to Captain Benwick (101); the imagination and awareness to smile at those about her – at Henrietta, for instance, or the Crofts (103; 92, 128); and the thoughtfulness to find 'more than amusing' Captain Harville's domestic accommodations, which provoke some wistfully melancholic reflections in her (98). Even her own improvement in looks, the admiration of Mr Elliot, his surprise at discovering her identity, occasion her nothing stronger than the mild entertainment of *amusement* (124, 143), for her heart is not free, hopeful or young enough to be fluttered by such things. And, towards the end of the novel, secure in a happiness known as yet only to herself and Frank, she has the *amusement* of meeting the Wallises with an understanding (gained from Mrs Smith) of their mistaken assumptions about an imminent marriage between herself and Mr Elliot (246). These moments are symptoms of the richly and often poignantly private world of *Persuasion*, and the detachment they testify to has its profounder analogue in the way in which Anne, of a retiring disposition accentuated by a continuing but necessarily concealed sorrow, has become detached from her world; those around her are universally ignorant of her feelings, and largely indifferent to them. There is a consequent disjunction between her own private emotional drama and the external events and social contexts in which it occurs. Her griefs, anxieties and even her happiness occur at a tangent from the focus of interest of those around her, who are unaware of what she feels; and the near autonomy of her emotional life blossoms finally into a radiant self-sufficiency of happiness that is blissfully independent of the external world ('Anne saw nothing, thought nothing of the brilliancy of the room. Her happiness was from within': 185), through which she moves glowing with a content it is quite unaware of and irrelevant to.

The antonyms of *spirit(s)* are as various as the implications of the word itself. *Languor* is one of the most frequent. *Languid*, according to Crabb, belongs with, but is more extreme than, *faint*, and indicates that 'which has lost its spirit'. Lady Bertram, totally without energy of mind or body, speaks characteristically in a 'tone of calm languor, for she never took the trouble of raising her voice' (*MP* 218; cf. 283, 338). Marianne finds the behaviour of Elinor and Edward very "cold . . . composed . . . languid" for supposed lovers (39): that is, **spiritless**, lacking in ardour. Mrs Smith, with her resilient elasticity of spirits, has 'moments only of languor and depression' (*P* 154) – is only occasionally **dispirited** or **listless**. 'Languor and . . . solitude' contrast with the animation, bustle and *brilliance* of a last evening's ball (*MP* 283): a dullness inducing a lowness or dejection of spirits. And the opposite of *brilliant* and *lively* talk occurs in the desultory, predictable and incongruously 'very, very languid remarks on the probable Brilliancy of the Ball' (*MW* 323). It is a mark of the volatility of Marianne's spirits that her emotional trauma leaves her without any resilience of spirit to bear her up. There are moments when 'her spirits' are 'quite overcome' to such an extent that she is not even able to sustain tolerable composure in public (*SS* 236); and the contrast with her former *eager* and *animated* self is accentuated, when she becomes not only out of spirits, but, as a consequence of her fever, also **lethargic**, 'weary and languid', 'languid and low' (307, 308) – where the para-medical sense of the word[13] makes her deterioration in health parallel that in her spirits.

Dull is a word often used to characterize the unanimated or unanimating in various ways. It can have much the same meaning of **boring**, **uninteresting** as it has today: as with those *dull* history books Catherine wondered that anyone's *courage* [heart, spirit[14]] would serve them to write (*NA* 108–9). As applied to persons, it is used especially of those whose conversational powers are the very reverse of *brilliant* or *lively*. In *Marriage* (430) *dull* opposes the vogue Gallicism *spirituel* (lively, witty, sprightly), and Evelina says she would prefer the company of 'dullness itself' to that of the would-be 'sprightly' Mr Smith, who is 'desirous of appearing a man of gaiety and spirit' (*Evel.* 178). In *Emma* the word is applied bad-temperedly by the home-loving John Knightley to a prospective evening engagement offering "nothing to say or hear that was not said and heard yesterday, and may not be said and heard again tomorrow" (113).

Deficiency of conversational vitality is found in its extremest form in those who say nothing at all. Hence *dull* can indicate a quantitative as well as a qualitative defect. Mary Musgrove, too self-engrossed to detect any causes of silence other than constitutional phlegm or bad manners, declares of Captain Benwick: "He is one of the dullest young men that ever lived. He has walked with me, sometimes, from one end of the sands to the other, without saying a word" (*P* 132). Edward Ferrars, shy and 'not in spirits' (*SS* 90), incurs the epithet for similar reasons: 'His gravity and thoughtfulness returned on him in their fullest extent – and he sat for some time silent and dull' (95). For both *grave* and *silent* can collocate with *dull*. Colonel Brandon Marianne finds wanting in *brilliance*, *ardour* and *spirit*; and Charlotte Palmer puts this more simply, when, with her habitual cheerful self-contradiction and vapid use of the word *charming*, she declares: "He is such a charming man, that it is quite a pity he should be so grave and so dull" (*SS* 115).

Absence of liveliness can also be indicated by *dull* as it means **glum, dejected, low-spirited**:

They said, that he had always appeared very low-spirited, but, for the last month, he had been *duller* than ever.   (*Evel.* 177)

Lady Emily was too dull herself . . . to take any notice of Mary's
dejection.   (*Mar.* 387; cf. *DJ* V.8)

Emma attributes the dullness of the Box Hill outing in large part
to the behaviour of the man who would generally guarantee 'great
spirit' (262) to a social occasion: Frank Churchill, whom she has
never seen 'so dull'. He is 'silent . . . said nothing worth hearing
. . . admired without intelligence. While he was so dull . . .' (367).
The effects are inevitable. Dull company produces nothing but an
occasion of 'downright dulness'. But that quantity and cheerfulness of talk are not incompatible with *dullness* is proved by Miss
Bates, from whose mouth there issues a constant spate of mun-
danities, and whose *dullness* is (on this same occasion) the subject
of a piece of *liveliness* from Emma that the heroine comes sorely to
regret – though surely only a saint could have resisted such
temptation. Frank Churchill jestingly demands that everyone
should say something *clever* or *entertaining* – or three things of an
opposite nature, "three things very dull indeed". Miss Bates
declares she will have no difficulty with the latter, and the unlucky
jest occurs when Emma responds that her difficulty will be rather
in limiting herself to "only three" (370).

It will be observed that *dull* is here conceived as the opposite not
only of *entertaining*, but also of *clever*: the negation of wit, in
short. *Dull* in the sense of **obtuse**, **imperceptive** makes a famous
appearance in Wordsworth's sonnet on Westminster Bridge: 'Dull
would he be of soul who could pass by / A sight so touching in its
majesty'; and the related sense **unintelligent, stupid** is one im-
mortalized in the goddess Dulness, the deity of fools and dunces in
Pope's *Dunciad*. This sense also occurs, significantly, in *Emma*.
For it is Emma's fate to be surrounded by people considerably less
clever than she is. It is not for nothing that her troubles, together
with the novel itself, begin with the removal of Mrs Weston, who
(apart from Mr Knightley) must have been the only person with
whom she could converse on equal terms. Her new companion,
Harriet, is no brighter than Miss Bates. Mr Elton's charade, whose
answer Emma fairly immediately guesses, has to be explained to
her after she has herself puzzled over it to no effect 'in all the
confusion of hope and dulness' (72) – that is, lack of understanding or penetration.

Persons can thus be the *dull* reverse of stimulating company by being taciturn, glum, boring or dull-witted. The adjective can also be applied to them to negate entertainment in a subjective way: meaning 'lacking anything to amuse oneself with', 'lacking entertainment' (cf. *BLJ* 2.50, 105). When the heroine of *Catherine* is prevented by toothache from attending a ball, her aunt hopes she may find a book to "amuse herself with", for the poor girl "must otherwise be very dull" (*MW* 220): that is, **bored, unentertained**. *Dull* in this sense is used especially of those who lack the entertainment of company, who have no or limited opportunities for social intercourse:

> I was very glad of your letter this morning, for, my mother taking medecine, Eliza keeping her bed with a cold, and Choles not coming, made us rather dull and dependant on the post.   (*JAL* 240; cf. 235)

Margaret Lesley, in the mock epistolary novel *Lesley Castle*, reveals how often the **unoccupied** sense of *dull* could imply **lacking company**:

> But tho' retired from almost all the World, (for we visit no one but the M'Leods, the M'Kenzies, the M'Phersons, the M'Cartneys, the M'Donalds, the M'Kinnons, the M'lellens, the M'Kays, the Macbeths and the Macduffs) we are neither dull nor unhappy; on the contrary . . . not an hour in the Day hangs heavy on our hands. We read, we work,[15] we walk . . .
> (*MW* 111)

Margaret might be supposed *dull* because (she is pleased to think) she **lacks society**; but she congratulates herself on not being so shallow as to be, without company, **unoccupied**.

The word is thus quite frequently used of persons from whom congenial company has recently departed. Mrs Jennings, a woman nothing if not gregarious, adds her own lively simile to represent the horrors of such *dullness*: "Ah! Colonel, I do not know what you and I shall do without the Miss Dashwoods . . . Lord! we shall sit and gape at one another as dull as two cats" (*SS* 280). Her predictions are not wide of the mark, for when the Dashwoods do depart from Cleveland, the two are left to 'feel their own dulness, till Mrs. Jennings was summoned to her chaise to take comfort in the gossip of her maid for the loss of her two young companions' (341). Lady Catherine similarly, on the departure of her nephews from Rosings, sends a gracious message to the Parsonage announcing that 'she felt herself so dull as to make her very desirous of having them all to dine with her' (*PP* 210). And Mrs Bennet finds herself 'very dull for several days' (330) after the departure of her newly-married favourite daughter, Lydia – though the parting occasions comically little reciprocal sensibility in the young lady herself. Perhaps the most pointed use of *dull* to refer to that sensation of flatness which is induced by the withdrawal of company one has enjoyed comes in *Mansfield Park* – when Henry Crawford returns for a fortnight to his Norfolk estate, 'a fortnight of such dulness to the Miss Bertrams, as ought to have put them both on their guard, and made even Julia admit in her jealousy of her sister, the absolute necessity of distrusting his attentions, and wishing him not to return' (114). Similarly, feeling *dull* in his absence is, in Emma's eyes, evidence that she must be in love with Frank Churchill (262).

As applied to places or locations, *dull* indicates the opposite of *lively* and *gay* in their social senses: that is, **absence or poverty of society** on offer (*SS* 123; *NA* 115). In a nice counterpart to the *liveliness* (social business) of Mr Collins's room (from which he could watch the carriages go by), there is the situation of Delaford, which Mrs Jennings is delighted (for Marianne's sake) to announce is "never dull", for, since it is near the turnpike road, "you may see all the carriages that pass along" (*SS* 197) – a facility one suspects Marianne is not likely to appreciate or utilize. The two words are used in contrast with one another by Mary Musgrove in her comments upon Captain Benwick's declining the invitation to stay with them: "I suppose he was afraid of finding it dull", she says with offended resentment; "but upon my word I should have thought we were lively enough at the Cottage for such a heart-broken man as Captain Benwick" (*P* 130): they could surely offer company enough, that is, for one in a condition usually associated with an instinct to shun society. A dull season or place is one that offers no or few social engagements. Mary, with her constitutional tendency to feel herself ill-used, shows herself petulantly defensive and resentful about what she seems to regard as her less lively situation in the country; her irritable quickness to fancy Uppercross slighted by Captain Benwick is matched by the sulkily accusing tone of her letter to Anne:

"I make no apology for my silence, because I know how little people think of letters in such a place as Bath. You must be a great deal too happy to care for Uppercross, which, as you well know, affords little to write about. We have had a very dull Christmas; Mr. and Mrs. Musgrove have not had one dinner-party all the holidays. I do not reckon the Hayters as any body."   (162–3; cf. *PP* 237, 215; *MP* 199; *SS* 34)

That last sentence crossly justifies the term *dull*, for it carried in such contexts heavy implications of 'not seeing anybody'.

Analogous with *dull* is *stupid*. In Jane Austen's English, the adjective had not yet diverged from the related noun *stupor*,[16] and *stupid* as used by her may be glossed 'afflicted with or inducing stupor': that is, **lethargic, dull, boring, leaden**. It too can be applied to persons and to social occasions, and, like *lively* and *dull*, to reading matter (conversation and company at one remove). *Stupid* literature is dull, heavy, turgid stuff. When John Thorpe calls some of the Gothic romances mentioned by Catherine "stupid", he is using the word in opposition to those he finds "amusing enough" (*NA* 48–9; cf. *JAL* 304); he is not nearly clever enough to find them stupid in the modern sense. Catherine, who found history *dull*, cannot believe General Tilney is really going to sit up all night reading 'stupid pamphlets' (187): activities of a more thrillingly macabre nature are what her imagination, fed by distinctly more exciting reading, foresees. In this sense of **dull, boring**, *stupid* can be applied to a variety of such other things as places, letters or topics of conversation (*Evel.* 334; *Mar.* 6; *BLJ* 2.216, 245, 3.92).

Social occasions that are *stupid* are similarly dull, boring, ordinary, spiritless affairs. Exclamations of ennui and irritation such as 'Another stupid party' and 'I never was at a stupider Ball' are frequent in the *Letters* and minor works (*JAL* 128, 131; *MW* 120, 225). When no new acquaintances are made or when the conversation is flagging or unremarkable, the occasion is judged *stupid* (*JAL* 40, 126, 348; *MP* 199; *PP* 166). Anne Elliot, who moves through the public world of *Persuasion* with griefs and joys so intensely private, becomes, even with her *gentle* nature, as her personal emotional drama reaches its hidden climax, irritated and frustrated by the irrelevancies of her social context: even company normally congenial becomes distracting (178), and especially wearisome is the 'elegant stupidity' (genteel dullness and vacuity) of the private parties in which her father and sister delight (180).

As applied to people, the adjective has a slightly greater variety of nuances. Here too it can mean boring or **uninteresting** (*SS* 247; *MP* 138; *PP* 14, 74). Mr Collins, ponderously empty of any personal asset that might render his company agreeable, is the epitome of *stupidity*, as Elizabeth, whose very exasperation takes a *lively* turn, indicates:

> "I have a very poor opinion of young men who live in Derbyshire; and their intimate friends who live in Hertfordshire are not much better. I am sick of them all. Thank Heaven! I am going to-morrow where I shall find a man who has not one agreeable quality, who has neither manner nor sense to recommend him. Stupid men are the only ones worth knowing, after all."   (*PP* 154)

Henry Crawford, however, is probably using the word in a slightly different sense when, by now attracted to Fanny, he refers to the perpetual tasks imposed on her by Lady Bertram's *stupidity*, and her patient submission to "that stupid woman's service" (*MP* 296). Here **lumpish** might provide the closest equivalent in sense and gallantry to the epithet chosen by Henry, which obviously refers to the phlegmatic inertia of mind and body characteristic of Lady Bertram as well as to her vacuity. Lady Bertram in fact uses the epithet of herself on that anti-climactic morning after the ball: "I feel quite stupid . . . Fanny, you must do something to keep me awake. I cannot work. Fetch the cards, – I feel so very stupid" (283). The sense, if not the tone, is similar: she feels **apathetic, leaden, lethargic** (cf. *Evel.* 325); though it is amusing to find her apparently surprised by and discontented with a *stupidity* that would have been recognized as a pretty perpetual condition with this least animated of all Jane Austen's characters.

Apathetic, lethargic is also the sense in which Emma uses the word, in close proximity to *dull*, when she contrasts her present listless discontent with the 'indescribable spirit' Frank Churchill's presence had given to the previous fortnight (262). In the same novel, the adjective is used repeatedly, together with *dull*, to characterize that outing to Box Hill, which is as oppressively unenjoyable as only parties which fail of the express purpose of enjoyment for which they are formed can be. Emma 'had never seen Frank Churchill so silent and stupid' (367). For his own reasons, Frank does grow more lively, only to become aware of a similar pervading *stupidity* around him: "Our companions are excessively stupid. What shall we do to rouse them? Any nonsense will serve. They *shall* talk" (369). The reference is to a phlegmatic lack of response manifesting itself primarily in uncommunicativeness. Cheery Mr Weston gladly lends a third tongue to the efforts of Frank and Emma, but his conundrum has no effect in producing any more general enlivenment, for 'some looked very stupid about it' (371): that is, **unmoved, unresponsive**.

Stupid is used in social contexts as a rebuking reference to words or behaviour which express disinclination to 'enter into the spirit' of the proceedings. When Mrs Gardiner suggests a visit to Pemberley, Elizabeth in some embarrassment feigns ennui at visiting great houses: 'after going over so many, she really had no pleasure in fine carpets or satin curtains'. Though it is not in this case genuine, such an attitude is most irksome and unhelpful in a party on holiday, and Mrs Gardiner accordingly 'abused her stupidity' (*PP* 240). It is in similar contexts that the word is twice used of Darcy, whom not even his worst enemies could call *stupid* in the modern sense. When he attends the Meryton ball only to take no part in it, his friend says impatiently: "Come Darcy . . . I must have you dance. I hate to see you standing about by yourself in this stupid manner. You had much better dance" (11; cf. 180). Darcy's aloofness from the proceedings, expressing lack of response to them, makes him a leaden presence that others find dampening. One should dance at balls and converse in company. To be bad at either is a misfortune; but lack of any participatory response constitutes a *stupidity* that is hugely obstructive to social spirit.

Phlegmatic, slow of response is what Henry Tilney means by the word when, in reply to Catherine's surmise that novels would not be "clever" enough for male taste, he says:

> "The person, be it gentleman or lady, who has not pleasure in a good novel, must be intolerably stupid. I have read all Mrs. Radcliffe's works, and most of them with great pleasure." (*NA* 106)

The passage should be noted by those who view *Northanger Abbey* as an exposé of the inanity of the popular novels of the day; for Henry's is the most authoritative voice in this work.

The meaning **obtuse, dull-witted** is also found. Mr Palmer puns on both *stupid* and *dull* when he says in exasperation at the bad weather:

> "Dulness is as much produced within doors as without, by rain. It makes one detest all one's acquaintance. What the devil does Sir John mean by not having a billiard room in his house? How few people know what comfort is! Sir John is as stupid as the weather."   (*SS* 111)

Here the sense **dull**, **boring** (Sir John is being compared with the weather) combines with **obtuse** (his lack of insight into "comfort"). The same pun (**dull/tiresome** and **uninspired/obtuse**) is made rather more wittily by Byron to vent a similar fit of spleen:

> . . . we have had lately such stupid mists – fogs – rains – and perpetual density – that one would think Castlereagh had the foreign affairs of the kingdom of Heaven – also – upon his hands.   (*BLJ* 5.86)

Of the non-derogatory antonyms of *spirit(s)*, *gentle* is the most important. This is the word used to characterize the two heroines Anne and Fanny, and the one used by Anne when she wishes to indicate without denigrating the opposite of a *lively* temperament (*P* 74). Similarly, Emma Watson, on being warned by her eldest sister that her refined habits will be subjected to the "wit" and laughing "ridicule" of another sister, Penelope, who has "great spirits, and never cares what she says", asks of the remaining sister, "Margaret is more gentle I imagine?"; to which the answer is, "Yes – especially in company; she is all gentleness & mildness when anybody is by" (*MW* 318–19). When one foresees becoming the object of another's wit and merriment, one is not likely to think of the negation of those talents with any distaste; so it is natural that Emma should indicate a temperament of an opposite kind by choosing a word that brings into focus its positive qualities.

To be able to combine the charms normally conceived of as belonging to dispositions antithetical to one another is the deadliest and most fiendish of the wicked Lady Susan's many powers of pleasing. As Mrs Vernon says, 'she possesses an uncommon union of Symmetry, Brilliancy and Grace': a fearful symmetry indeed. Lady Susan has at her command both the sparkling wit and animation that makes for *brilliant* company and, when it suits her to assume it, the *grace* of an 'address ... gentle, frank ... affectionate', and a 'voice & manner winningly mild' (*MW* 251).

The contradistinction from *lively* is a contextual specialization of the general sense of *gentle* (as applied to *temper*), which was then broader and more serious than today. Like Middle English *gentil*, it connoted sensitivity and sympathy, and covered the whole range of what we would today call **humane** emotions and reactions. Shelley can use 'gentle feelings' to denote all that is the opposite of cruelty and greed, refer to Epicurus as 'the most humane and gentle among the ancients', and to God as 'all that is gentle and beneficent and compassionate' (*SP* 85, 87, 180, 203). A 'liberal mind and gentle temper' can summarize the essence of the 'Christian spirit' (*Mar.* 39). Byron can cite the most moving passages of *La Divina Commedia* as evidence that Dante did not lack 'gentle feelings' (*BLJ* 8.39). The word comprised and connoted all non-self-assertive and non-antagonistic response: affection, pity, kindness, considerateness, deference to the pleasure or will of others. *Gentleness* 'amalgamates freely with the will of another' (Crabb), and collocates with *sweetness, goodhumour, tenderness, compliance, obedience, modest, attentive, soothing*, opposes such words as *obstinate* and *stubborn*, and is seen as an essential constituent of 'a true feminine character'.[17] Since it is a virtue that is quick to yield and oblige, it can also oppose that *fortitude* (cf. *Evel.* 217) Frank Wentworth judges Anne to have wanted, though he becomes convinced of her being 'the loveliest medium of fortitude and gentleness' (*P* 241); and the care that is taken in that novel to distinguish the compliant sympathies implied by *gentleness* from such yielding as issues from weakness can be paralleled in one of the illustrative quotations (from Blair) cited by Crabb in his *Synonymes*, in which it is stressed that the former "stands opposed, not to the most determined regard to virtue and truth, but to harshness and severity, to pride and arrogance".[18]

The word is also used to refer to the susceptibility that prompts these more generous emotions, and so can be equivalent to or coupled with 'tender-hearted' (*Evel.* 19; *SCG* V.487): 'It was the

easier for me to attribute to the gentleness of my heart, the instant
sensibility' (*SCG* III.171). When Mrs Thrale declares that she
cannot make Fanny Burney weep to order – as she can the
ludicrously tear-prompt Sophie Streatfield – two of the assembled
guests reply that Fanny is, however, "gentle enough" and so "can
cry . . . on any proper occasion" (*FBD* 36). Hence *gentle* can also
be used as a kind of transferred epithet of states or actions that
arise from sensibility and/or affection, and be roughly equivalent
to 'tender': one may hear of 'a gentle sigh', 'a gentle tear', which
could in turn testify to what was coyly called 'the gentle passion'[19]
(that is, love; cf. *SCG* VI.53: 'I soon found, that my admiration of
her fine qualities was likely to lead me into a gentler, yet a more
irresistible passion'). We could scarcely today collocate *gently*
(meaning 'in a moved manner') with the verb *cried*, as Fanny
Burney could (*Evel.* 384).

Since wit and teasing often require some real or feigned heart-
lessness, they may grow less readily in the *gentle* soil. And in *Sir
Charles Grandison* the *lively*, humorous, teasing Charlotte is
consistently contrasted with her less entertaining and softer-
hearted sister, the *gentle* Caroline.

Gentle, therefore, may indicate in a commendatory fashion
a pleasing absence of the louder and sharper tones sometimes
assumed by some forms of *spirit(s)*. It has kindness, grace,
modesty and mildness rather than *brilliancy* or *liveliness*. It is a
word used of those quieter, tender-hearted and vulnerable females
whose manner attracts by charms other than those of Marianne,
Elizabeth or Mary Crawford: Elinor Tilney, Georgiana Darcy,
Isabella Knightley (*NA* 140; *PP* 261; *E* 92) and Mrs Weston. So
when Mr Elton remains, for his own spiteful reasons, ostentatiously
unpartnered at the Crown Inn ball,

> The kind-hearted, gentle Mrs. Weston had left her seat to join
> him and say, "Do not you dance Mr. Elton?"   (*E* 327)

Mrs Weston, that is, does not, in jest or earnest, attack: she
neither rebukes nor rallies with a witticism (as Bingley does Darcy
on a similar occasion), but speaks with the mild and considerate
concern natural to the *gentle* character.

4 Manners

> The master of the ceremonies introduced her to a very gentle-
> manlike young man as a partner . . . [He] was rather tall, had a
> pleasing countenance, a very intelligent and lively eye, and, if
> not quite handsome, was very near it. His address was good, and
> Catherine felt herself in high luck. (*NA* 25)

Henry Tilney's success in capturing Catherine's heart fairly immediately is not difficult to account for. She is young and naive and
moving in fashionable circles for the first time; he is nice-looking,
and has head and spirits enough to interest. But the promptitude
of the favourable impression he makes is also due to a *gentlemanlike* air and the possession of *address* (a social manner calculated to
please). The term *manners* can also be used of this latter quantity –
though it can be misleading, as the word in the plural today refers
to a much more restricted aspect of one's social deportment than it
does in the singular. When Jane Austen comments on *manners*,
she is referring not necessarily to the presence or absence of
punctilious civility, but to whether or not someone's general
manner is likely to recommend him or her (though, if it is, some
degree of courtesy often enters into the matter). When Elizabeth
Bennet says to Jane, "And so, you like this man's sisters too, do
you? Their manners are not equal to his" (*PP* 15), she does not
mean that Bingley's sisters are less observant of common polite-
nesses than he. She means that their manner, somewhat haughty
and reserved, is less calculated to please than Bingley's good-
natured ease, which constitutes the happy facility of *address*
possessed by this most likeable of Jane Austen's likeable young men.
  The stamp of the *gentleman* or *gentlewoman*, however, should
also be discernible in one's general presence and behaviour.
Gentleman and its derivatives had a variety of related implications:
Gentleman (1) At their simplest, they are merely markers of social

rank, distinguishing the gentry from the non-gentry. *Ladies* (originally the female counterparts of *lords*) and *gentlemen* were still status terms, not the mere polite synonyms for 'men and women' they have become. Thus, in *Sense and Sensibility*, 'a man on horseback' seen by Elinor and Marianne is further distinguished, as he approaches (by his dress and mount, presumably), as a 'gentleman': that is, a member of the gentry (86; cf. *E* 30; *MP* 211, 241). There were distinctions of rank within that of gentleman, but the distinction between the gentry and the non-gentry was the main one and the one of which those who claimed to be *genteel* were most jealously, touchily and proudly conscious. Thus Elizabeth can reply to Lady Catherine's objections against the social inequality of a match between her and Darcy by retorting that: "He is a gentleman; I am a gentleman's daughter" (*PP* 356). Lady Catherine does not question the validity of this reasoning; she counterattacks rather by pointing to Elizabeth's inability to pronounce herself the daughter of a *gentlewoman*.

Their identity as *gentlemen* and *gentlewomen* considerably influenced the self-respect of the gentry. For the rank also connoted various kinds of standards:

Gentleman (2) Standards of life-style, and the financial means to support genteel levels of comfort, elegance and independence (*MP* 7; *P* 105, 199):

> . . . do you think [£3,000] would enable me to see all Italy in a gentlemanly way? (*BLJ* 4.171)

Emma is pleased to see Mr Knightley arrive at the Coles's dinner-party in his carriage, instead of walking, as he usually does:

> "This is coming as you should do," said she, "like a gentleman." (*E* 213)

Mr Knightley replies by rallying her about the snobbish notions of gentlemanliness that underlie her commendation.

Gentleman (3) Standards of cultivation, decorum and good-breeding – which included a 'gentleman's education' (*PP* 200); refined accomplishments such as dancing (*MP* 250; *E* 326); well-groomed appearance and well-bred manner – as possessed, for instance, by Colonel Fitzwilliam, 'in person and address most truly the gentleman' (*PP* 170–71), but not by John Thorpe, who behaves as if he feared to be thought 'too much like a gentleman unless he were easy where he ought to be civil, and impudent where he might be allowed to be easy' (*NA* 45). *Gentlemanlike* manners are those which combine reticence and friendliness to form that well-bred ideal that is neither stand-offish nor over-familiar, and which may thus be contrasted with pride on the one hand or presumption on the other (*NA* 45, 130; cf. 95). (1) and (3) are used in mutual confirmation at Anne's first meeting with Mr Elliot:

> It was evident that the gentleman, (completely a gentleman in manner) admired her exceedingly.   (*P* 104; cf. 141, 196)

(1), (2) and (3) predominate in *Emma* and *Persuasion*, two novels which contain characters intensely conscious of rank.

Gentleman (4) Standards of honour, liberality and integrity – as when Mr and Mrs Morland judge that General Tilney, in forcing a young girl who had been his guest to make a long and un-accompanied journey home, 'had acted neither honourably nor feelingly – neither as a gentleman nor as a parent' (*NA* 234). The semantic overlap between moral and social distinction in fact dates back to the Middle English use of the term *gentil*, which could be applied to nobility of behaviour or of rank; and the '*gentil* is as *gentil* does' argument existed even then, and is repeated, for instance, by Chaucer in 'The Wife of Bath's Tale', in which the old woman contends that those who do not act in a *gentil* (honourable and humane) way do not deserve to be considered *gentils*, what-ever their birth.[1] And *gentleman* (1) and (4) could similarly be played off against each other – as, for instance, by Thackeray when he contrasts the modesty, honesty and humanity of true *gentlemen* and *gentlewomen* with the external attributes enjoyed by many others who usurp those names (*VF* 649, 695, 720).

These most serious standards of the *gentleman* are invoked – in very different ways – by Elinor Dashwood and Mary Crawford. "I know", Mary says to Henry, "that a wife you *loved* would be the happiest of women, and that even when you ceased to love, she would yet find in you the liberality and good-breeding of a gentleman" (*MP* 296): a remark with an odd mixture of worldly wisdom ('when', not even 'if', he falls out of love with his wife) and real appreciation of humane and civilized decencies. When

Willoughby sends that terrible letter to Marianne, Elinor is horrified that he could be 'capable of departing so far from the appearance of every honourable and delicate feeling – so far from the common decorum of a gentleman, as to send a letter so impudently cruel' (*SS* 184). There was nothing abusive or coarse in the wording of the letter, as might be implied by the modern trivialized sense of the word *gentleman*. On the contrary, its cruelty lay precisely in the icy formality and politeness that implicitly disavowed any intimacy between himself and Marianne. It was unworthy of a *gentleman* in its cowardly treachery and unscrupulous hurtfulness: its want of honour and humanity.

The resonance of the word actually becomes a feature of the plot in *Pride and Prejudice*, where its utterance in indignation by Elizabeth to Darcy serves to change the current of all his powerful pride of birth (which is not a superficial pride) and make it run with instead of against his regard for her. As he explains on the occasion of his formal proposal, that pride had been something he had had to struggle against (189). His statements on this subject show such a hurtful disregard for her self-respect in his preoccupation with his own that Elizabeth refuses him more un-gently than she would have done had he, in her words, "behaved in a more gentlemanlike manner" (192). Since he had not had the *gentlemanly* delicacy (cf. *MP* 321) to spare her feelings, that is, she had not felt it incumbent upon her to spare his. That rebuke makes an indelible impression on Darcy, as he later confesses (367). His deep mortification makes him determine to prove to her and to himself that he is not "devoid of every proper feeling" (368) and can act with that *gentlemanly* generosity, courtesy and considerateness he later displays.

The related word *gentility* gave the official verbal stamp validating a passport into respectable society, certifying satisfaction of certain minimum levels of civilized decency in life style and/or behaviour.[2] Persons of *gentility* have their opposite in "low company" (*SS* 94; *VF* 201). And the related adjective *genteel* at its simplest denoted a social class, contradistinguishing members of that class from their servants and from tradesmen:

> ... must [the witness to a signature] necessarily be genteel? would not a servant or a merchant do?   (*BLJ* 5.191)

The word also figured as the middle term of a scale of social polish and grace ascended by *smart* (**chic**, **modish**) and *genteel* ('not vulgar') degrees to the envied acme of *elegance* (**refinement**), which was the stamp of 'real class' the socially self-conscious would have murdered for. The relative ranking of the three terms is evident from several passages in *Sense and Sensibility*. The manners of Lady Middleton 'had all the elegance which her husband's wanted' (31; cf. 32, 228), and *elegance* is practically the only thing in the world she is interested in. She is, therefore, apprehensive at the prospect of a visit from the Steele sisters, 'two girls whom she had never seen in her life, and of whose elegance, – whose tolerable gentility even, she could have no proof' (118). The distinction implied between *gentility* and *elegance* is confirmed when the Steeles arrive on the scene. They are observed to be 'by no means ungenteel or unfashionable' (119), though Lucy is soon perceived by Elinor to have no real 'elegance or grace' (120, 124). She is surprised at how quickly they manage to flatter their way into Lady Middleton's good graces, even though 'Lucy was certainly not elegant, and her sister not even genteel' (231). Anne, with her 'vulgar freedom and folly' (124), is plain common – 'not even genteel'. Lucy is shrewd enough to have picked up some *gentility*, but in fact neither sister can achieve much beyond *smartness*. 'Their dress was very smart' (119), we are informed at their introduction into the story, and Elinor notes in Lucy 'a smartness of air, which though it did not give actual elegance or grace, gave distinction to her person' (120). One may compare the 'inelegant smartness of his air and deportment' noticed in the horribly vulgar Mr Smith in *Evelina* (219).

In fact, *smart* is a word used mainly, not only *of* the vulgar who nevertheless have social pretensions, but also *by* them: that is, it was a lowish word selected by the inelegant or ungenteel where their social betters would use 'fashionable' or 'genteel'. *Smart beaux* are forever on Anne Steele's tongue and mind (though they are hastily rephrased into "genteel young men" (123) by her cuter little sister); and her inquisitive stares at Marianne's dress generally ended in the assertion that 'upon her word she looked vastly smart, and she dared to say she would make a great many conquests' (249). Lady Middleton's much less *elegant* husband, Sir John, apologizes to the Dashwood girls for being 'unable to get any smart young men to meet them' at Barton Park (33): that is, fashionable young bucks, which, in his endearing vulgarity, he assumes would be the sort of company Elinor and Marianne would prefer to that of old squares like himself. Miss Gray is described by the narrator as, in appearance, 'a very fashionable looking young woman' (176); the warm-hearted but very vulgar Mrs Jennings, however, expresses herself differently: "a smart, stilish girl, they say" (194). And the word receives the emphasis marks regularly given to the vulgarisms of the Branghtons in *Evelina* (186).

When used by the genteel, it tends to suggest a sniff at rather vulgar notions of what constitutes social distinction. Thus Edward reports that his own preferred profession of the church "was not smart enough for my family" (*SS* 102), who would have preferred him to drive around in "knowing gigs" or cut a "dashing and expensive" figure in the navy (103). Edward is clearly using the word *smart* to discredit the criteria of stylishness he is reporting. Similarly, when Elinor envisages Lucy married to Edward and 'uniting at once a desire of smart appearance, with the utmost frugality, and ashamed to be suspected of half her economical practices' (357), she is clearly, with wry irony, using the word (which she probably feels Lucy herself would use) to depreciate Lucy's own ideas of what makes for social standing – a sort of keep-up-with-Lady-Jones chicness in appearance and life style.[3]

Elegance is basically a word relating to style or manner that shows grace and distinction. Marianne, who sets as much store by elegance of execution as by *spirit*, asks eagerly of Willoughby whether he danced "with elegance, with spirit?" (*SS* 45). And she applies the word to verbal style when she laments that, "Every body pretends to feel and tries to describe with the taste and elegance of him who first discovered what picturesque beauty was" (97). The word is applied to mode or manner of verbal description, in an ironic way, by the narrator herself: 'Marianne's preserver, as Margaret, with more elegance than precision, stiled Willoughby ...' (46) – where, again, the reference is to a manner possessing style and graceful distinctiveness. A written style that is *elegant* (cf. *FBD* 73, 76; *SCG* VII.400) finds its antithesis in a *vulgar* one (*BLJ* 3.107), *vulgar* in such contexts meaning, not 'coarse', but 'common, ordinary, undistinguished' (a sense closer to its original meaning of 'relating to the people') – as in Reid's comment (which occurs in the course of some literary criticism by him) that,

'Nothing is more vulgar than to say that we must all die' (*Lectures on the Fine Arts*, 34).

The extension of meaning from 'manner formally pleasing' to 'manners that show good form', from gracefulness to the social graces, is not hard to trace. The *OED* points out that the etymological meaning of *elegant* is 'choosing carefully or skilfully' (it is related to 'electing'). And *elegant* is often loosely equivalent to 'classy', 'of or belonging to the social élite' (one may compare the emphasis acquired by the word *select* today, in such expressions as 'a select gathering'). Mrs Jennings, who resides every winter at Portman Square in London, is said to have done so 'Since the death of her husband, who had traded with success in a less elegant part of the town' (*SS* 153). The snobbier and more superficial senses of the **refinement** elegance connoted are much associated with the *elegant* Lady Middleton. The word is virtually equivalent to 'social prestige' in the following instances. Though quite happy to give impromptu balls in the country, she is unhappy about doing so in London, because there 'the reputation of elegance was more important and less easily attained', and 'it was risking too much for the gratification of a few girls, to have it known that Lady Middleton had given a small dance of eight or nine couple, with two violins, and a mere side-board collation' (170–71). And, though finding Willoughby's behaviour "very shocking", she decides she will not ignore his future wife, since 'Mrs. Willoughby would at once be a woman of elegance and fortune' (216). Then there is her 'great dislike of all such inelegant subjects of raillery as delighted her husband and mother' (62) – where *inelegant* means 'unsuited to refined society, coarse, vulgar' – which latter terms were antonyms of elegant.[4]

But *elegance* can refer in a less crude way to a social self-possession, good-breeding and **refinement**, **grace** and **polish** in the manner(s). Crabb links *elegance* with *gracefulness*, treating the former as a superior degree of the latter (what is *graceful* excites pleasure, what is *elegant* 'admiration'), and sees it as the hallmark of 'superior class' in more than a merely external sense: it is the 'consequence not only of superior birth and status, but also of superior natural endowments'. *Elegance* occurs as a synonym for *refinement* and is collocated with *nicety* of taste in Gerard (116, 117). The *OED* gives (*sv elegant* 6b) 'Refined in manners and habits', and Johnson defines *polish* and *polite* as, respectively, 'to make elegant of manners' (*verb* 2) and 'elegant of manners' (*adj.* 2). *Elegance* of this kind is a quality present in the Dashwood household itself: Willoughby, on first being introduced into it, notices at once the 'sense, elegance, mutual affection, and domestic comfort of the family' (46). He registers, that is, qualifications under head and heart, and the refinement, cultivation and polish that went by the name of *elegance*. *Elegance* is likewise one of the first things they notice about him: Mrs Dashwood would have felt well-disposed toward anyone who had been kind to Marianne, even had he been 'old, ugly, and vulgar'; but in this case, 'the influence of youth, beauty, and elegance, gave an interest to the action which came home to her feelings' (42). None of these three attributes relates to what is called elsewhere more "solid worth", but they summarize at once a man guaranteed to recommend himself to a family of women. It is this quality of real refinement and good-breeding that Lucy Steele lacks, for all her anxiety to appear *genteel*, and which, for instance, Catherine sees Elinor Tilney to possess more of than Isabella Thorpe (*NA* 56).

The word figures large in that very quality conscious novel, *Emma*.[5] Emma detects in the fulsome compliments of Mr Elton a want of refinement and nicety of taste and tact, which she puts down to 'error of judgment, of knowledge, of taste, as one proof among others that he had not always lived in the best society, that with all the gentleness of his address, true elegance was sometimes wanting' (134–5). By a well-established convention of art, a similar slight coarseness is detected by her even in his brand of good looks:

> He was reckoned very handsome ... though not by her, there being a want of elegance of feature which she could not dispense with. (35)

Reflected through that horrid caricature of herself, Mrs Elton, Emma's value for *elegance* takes on all the *in*elegant, vulgar snobbery latent in the word (cf. 301). Mrs Elton's *elegance* gets what it deserves in its parodic refraction through the mouth of Miss Bates, who, with respect to the prospective employers of Jane, has obviously received from Mrs Elton only the overwhelming impression of a frightfully good class of family with a frightfully good class of children:

"Except the Sucklings and Bragges, there is not such another nursery establishment, so liberal and elegant, in all Mrs. Elton's acquaintance . . . .. A style of living almost equal to Maple Grove – and as to children, except the little Sucklings and little Bragges, there are not such elegant sweet children anywhere."
(382)

Emma is nicer in her criteria for *elegance*, and sees at once that Mrs Elton herself has 'ease, but not elegance' (270): that she has no real refinement or polish, snob though she is.

It is also in *Emma* that one finds the most emphatically *elegant* person in the whole Austen canon (and the emphasis is placed by no less a person than Emma herself, who plainly has pretty exacting standards in such matters): Jane Fairfax. Emma, rather despite herself, is impressed by the **distinction** in Jane's person, presence and deportment:

> . . . she was particularly struck with the very appearance and manners, which . . . she had been depreciating. Jane Fairfax was very elegant, remarkably elegant; and she had herself the highest value for elegance . . . . It was a style of beauty, of which elegance was the reigning character, and as such, she must, in honour, by all her principles, admire it: – elegance, which, whether of person or mind, she saw so little in Highbury. There, not to be vulgar, was distinction, and merit.   (167)

She likewise insists on the word to Frank Churchill when commending Jane's manners and behaviour:

> ". . . she is a very elegant young woman . . . . If you were never particularly struck by her manners before . . . I think you will today."   (194)

Emma is something of a snob, of course, but (unlike Mrs Elton) she is a discriminating snob, and she knows real class when she sees it. What she admires in Jane is neither wealth nor rank (for Jane has neither, and Emma is much her superior in both), but grace and distinction of person and presence; without being either refeened or snooty, the girl is evidently a really classy piece.

As suggested by Emma's reflections on Mr Elton, *elegance* is an acquired, not an innate, virtue (though some innate capacity *to* acquire it is probably necessary), and exposure to 'the best society', to civilized and refined company, is required to produce it. Jane, one may recall, has been brought up in the home of the Campbells, where she enjoyed an 'excellent education' and shared in all 'the rational pleasures of an elegant society', where 'her heart and understanding had received every advantage of discipline and culture' (164), and where she had received all the 'advantages of connection [and] improvement to be engrafted on what nature had given her' (163) which her Highbury home could not have furnished.

Elegance can be overrated, and without spirit(s), heart or head it is what the *elegant* Lady Middleton (a thoroughly lightweight woman, of cold heart, weak understanding, and spirits never elated or depressed: 31, 55, 229) is often called: *insipid*. But that is not to say it has *no* value. Marianne is said to err only in placing 'too great' an emphasis on it (*SS* 201). The social refinement and nicety of taste possessed by the *elegant* guard them from the nosiness, impertinence, tactlessness, indiscretion and all the many other kinds of offensivenesses and irritations inflicted on the Dashwoods by the less *elegant* relations of Lady Middleton. She is too well-bred to make vulgar jokes about their *beaux* or impertinent inquiries into their private affairs. As Elinor perceives (62), her restraint comes from her *elegance*, not sensitivity; but that is better than it coming from nowhere; and if her society is *insipid*, it is at least not painful.

Complaisance (willingness to please, obliging compliance) is an aspect of social manner that often involves restraint of vexation and ill-humour in the cause of a civilly pleased and cheerful exterior (cf. *NA* 88, 237; *P* 16).[6] This may require some *exertion*. The latter is a word often used at this period of the suppression or control of feelings in the presence of others, in the interests of prudence, social complaisance or considerateness. The idiomatic association of the word with emotional self-control and social effort is not confined to Jane Austen.[7] It is a word particularly prominent in *Sense and Sensibility*, where it is used to contrast the self-control of Elinor with the indulgence of her feelings evident in Marianne. *Energy* and *animation* are qualities one comes to associate with the latter. *Exerting* herself, on the other hand, expending an energy that requires effort, is what Elinor characteristically does. She is doing it even by the end of the first chapter. Marianne and her mother 'gave themselves up wholly to their sorrow':

> Elinor, too, was deeply afflicted, but still she could struggle, she could exert herself. She could consult with her brother, could receive her sister-in-law on her arrival, and treat her with proper attention; and could strive to rouse her mother to similar exertion . . .   (7; cf. 141; 159)

Elinor's supreme efforts of *exertion* occur, of course, in her conversations with Lucy, when she feels it due to prudence, dignity and principle to disguise the really deep personal distress and mortification Lucy's communications about Edward cause her (130, 134). She later tells Marianne that the composure and self-command Marianne has, in effect, been rather despising her for were not the effects of insensibility, but of "constant and painful exertion" (264). Marianne herself confesses regretfully to having neglected all the social duties attended to by her sister, to whom she left "every exertion of duty and friendship" (346). And it is "Exert yourself!" that Elinor cries to Marianne at the climax of the novel, when Marianne is prostrate with affliction, giving way to a 'torrent of unresisted grief' (185).[8]

Exertion often involves curbing, inwardly and outwardly, the indulgence of distress, for one's own sake and that of others – for that nexus of interconnected reasons Emma is really rather eloquent on, when she urges Harriet to stop moping over Mr Elton. Harriet should do so, not only out of consideration for the painful self-reproach it must occasion Emma, but for other and wider reasons:

> "I have not said, exert yourself Harriet for my sake, think less, talk less of Mr. Elton for my sake; because for your own sake rather, I would wish it to be done, for the sake of what is more important than my comfort, a habit of self-command in you, a consideration of what is your duty, an attention to propriety, an endeavour to avoid the suspicions of others, to save your health and credit, and restore your tranquillity."   (268)

Emma herself is capable of such *exertion*. When Harriet confesses her love for Mr Knightley, and her impression that it is reciprocated, the 'bitter feelings occasioned by this speech, the many bitter feelings, made the utmost exertion necessary on Emma's side' – and Emma can rise to the occasion (411). It will be evident that the social reasons dictating *exertion* are often not of the superficial 'the show must go on' type, but ones that involve acting honourably and generously in a relationship. But the word can be used of any kind of social effort: taking the trouble to be polite or kind or cheerful or 'useful' are termed *exertions* (*P* 100, 126; *E* 9).

The social considerations that can prompt *exertion* may be of several types. The most obvious is the need for common civility under trying circumstances. Thus Sir Thomas, tired after a long journey home after a long absence, and not much pleased to find his house turned upside down or Mr Yates in it, feels it due to his own self-respect to be hospitable, and even 'exerted himself so far as to speak a few words of calm approbation in reply to an eager appeal of Mr Yates as to the happiness' of the staging arrangements (*MP* 183) – a heroic exertion, for which Sir Thomas's self-command deserves all credit. The need to go through the ordinary social decencies with composure, sometimes reinforced by a disinclination to attract unwanted attention to one's state of mind, often dictates the exertion of pulling oneself together – or what is called 'recollecting oneself', which means recollecting the part one must play in civilized social intercourse. *Exertion* may also be required in the handling of social situations, to make them go off smoothly (*JAL* 132), or to pass off awkward moments (*PP* 269, 337).

These associations of the word add a nuance to the account of the farewells at Rosings to Elizabeth and her party. Lady Catherine condescendingly wishes them a good journey, 'and Miss De Bourgh exerted herself so far as to curtsey and hold out her hand to both' (*PP* 214); here, the physical and social senses of the word are punningly combined to make this limp girl's bodily feebleness and languor expressive of a constitutional indisposition to effort that is more than merely physical.

Pretty and *pretty behaved* are terms commendatory of what is taken to show graceful propriety in speech or behaviour. But there are marked distinctions in how it is used as between more and less sophisticated speakers. Jane Austen herself uses it in an ironically perfunctory or faintly quizzical way, as when she wrote to her sister:

> We have called on Miss Dusautoy and Miss Papillon, and been very pretty. (*JAL* 391)

Similarly, when Edward Ferrars proposes to Elinor, he refers very properly to his doubts and suspense, despite the fact that he cannot have expected 'a very cruel reception'; but 'It was his business, however, to say that he *did*, and he said it very prettily' (*SS* 366; cf. *PP* 330; *NA* 33). Jane Austen's more sophisticated and intelligent characters use the word with similar knowing, invisible but audible inverted commas round it. It is used straight only by the less sophisticated – especially the old-fashioned, the socially relatively humble or rusticated, and the downright vulgar.[9] It suits the homely common sense of Mrs Morland, who refers to the Tilneys as "very pretty kind of young people" (*NA* 236). Otherwise, it is used seriously mostly only by such vulgar characters as Mrs Bennet, Anne Steele (*SS* 149) and Mrs Jennings. Mrs Bennet can afford to commend such *prettiness* in the Long nieces, since it fortunately does not extend to their looks: "very pretty behaved girls, and not at all handsome: I like them prodigiously" (*PP* 342). The honest Mrs Jennings uses the word of the utterly disingenuous letter from Lucy, who is careful to express all the right sentiments she never feels:

> ". . . how prettily she writes! . . . That sentence is very prettily turned . . . How attentive she is to every body! . . . It is as pretty a letter as ever I saw, and does Lucy's head and heart great credit." (*SS* 278)

The chapter end that follows the speech is beautifully placed, constituting a demurely telling 'no comment' (such as Elinor herself doubtless gave). In fact, the distinction in usage is well illustrated by the tone in which Elinor had herself mentally applied the word to Lucy's equally disingenuous account of her relationship with Edward:

> "All this," thought Elinor, "is very pretty; but it can impose upon neither of us." (148)

The most persistent non-ironic user of the word (in this sense) is, however, the old-fashioned Mr Woodhouse, on whose lips it forever is, where it serves to emphasize his rather old-womanish naiveté, his simplistic notions and the corresponding narrowness of his vocabulary, and his unsophisticated, undiscriminating good will. For him, the housemaid at Randalls is "a civil, pretty-spoken girl . . . she always curtseys and asks me how I do, in a very pretty manner" (*E* 9); Mr Elton is "a very pretty young man to be sure" (14); Isabella's calling her first son after him he thinks "very pretty of her" (80); "it was an exceeding good, pretty letter" that Frank wrote to Mr and Mrs Weston (96); again referring not to looks but to behaviour, he judges Harriet "just such another pretty kind of young person" as Jane Fairfax (104), who is "a very pretty sort of young lady, a very pretty and a very well-behaved young lady" (171) – Emma's word for her, of course, is *elegant*, but the vaguer, simpler term suits the less precise reflections of her father. Despite his faddiness about food, noise and draughts, Mr Woodhouse does not seem in other respects very hard to please, for he can even apply his favourite epithet to the dire Mrs Elton – with some reservations:

> ". . . she seems a very pretty sort of young lady . . .. She speaks a little too quick. A little quickness of voice there is which rather hurts the ear. But I believe I am nice; I do not like strange voices . . . However, she seems a very obliging, pretty-behaved young lady, and no doubt will make him a good wife."   (279)

Nice is here used in its earlier sense of 'finely discriminating, fastidious'. Mr Woodhouse's immediate and endearing retreat from criticism by referring the detected fault to his own *niceness* heightens the comedy of his verdict on Mrs Elton as "pretty-behaved", which only a taste not at all *nice* could pass. That he can lump together the manners of Harriet Smith, Jane Fairfax and Mrs Elton under the one benign heading of *pretty* may reflect some credit on the old man's good-natured heart, but little on his head. The contrast in usage between Mrs Jennings and Elinor repeats itself here, for Mr Woodhouse's more sophisticated daughter uses the word only with a sort of wry knowingness not at all apparent in him; Mr Elton's verses may be entered into Harriet's book, for with the final couplet omitted "a very pretty gallant charade remains, fit for any collection .... A poet in love must be encouraged in both capacities, or neither" (77).

Gentle, a word related to *genteel*, originally meant 'well-born', and could still be used in this straightforward sense.[10] It very early came to have a depth and breadth of secondary connotations, relating to the refinement of feeling those of *gentle* birth were ideally supposed to possess; and those familiar addresses to the 'gentle reader' are complimentary assumptions as to the soft-heartedness and susceptibility the word connoted as regards disposition.[11] With relation to manners, it was used more frequently and in a broader way than it is today to indicate a behaviour softened by due care not to hurt or offend. Crabb relates *gentle* manners to *soft* ones; but where the latter are most suited to a feminine deportment, *gentleness*, which it is 'the object of polite education to produce', is appropriate to both sexes; it acts lightly upon, and is easily acted on by, others – slow to pressurize, to ridicule, to upbraid, and considerably quick to comply, sympathize, defer and respect. It collocates with such words as 'soft-mannered', 'civil', 'attentive', 'unassuming' and 'soothing'.[12] Elizabeth notices it as something new in the reformed Darcy: 'never had he spoken with such gentleness as on this unexpected meeting' at Pemberley (252). The word describes not a tone of voice, but that in Darcy's manner which now shows him to be consulting with care the sensibilities of his companions, and which stands in contrast with the former pride that had suggested indifference or contempt (cf. 263). The same contrast occurs at Elizabeth's first meeting with Georgiana, whom she has heard to be 'exceedingly proud', but who is immediately perceived to have 'manners perfectly unassuming and gentle' (261).

Gentleness figures most conspicuously, however, as a feature of the pleasing manner(s) of those male characters who are something of womanizers, and whose winning *address* conceals a defective *temper*. Wickham has it off perfectly, though Elizabeth comes to detect 'in the very gentleness which had first delighted her, an affectation and a sameness to disgust [arouse distaste] and weary' (*PP* 233; cf. 234). *Gentleness* is likewise one department of manners in which Emma opines that Mr Elton might actually score higher than Mr Knightley with his "downright, decided, commanding sort of manner". Mr Elton's have more "gentleness", and have been "particularly gentle of late" with "additional softness" (34). She learns, as Elizabeth had, that this is all flannel, and that he is one of those who *can* combine 'gentle manners and a conceited head' (136). *Gentleness* is at odds with conceit, as with pride, because it indicates a manner pleasingly unassuming, attentive and toned down, which gratifies by the care and esteem for the interlocutor it implies.

More literally 'toned down' is the *gentleness* of Henry Crawford which Fanny finds such a relief to her shattered ears and nerves in her Portsmouth home, with its 'little intermission of noise or grog' (413). The contrast brings Henry as near to winning her over as he ever gets. The occurrence of the word in this context forcibly reminds one of its etymology in 'good birth' and the civilized and refined habits of feeling and conduct that was assumed to entail. For Fanny, of course, learns in Portsmouth to value the *genteel* ways of the *gentleman's* house in which she had recently experienced such distress. Henry is practically the only *gentleman* she encounters in Portsmouth, a place calculated to reveal the value of that good breeding that can tone down the accent and the manners and train them to ride less clamorously roughshod over the ears and feelings of others:

> Not considering in how different a circle she had been just seeing him, nor how much might be owing to contrast, she was quite persuaded of his being astonishingly more gentle, and regardful of others, than formerly. (*MP* 413–14)

The ideal manner(s) are those which make for agreeable company. Hence they tend to be those which combine the discretion and poise of *elegance* with what is termed *ease, openness, plainness, simplicity*. Three heroines are particularly attracted to their destined partners by what they see as peculiarly excellent manners – and what the happy men excel in is one of the latter qualities rather than the former. Jane Bennet exclaims to Elizabeth of Bingley: "I never saw such happy manners! – so much ease, with such perfect good breeding!" (*PP* 14). The novel does nothing to contradict her, depicting in Bingley an uncommonly attractive and engaging relaxed, good-natured *ease* of manner. *Ease* can be overdone or ill-timed, of course (*NA* 45; *E* 270, 279, 324); but manners described as good nearly always combine civility with that *ease* the shy Edward Ferrars so much envies (*SS* 94).[13]

Anne Elliot can admire and approve the *manners* of Captain Harville and Mr Elliot, but always feels that those of Frank are superior (*P* 97, 143). Since the former are termed *gentlemanly* and *polished*, it is obviously not on that count that Frank outscores them. There is a quality of *openness* and *warmth* missing in Mr Elliot (161), and (though she does not at this point allow herself to be quite explicit as to whom she is comparing Mr Elliot with) it is this that Anne values in the aptly named Frank. *Open* in this novel occurs consistently among the qualities of the naval world (as represented by Admiral and Mrs Croft, Frank, Captains Harville and Benwick) in contradistinction from the drawing-room world of Sir Walter, Elizabeth and Mr Elliot (32, 48, 61, 63, 161), the contrast between which helps to orientate Anne and the reader and provides a partial scheme for the clarification of the values at issue in this work.

And the person whose manners are pronounced to be very perfection by that connoisseuse of good form, Emma Woodhouse, is the blunt, forthright Mr Knightley – whose manners she prefers to the overdone gallantries of Mr Elton. "You might not see one in a hundred, with *gentleman* so plainly written as in Mr. Knightley" (33), she declares. This, of course, is a narrative hint that Emma is really in love with him; but it also provides one of the reasons why. Mr Knightley, with his 'plain, unaffected, gentlemanlike English' (448), is the man who really satisfies her high standards. And if *plain* can collocate quite happily with *gentlemanlike*, so can *simplicity* with that *elegance* Emma sets so much store by. "Mrs. Weston's manners", she asserts pointedly to Mrs Elton (who has just been condescendingly commending them), "were always particularly good. Their propriety, simplicity, and elegance, would make them the safest model for any young woman" (278).

The sheer frequency and evaluative emphasis with which Jane Austen uses such words as *manners, genteel, propriety, decorum, decency* and *respectable* may in fact be misleading as to what she really values, which is not the snooty primness with which such words are associated today. They are all ones which have radically changed in meaning and/or register since her time. *Propriety* and *decorum* referred to a quality of **appropriateness** or fittingness which was appealed to as determining what the context required as the right, not merely the polite or conventional, thing to do. When Emma commends the *propriety* of Mrs Weston's manners, she means that she behaves and speaks in a manner appropriate to the situation. [14] *Decorum* (deriving from the Latin verb *decere* [= to be fit/seemly]) similarly invokes the notion of **fitness** in a much less trivial way than it does today. The words that express Elinor's indignation at the cruelty of that frigidly polite letter of Willoughby's to Marianne illustrate the serious resonance the latter word could have:

> . . . nor could she have supposed Willoughby capable of depart-
> ing so far from the appearance of every honourable and delicate
> feeling – so far from the common decorum of a gentleman, as to
> send a letter so impudently cruel.   (*SS* 184)

Decorum here evidently appeals to something much more impor-
tant than mere conventions of polite behaviour; it should be (and was[15]) strictly distinguished from mere *punctilio*. This letter's cruelty lies precisely in its deliberately distancing politeness – so very **inappropriate** to the relationship between the writer and the addressee; and *decorum* appeals by contrast to the *gentleman's* obligation to adopt, in whatever circumstances, such behaviour as responds most fittingly (here, honestly and honourably) to them; though neither word could today be invoked to express the deep moral revulsion that inspires this passage.

Similarly, Fanny's reflections at the end of *Mansfield Park* will sound unwarrantedly prim and priggish if the essentially much straighter meaning of *respectable* ('worthy of respect') is not remembered. Convinced that Edmund will marry Mary Crawford, she prays, "God grant that her influence do not make him cease to be respectable!" (424). She does not mean she hopes Edmund may not acquire any of those interesting naughtinesses that 'nice people' don't approve of; what she fears, in fact, is that his values may become such as can be implied by *respectable* today – those of status and fashion – and that he will become selfish and unprincipled. This is clear from what follows on the statement that 'Fanny was disposed to think the influence of London very much at war with all respectable attachments':

> [Mary's] attachment to Edmund had been respectable, the most
> respectable part of her character, her friendship for herself
> had at least been blameless. Where was either sentiment now?
>   (433)

MUND!

Mary's disinterested affection for ~~Edward,~~ marriage with whom could provide her with none of the social prestige and jet-setting life style for which she has some taste, was worthy of serious respect.

The values of *propriety, decorum* and *respectability* can, naturally, be appealed to in a tactical, superficial or narrow-minded way by the less intelligent characters. But the narratives tend to champion the more serious meanings of the words and to resist their incipient trivialization. [16] *Respectable* can thus be used in defiance of that esteem or disesteem that results merely from social status (which diminished *respect* the word was already occasionally reduced to imply). When Emma pays the penitential *attention* of a visit to the Miss Bates she was cheeky to, the cramped quarters of the humble and indigent pair cannot prevent the privileged Miss Woodhouse from finding them 'truly respectable' in their selfless happiness (418). More significantly, Elizabeth Bennet can draw on the moral weight of the word and cast it, in private soliloquy, in the teeth of any *respect* due to the rank of the man who had raised objections to her sister's connections:

> "Neither could any thing be urged against my father, who . . . has abilities which Mr. Darcy himself need not disdain, and respectability which he will probably never reach."   (*PP* 187)

In the same way, the superficial pleases and thank-yous implied by 'good manners' today form only a small part of what Jane Austen means by the term. Manners should indeed be civil, but if they are really good they will also include *ease, openness* and *simplicity*, the *formal, reserved* and *affected* opposites of which were no more appreciated in manner(s) then than they are now.

Manners that oppress by a rigid observation of forms are often signalled by the word *formal*. The adjective is associated especially with the pompous Mr Collins, whose 'air was grave and stately, and his manners very formal' (*PP* 64; cf. 155). He cannot perform even a casual gesture without that ceremonious studiedness typical of him:

> "I am not now to learn," replied Mr. Collins with a formal wave of the hand, "that it is usual with young ladies to reject the

addresses of the man whom they secretly mean to accept, when he first applies for their favour." (107)

Elsewhere, the term is associated with stiffness, coldness, gravity (*PP* 16, 340; *MP* 273). We tend to have such a caricatured notion of the 'drawing-room world' of this period that it is perhaps worth emphasizing that *formality* was distinctly out of fashion. Such committed devotees of the fashionable world as, in their different ways, Mary Crawford and Elizabeth Elliot regard what is *formal* as being in rather *bad* form (*MP* 211; *P* 215; cf. *E* 302; *FBD* 179; *Evel.* 284; *Mar.* 49). *Formal* could be used of anything – manners, style of dress, accoutrements – that had an over-arranged or studied air, and is glossed by *ceremonious* (which referred, not to 'elaborately polite' manners, but to 'stiffly correct' ones) by Crabb, who opposes it to *easy*.

Formality may also be applied to what is seen as an old-fashioned over-concern with propriety in rather larger questions of behaviour: 'precise, formal notions of . . . conduct' (*Mar.* 428). Willoughby comments of his aunt's discovery of an early seduction of his:

> "The purity of her life, the formality of her notions, her ignorance of the world – every thing was against me." (*SS* 323)

– where there is surely some self-excuse in the choice of the word: no very great degree of primness would be required to find the part Willoughby had played by the unfortunate Eliza pretty disgraceful. Those who are young, impatient of constraints and want to enjoy themselves are very liable to bestow the word *formal* on those with a tiresomely stricter sense of propriety than they have. When Jane and Elizabeth prudently dismiss the waiter, as Lydia's conversation at the inn shows signs of becoming especially unguarded, the irrepressible Lydia comments dismissively, "Aye, that is just like your formality and discretion" (*PP* 220). The wonderfully shameless Lady Susan writes sympathetically to a friend whose social pleasures have been curtailed by the need to nurse her husband through an attack of gout:

> My dear Alicia, of what a mistake were you guilty in marrying a Man of his age! – just old enough to be formal, ungovernable & to have the Gout – too old to be agreeable, & too young to die. (*MW* 298)

Precise carries rather similar connotations of over-correctness in notions of behaviour, in both a superficial and a larger sense. Mary Crawford is relieved to find in Mrs Grant a sister without the extremes of either 'preciseness or rusticity' in her manners (*MP* 41) – that is, one whose air has neither the entire lack of polish nor the awkward over-scrupulousness she might have expected in someone not much used to mixing in fashionable society. And, with regard to behaviour in the larger sense, Mrs Norris can use the word with the same rhetorical aim of making scruples look over-fussy as motivated Willoughby, Lydia and Lady Susan in their selection of *formal*; wanting to indulge Maria and Julia, she dismisses Edmund's disapproval of the planned play-acting by declaring, "We must not be over precise, Edmund" (141).

Reserve[17] was a more complex word than it is today, graduating through (1) an unfortunate circumstantial necessity and (2) a more habitual defect of manner(s) to (3) downright disingenuity and concealment.

Reserve (1) This is the opposite of that *confidence* which in Jane Austen refers not simply to 'trust', but to the act or habit of confiding in someone. Emma, on hearing that Harriet is to marry Robert Martin, is relieved that 'all necessity of concealment from Mr. Knightley' will soon be over; she 'could now look forward to giving him that full and perfect confidence which her disposition was most ready to welcome as a duty' (475). Mrs Gardiner is surprised that Elizabeth should apply to her for an explanation of Darcy's part in Lydia's marriage, for she 'had been persuaded that affection and confidence subsisted between Mr. Darcy and [Elizabeth]' (*PP* 327). *Confidence* in these contexts refers, not to 'trust' in a general way, but to the confiding of information, to a relationship in which one party has no secrets from the other. *Confidence* of this kind is generally treated as a luxury rather than a virtue – a luxury particularly associated with the sibling relationship, in the context of which the words *confidence* and *reserve* are frequently found opposed:

> Jane could have no reserves from Elizabeth, where confidence would give pleasure; and instantly embracing her, acknowledged . . . that she was the happiest creature in the world.
>
> (*PP* 346; cf. *SS* 169–70)

Reserves here means 'secrets', and *confidence* the act of confiding the engagement to Elizabeth. Most distressing to Fanny is the 'mutual reserve' created by Henry's suit to her between herself and Edmund, the lover (eventually) with whom she has had the unusual privilege of enjoying that perfect *confidence* siblings can indulge in. This distresses Edmund too:

> She had been used to consult him in every difficulty, and he loved her too well to bear to be denied her confidence now . . . . Fanny estranged from him, silent and reserved, was an unnatural state of things. (*MP* 345)

Here again, *confidence* refers to Fanny's confiding in him on the present occasion, and *reserved* to her not doing so.

Outside such relationships, 'perfect unreserve' is usually more desirable than possible; it may be remarked that Mrs Weston (of whose relationship with Emma that phrase is used: *E* 6) has been virtually a mother to Emma – though much younger than her real mother would have been, and the relationship is probably nearer to that of an older with a younger sister. The bosom friendships between females that were something of a cult among young ladies Jane Austen often burlesques in her early works, and portrays one such with subtler comedy in *Northanger Abbey*. For a "friend to whom you can speak with unreserve" (*NA* 207) is a rare solace – such as is most genuinely enjoyed in Charlotte Lucas by Elizabeth Bennet. Elizabeth's last act of 'perfect unreserve' with Charlotte, however, is "Engaged to Mr. Collins! my dear Charlotte, – impossible!" (*PP* 124). She at once recollects herself, however, realizing that she can no longer place complete *confidence* in Charlotte. And though the two remain firm friends, and their correspondence is 'regular and frequent', that 'it should be equally unreserved was impossible' (146); for there is now one major subject on which Elizabeth's feelings must be held back from Charlotte – to wit, Charlotte's husband, her very much worse half.

Though the *reserves* that simply indicate **keeping one's counsel** on specific matters (cf. *PP* 324) may be always undesirable, they are not inevitably wrong. For (even between friends and siblings) there can be prudent and seemly *reserves* (*SS* 150; *P* 15; *E* 403). Thus Mr Knightley replies to Emma's charge that Jane Fairfax is *reserved*:

"... you will soon overcome all that part of her reserve which ought to be overcome, all that has its foundation in diffidence . ... What arises from discretion must be honoured." (171)

There are some matters on which Jane's feelings (disinclination for governessing, frustrations and vexations with her well-meaning aunt and grandmother) could not properly be given expression.

Reserve (2) Mr Knightley, in diagnosing Jane's *reserve* as mixed diffidence and delicacy, is engaged in some special pleading; for when used as a term to characterize manner(s) in a more general way, *reserved* was fraught with more opprobrium than its modern equivalent, and was usually carefully distinguished from shyness (*SS* 94–5; *P* 100; *PP* 267). It designated not simply an unforthcoming demeanour, but one that positively repels rather than invites freedom (it frequently collocates with *cold* or *proud*). Where shyness is the effect of lack of confidence in oneself, *reserve* comes from lack of faith in one's interlocutor, who is thus made to feel that (s)he is not liked, trusted or esteemed enough to be spoken to freely: Darcy's manners, 'haughty, reserved, and fastidious . . . were not inviting' (*PP* 16; cf. 171, 263). The opposite of *inviting* or *attractive* is *repulsive* (which in Jane Austen does not mean 'nauseating', but metaphorically 'pushing back'), a word much used to characterize *reserve*. Edmund admits that Sir Thomas's "reserve may be a little repulsive" to Mary (*MP* 199; cf. 19) – that is, such as to repel rather than to invite freedom. Lady Middleton, whose non-committal nothings are dictated by an interest in *elegance* that far exceeds any real interest in persons, is also called *reserved* (*SS* 31, 55), and Elinor finds her 'cold insipidity . . . so particularly repulsive' (34) as to make even the silent gravity of Colonel Brandon and the noisy laughter of Sir John attractive by contrast. Frank Churchill similarly agrees with Emma, with respect to Jane's *reserve*, that it is a "most repulsive quality" (203), in which there is "safety", but no "attraction" (the opposite of *repulsion*). Jane has her special reasons for wishing to repel attempts to 'draw her out', and her consequent *reserve* forms throughout the novel the one real justification for Emma's distaste for her company, whatever other motives which might not bear too strict an investigation the latter may have. Even in moments of self-examination of those motives, Emma cannot get past Jane's "coldness and reserve" (166). Nor can a serious attempt to be more magnanimous survive an evening in Jane's company:

> She was, besides, which was worst of all, so cold, so cautious! There was no getting at her real opinion. Wrapped up in a cloak of politeness, she seemed determined to hazard nothing. She was disgustingly, was suspiciously reserved.   (169)

Disgust in Jane Austen means, strictly, **distaste**; though **offensive** is what *disgusting* often implies. Emma is not using a meaningless hyperbole; she means that Jane's *reserve* **offends** by its implied mistrust. Nor does *suspiciously* here indicate that it is such as to give one suspicions about what she may be holding back (though it certainly has the effect of prompting Emma to speculate on that); the word relates subjectively and not objectively to Jane's manner, associating itself with that 'cautious' determination to 'hazard nothing', and gives justificatory weight to the adverb *disgustingly*: she behaves as if she were suspicious of you, and that cannot but provoke strong distaste.
Reserve (3) The second sense could, however, combine with the first to suggest **concealment**, not simply of thoughts and feelings, but of *facts*, allowing a *reserved* want of *openness* of manner to pass into a want of that openness that is plain dealing in moral conduct. *Reserve(s)* thus occurs as a synonym for **secrets** and often collocates with *mysteries* (itself frequently a derogatory term):[18]

> Take care never to seem reserved and mysterious, which is not only a very unamiable character, but a very suspicious one too.

counsels *The Young Man's Companion* (12). The opposition between *open* and *reserved* is common, and the contexts make it clear that it tends to be a value judgement about honesty and frankness, not simply a more neutral indication of an introvert or extrovert character (e.g. *SS* 48, 81, 170, 337). It is thus significant that the two persons with whom the term is most emphatically associated are Edward Ferrars and Jane Fairfax, both of whom are, of course, in fact concealing something (in each case, an engagement), and are therefore being *reserved* in the specific sense of 'holding something back'. Consciousness of this has added a constraint to manners in neither case naturally lively, and has hardened diffidence into what others see as an offensive *reserve*. In each case there is some interplay between the second and third dimensions of the word: between 'holding back' (the basic meaning of *reserve*) in the expression of thoughts and feelings and 'holding some*thing* back'. When Edward wishes his shyness could be replaced by "easy and graceful" manners, Marianne responds:

> "But you would still be reserved . . . and that is worse."
> Edward stared – "Reserved! Am I reserved, Marianne?"
> "Yes, very."
> "I do not understand you," replied he, colouring. "Reserved!
> –how, in what manner? What am I to tell you? What can you
> suppose?"   (*SS* 94–5)

Edward's relatively unembarrassed acknowledgement of his shyness is in stark contrast with his reaction to the "worse" charge of *reserve* – in which he plainly senses some imputation of concealment ("What am I to tell you?"). And, though Marianne probably intends to charge him with being *reserved* only in my category (2) sense (manners), there is every reason for Edward to jump guiltily to the word's extremest implications: for he is in fact concealing from the woman he loves the rather pertinent information that he is engaged to another.

These implications are similarly present when Mr Knightley refers on a second occasion – much less sympathetically than he had on the first – to Jane Fairfax's *reserved* manner. He rationalizes his changed attitude by claiming that the reserve is *more* than it was. But his thoughtful dwelling on the words *open* and *reserved* allows the reader to wonder whether he is not now pushing them toward their category (3) status as descriptions of moral conduct (honesty v concealment), and whether his "more" should not, therefore, more properly apply to the implications of the terms, even though their ambiguity allows them to be taken merely in the same category (2) sense of manners as previously (for Mr Knightley is more scrupulous than is Emma about communicating potentially slanderous suspicions):

> "She has not the open temper which a man would wish for in his
> wife . . . . She is reserved, more reserved, I think, than she used
> to be – And I love an open temper."   (*E* 288–9)

Reserve, then, is at best *repulsive*, and hence more *disgusting* than such *elegance* as Lady Middleton's, or even Jane's, can atone for; and, since *openness* could characterize not merely manner(s) but also moral conduct, its want of that could suggest something worse – as it does to the integrity and astuteness of Mr Knightley, and to the guilt of poor Edward Ferrars. Hence Anne, reflecting on Mr Elliot's lack of Frank's *openness*, finds herself concluding that the former is someone not only whom she cannot warm to, but also whom she cannot trust (*P* 161).

Into the category of behaviour that offends, by contrast, through too much freedom fall *impudence, impertinence* and *insolence*, which are today nearly synonymous terms for cheekiness. In Jane Austen's usage they are closer to their respective etymologies and are used to indicate very different kinds of offensiveness. *Impudent* derives from the Latin word for 'shame' or 'modesty' (*pudor*), and still carried much of its etymological meaning of **shameless** or **immodest**. And (though it could be used fairly playfully to refer to 'cheek', 'nerve' or any sort of cool unshame-facedness) it could thus be deployed to vent more serious indignation than it can today – as with Elinor's at the letter to Marianne from Willoughby; she cannot imagine how he could have departed 'so far from the common decorum of a gentleman, as to send a letter so impudently cruel' (*SS* 184).

Impertinent[19] refers etymologically to what does not pertain or belong, and is used to indicate various different kinds of rudeness that involve some kind of 'intrusion' or officious 'interference' that is offensively uncalled for or uninvited and so lacks 'pertinence'. Presuming to give advice to someone who may be assumed to be better informed on the matter in hand than oneself is an especially typical kind of offensively irrelevant *impertinence*. Cassandra could thus receive the following playful apology from her younger sister:

> It is rather impertinent to suggest any household care to a housekeeper, but I just venture to say that the coffee-mill will be wanted every day while Edward is at Steventon, as he always drinks coffee for breakfast.   (*JAL* 68)

The word was also used of officious intrusion into the affairs of another where such intrusion could not be pertinent to the interests of that other – what we would call **interfering**. Thus Darcy can say of his efforts to separate Bingley and Jane:

> "I told him of all that had occurred to make my former interference in his affairs, absurd and impertinent."   (*PP* 371)

It was also applied especially frequently to nosy, over-familiar probing into the private and personal affairs of someone else, or into information which courtesy and considerateness should leave to be volunteered. Lady Catherine has a good deal of such autocratic presumption or 'dignified impertinence' (*PP* 166). *Impertinent* behaviour of this kind is that which is **presumptuous** and/or over-**familiar**. It is used in *Sense and Sensibility* primarily of the two *inelegant* Miss Steeles, notable both for their 'impertinence, vulgarity, inferiority of parts' (127). The 'vulgar freedom' of the elder is particularly commented on (124). Her curiosity to learn the name of Elinor's *beau* the latter finds 'impertinently expressed', but 'perfectly of a piece with her general inquisitiveness into the concerns of their family' (125); and Anne's presumptuous nosiness and over-familiarity are constantly referred to as *impertinent* (219, 249). This application of the word is used to comic effect by the shamelessly unprincipled Lady Susan, with reference to the embarrassing questions put to her by a lover:

> I like him on the whole very well ... but he is sometimes impertinent & troublesome. There is a sort of ridiculous delicacy about him which requires the fullest explanation of whatever he may have heard to my disadvantage.   (*MW* 268)

This comically exploits one of the most common applications of the word – to intrusiveness into another's privacy. The word could also be used of visitors who intrude themselves without regard to the convenience of the visitee (cf. *SCG* VI.48–9); this usage is also given a burlesque application in 'Love and Freindship' [*sic*] (the writer's friend has taken to systematic robbery in Macdonald Hall, and is one night interrupted in a manner most *im*pertinent to her purposes):

... as Sophia was majestically removing the 5th Banknote ...
she was suddenly most impertinently interrupted in her employ-
ment by the entrance of Macdonald himself ... Sophia ...
demanded in a haughty tone of voice, "Wherefore her retire-
ment was thus insolently broken in on?"   (*MW* 96)

Insolence is the rudeness of arrogance. Johnson defines it as 'Pride
exerted in contemptuous and overbearing treatment of others'. It
characterizes behaviour that is offensive by reason of contempt or
high-handedness, or in any way suggesting that its agent 'looks
down on' another, or treats him or her as an inferior (or, on
occasion, does not look *up* far enough – i.e., failure of proper
respect from an inferior: *DJ* XI.41; *Mar.* 204). It is used of those
two autocratic and overbearing women, Lady Catherine, whose
manners Wickham describes as "dictatorial and insolent" (*PP* 84);
and Mrs Churchill, whose pride Mr Weston declares to be carried
to the point of "arrogance and insolence" (*E* 310). Marianne
exclaims at Willoughby's letter, "Oh! barbarously insolent!" (*SS*
190) – for the cool formality with which it had affected to correct
misapprehensions in her about his intentions is calculated to
mortify and snub. She later admits that she was herself "insolent
and unjust" to all the inmates of Barton Park, associating this with
the "contempt" with which she had treated them (346). Catherine
Morland is bewildered and humiliated by 'the abruptness, the
rudeness, nay, the insolence' of her ejection from General Tilney's
house (*NA* 226). Elizabeth Bennet, who feels insulted by Darcy's
objections to her family, is naturally rather more inclined to see
arrogant *insolence* than honesty and justice in his letter of explanation: 'his style was not penitent, but haughty. It was all pride and
insolence' (*PP* 204). The *insolence* of patronizing condescension
can be just as offensive in the superiority it assumes as arrogance.
Frank Churchill is infuriated at the ostentatious liberties with Jane
Fairfax's first name taken by the Eltons, at "hearing it bandied
between [them] with all the vulgarity of needless repetition, and all
the insolence of imaginary superiority" (*E* 442). *Insolence* tends to
provoke more indignation than *impudence*, which may shock, or
impertinence, which may irritate; for nothing offends the *amour
propre* so much as the sensation of being demurred upon.

One of the opposites of *insolence* is *affability*. *Affable* has become today a horribly patronizing word, referring to a geniality toward which the implied attitude of the speaker is one of kindly tolerance. But it once had very different connotations. The word comes from Latin *adfari* ['to speak to'], and means literally 'able to be spoken to'. In earlier usage, it therefore referred to persons who were approachably 'addressable'. Johnson defines it as 'Easy of manners; accostable'. And he adds a piece of information important to proper appreciation of its use by Jane Austen: 'It is used of superiors'. Social superiors who are affable are those ready to condescend to be pleasant to their inferiors, who do not maintain a haughty reserve from them, but are 'approachable' (Johnson's 'accostable') and 'addressable' by them. Where insolence insults by treating as inferior, affability gratifies by renouncing a right to do so. Thus Jane Austen could write of her brother Charles and his fellow sailors:

> They were well satisfied with their Royal Passenger, whom they found fat, jolly & affable.   (*JAL* 120)

What in anyone else would be simply good-natured ease is, in the Duke of Sussex, son of George III, *affability*.

So those who use the word of another's behaviour toward them are thereby indicating their consciousness of a distinction in rank which is influencing their perceptions of that behaviour. In *Sense and Sensibility*, Lucy Steele uses it of Mrs Ferrars's treatment of her. She is delighted at how "exceeding affable" she found her. Her use of the word is very revealing. It suggests an awareness of social inferiority, and that her pleasure is the flattered pleasure of the social climber at any notice from the great. She also, of course, intends the word as a compliment to herself, under colour of a compliment to Mrs Ferrars – and as a jibe at Elinor, to whom Mrs Ferrars had been pointedly rude and *insolent* (236, 264). So she insists on the word with flattered and spiteful complacency:

> "Could any thing be so flattering as Mrs. Ferrars's treatment of me yesterday? So exceeding affable as she was! . . . Such kindness as fell to the share of nobody but me! – No pride, no hauteur . . . all sweetness and affability!"   (239)

Lucy's use of the word of Mrs Ferrars is, in fact, not unlike that in which Mr Collins applies it to another *insolent* woman: Lady

Catherine. He is immensely flattered by Lady Catherine's patronizing behaviour to him, and constantly refers with servile relish to
her great *affability* (*PP* 66, 157, 160). His own obsequious conceit,
however, reveals to Elizabeth, even before she has met this awful
woman, that behind what he sees as an *affable* Ladyship is an
"arrogant, conceited" one (84).

There is only one other instance of the word in *Sense and
Sensibility* – when it is used, coincidentally, of Lucy herself. The
servant who gives the news of her marriage to the Dashwoods says
it was just like Lucy to call him across the street and chat to him,
because "She was always a very affable and free-spoken young
lady" (354). Again the word is used to indicate an inferior's
pleasure at civility or friendliness extended from a social superior:
it is a servant speaking – one who has always found Lucy
'approachable' and unreserved. Some ironic undertone in this
reference to Lucy's affability with domestics may well have been
intended. That she should be pretty free and familiar with servants
would very likely have been perceived as a detail entirely con-
sonant with her real, though anxiously disguised, vulgarity.

In the case of Lucy and Mr Collins, it is a certain flattered
conceit that leads them to mistake arrogant condescension for
affability. But these flattered sensations may equally issue from
modesty, implying a (just or otherwise) sense of inferiority in the
speaker. Harriet Smith sees wondrous *affability* in the great Miss
Woodhouse toward such an insignificant girl as herself (*E* 25).
Emma is socially and intellectually genuinely Harriet's superior.
But when Mrs Elton's attentions to Jane are commended by Miss
Bates, the suspicion that the word is liable to incur when used by
those of much humility and little penetration (that the graciousness extended was in fact the "insolence of imaginary superiority"
(442), as Frank puts it) is immediately indirectly confirmed by the
narrative. Mrs Elton 'was quite one of her worthies – the most
amiable, affable, delightful woman – just as accomplished and
condescending as Mrs. Elton meant to be considered' (284–5). The
word *condescending* itself carried no derogatory overtones. Johnson has no entry for the participial adjective, but gives for the
equivalent *condescensive*, 'Courteous; willing to treat with inferiors on equal terms; not haughty; not arrogant' (cf. *Evel.* 240).
In the above passage, therefore, that word simply reflects Mrs
Elton's own view of her behaviour, so completely endorsed by

the guileless Miss Bates; but there is poetic justice in that happy accident of the semantic history of *condescending* that shows what there really is beneath the *affability* she is pleased to credit herself with.

Some other words that related to one's 'social self', the way one is perceived by others, should also be mentioned here. *Character* can often come into this category. A Greek-derived word, it refers etymologically to that which is 'cut or engraved' upon something, and today retains most of that sense when it is used in the plural to refer to letter shapes which are 'inscribed' in writing. The modern use of the word to refer to the distinctive 'stamp' of a disposition or temperament was, at this period, still emergent out of an earlier one in which that stamp was one externally delivered rather than innate: that is, one in which the word referred to one's **reputation, name** or **standing**. This earlier sense was still very much in use, and the word *character* therefore often refers to the report current of someone, their reputed worth. In one particular idiom, 'giving a character' to, for instance, a servant, meant giving them a reference (cf. *BLJ* 5.75, 6.171)[20] – a usage wittily reversed by Mrs Gardiner, when, in response to the glowing account of Darcy given by his housekeeper, she says with knowing amusement that the latter "did give him a most flaming character" (*PP* 258). But servants only needed in a much more precise way the guarantee of a *character* – (good) name or 'standing' – that was important also to their betters. Jane Austen uses the word both in its modern sense, but also, not infrequently, in that earlier sense. The term was, in fact, in a state of transition from external to internal reference, the person as objectively seen and as he subjectively is. Byron could thus pun on the two senses in *Don Juan*, in a passage satirizing the dull sameness of polite society, which shows

> a smooth monotony
> Of character, in those at least who have got any.
>
> (XIV.16)

That is, only those who have no **good name** or **respectability** to lose can escape the monotony which is the essential **nature** of genteel society.

In its earlier sense one's *character* was thus the measure of social *credit* one could command. This latter word, too, can refer to one's standing in society, the degree of respect it accords one. It occurs with reference to Lady Russell's inner struggle over the debts contracted by the Elliots between her 'integrity', which urges retrenchments, and her solicitude 'for the credit of the family' (*P* 11), which makes her reluctant to see its standard of living reduced in a way that might lessen the esteem in which it was held. This struggle in Lady Russell to preserve the family's *credit* in one sense while its credit in another is fast running out is observed with sympathetic irony. For though the originally related words *honesty* and *honour* had long consented to a mutually convenient separation, debts were commonly perceived as one of those areas in which the former levied its claim of minimal maintenance on the latter.[21] And Lady Russell is far too honest and *sensible* not to know that the family honour will be more injured by failure to honour its debts than by anything else, and that, though much is due to the self-respect of a *gentleman* who would wish to live as such, "there is still more due to the character of an honest man" (12): that is, to his good **name** *for* honesty. Lady Russell's dilemma provides striking illustration of the way in which moral questions often formulated themselves as questions of social standing: she is trying to reconcile two different kinds of propriety that both look ultimately to social evaluation – the *credit* and *character* of the Elliot family.

Darcy is another person much concerned with the dignity of himself and his family. He tells Elizabeth that he would not have pained her or himself with the explanations given in his letter, "had not my character required it to be written and read" (*PP* 196) – by which he means his good **name**, not his disposition. Elizabeth has accused him of conduct, with regard to Jane and Wickham, that would have been dishonourable, and he wishes to clear his **name** from such imputations. Although 'owing it to one's character' was something of a formula in the context of explanations that purported to set the record straight as to conduct which had been damagingly interpreted (cf. *MW* 290), and might therefore be used somewhat imprecisely, the strict illogicality of the usage here is interesting. For Darcy's name or reputation, in any general sense, is not at issue. His explanations are for Elizabeth alone – and indeed (at least as far as the Wickham part of them goes) obviously confidential and not to go further. It is just that Darcy has the habit of viewing himself objectively, of measuring his conduct against that which he would wish the world to find him. On his *character* in the modern sense he is a lot less sensitive, coolly acknowledging that his *temper* may have many defects (58). He is prompted to reform his ways, one may recall, by the mortifying realization that Elizabeth has felt his conduct to be unbecoming that of a *gentleman*. The pride of himself and of Lady Russell is inseparable from their conscience. This does not mean that either is 'concerned only with appearances'. Both are in fact characters of considerable integrity, with a deep concern to deserve and justify by their behaviour the respect of the world. Such people did not ask if they could 'live with themselves' if they did such and such; they consulted rather their social self-image and the ideals postulated by it, their *character* and *credit* and the ethos of the *gentleman* so powerfully invoked by Elinor Dashwood and Elizabeth to condemn the actions of Willoughby and Darcy.

Morality and concern for the respect of the world are often not easily distinguishable at this period. Words such as *credit, character, decorum, propriety* and *gentleman* carried both moral and social implications which a user of them – such as Lady Russell, who registers 'injustice and discredit' (*P* 16) simultaneously and almost synonymously – might have been hard put to it to disentangle. In that passage in which Emma tries to explain to Harriet why she should stop wearing her heart on her sleeve about Mr Elton (*E* 268, quoted on p. 90 *supra*), the appeal to Harriet's *credit* is really also one to what we would today call her '*self-respect*'[22]. In this matter, what has happened to the word *character* is symptomatic of a major cultural shift towards the internal and the subjective, for that term now locates inside someone the quantity that it formerly identified with the external name and report current of him or her. Concepts of self and morality have certainly undergone a 'desocialization' in their formulation and conceptualization. The deep concern with honour, name and reputation, with what the world will think, of earlier cultures tends to be regarded now (often disingenuously) with condescension or distaste, since it is commonly assumed that the only important verdict is the one you pass on yourself (though whether that is a safer or more impartial one is at least arguable). Our *characters* and our 'selves' we now identify with those private, inner, instinctive responses often at odds with what, in response to social constraints, we may externally do. But in an earlier idiom, to 'forget oneself' was to be distracted by inner feelings from maintaining a proper social role (cf. *MP* 170; *E* 130); while to remember who or where you were was to 'recollect yourself' and the behaviour required of you.

Words that singled out the individual from social context thus frequently figured as terms of disapproval. *Odd, strange* and, more especially, *singular* and *particular* could often bear a derogatory emphasis, connoting the undesirably irregular. *Odd* can serve as a pointed or playful or deliberately restrained understatement for what is felt by the speaker to be behaviour that is unbecoming or offensive. It can thus bear Lady Catherine's majestic disapproval on hearing from Elizabeth that all her sisters are 'out': "All? – What, all five out at once? Very odd!" (*PP* 165). Mr and Mrs Weston use the word of Mrs Churchill, making it clear enough that it is a decorous makeshift for a stronger one (*E* 120–21; cf. *SCG* VII. 295; *NA* 104); and the sensible Mrs Morland, determined not to 'make a fuss' about the humiliation visited on her daughter, refers with calm restraint to its having been occasioned by some "odd fancy" of the General's (*NA* 237). Much the same applies to *strange* (cf. *NA* 87, 89; *P* 39). Mrs Norris, objecting to Fanny's inclusion in the trip to Sotherton, is comically forced (since there is no real impropriety involved) to hunt the connotations of this word as hard as she can into virtual denotation of bad manners, pointing to

> their having assured positively Mrs. Rushworth that Fanny could not go, and the very strange appearance there would con-sequently be in taking her. . . . It must have the strangest appearance! It would be something so very unceremonious, so bordering on disrespect for Mrs. Rushworth, whose own man-ners were such a pattern of good breeding and attention, that she really did not feel equal to it.   (*MP* 78)

The wise would especially guard themselves against any un-wanted observation of or speculation on their private affairs: anything that might attract *remark*. The socially aware Emma is thus glad that Mr Elton's marriage will screen the less friendly relations with him inevitable after the embarrassing misunderstanding that has occurred: 'A *Mrs. Elton* would be an excuse for any change of intercourse; former intimacy might sink without remark' (182–3). In fact, this word often implies observations not of a neutral kind, but of an exposing and critical kind (cf. *BLJ* 6.59).

That one's private affairs should be exposed to public notice is undesirable – but so is any *singularity* that attracts it: anything that singles one out by its lack of conformity with the norms of behaviour observed by those regarded as decent-living people. It is part of the peculiar excellence of that paragon, Sir Charles Grandison, that, though he lives to his conscience and not to fashion, he is yet 'above singularity', which is 'usually the indication of something wrong in judgment' (*SCG* I.137, II.230, VI.124). Lady Russell, with her intensely socially conscious brand of morality, can reconcile herself to the economies she devises for Sir Walter by reflecting that similar measures have been forced upon other genteel families:

"There will be nothing singular in his case; and it is singularity which often makes the worst part of our suffering, as it always does of our conduct." (*P* 12)

Particularity[23] was also a word to raise a shudder. It refers etymologically to 'that which relates to a part' rather than to a whole, and *particular* was used 'in a sense of contempt' (Johnson, *sv adj.* 6) of conduct that singled out an individual and drew the wrong kind of attention to itself, which was 'peculiar so as to excite surprise or wonder' (*OED adj.* 7c). Concern to avoid this is not necessarily prudishly conformist in its motives. It is concern for her sister's privacy and dignity that causes Elinor, in *Sense and Sensibility*, to be often distressed at that unguardedly open behaviour so characteristic of Marianne. There is a symbolic incident early on, when Marianne, pining after Willoughby, spies a horseman (in fact Edward Ferrars) whom she instantly determines to be Willoughby, and whom she hastens towards – 'and Elinor, to screen Marianne from particularity, as she felt almost certain of its not being Willoughby, quickened her pace and kept up with her' (86). Elinor quickens her own pace to shield Marianne's from being something peculiar to the latter, and thus drawing unwanted attention to her and her excited emotional state.

The word could be used to mean 'relating particularly to an individual' in a non-derogatory way in connection with behaviour that revealed a partiality for one member of the opposite sex (cf. *MW* 355). At balls, *particularity* could be applied to the act of dancing repeatedly with the same partner; and in such contexts the meaning 'display of distinctive preference' merges with the more derogatory 'behaviour exciting attention and comment'. Jane Austen, however, does not use the word in such situations with any seriousness. Mrs Norris, for instance, appeals to it when Mrs Rushworth, at the Mansfield ball, gives it as her view that her son and Maria should have been excused the "common forms" (that is, as a virtually engaged couple, should have been permitted to spend the evening dancing with each other), and expresses surprise that her son should not have said as much. Mrs Norris rises superbly to the occasion, which requires her to combine flattery with justification of her favourite:

> "I dare say he did, ma'am. – Mr. Rushworth is never remiss. But dear Maria has such a strict sense of propriety, so much of that true delicacy . . . that wish of avoiding particularity!"
>
> (*MP* 117)

The comment has beautifully comic irony in immediate and general context: Maria's motives for not wishing to spend the whole evening in Mr Rushworth's arms have, of course, nothing whatever to do with a delicate sense of propriety, and a great deal to do with the reverse; and her subsequent career does not exactly suggest an over-sensitive abhorrence of any éclat. The word is used semi-seriously in a similar ballroom context in *The Watsons* (*MW* 334), and the young Jane Austen herself used it of her own behaviour on a comparable occasion with mischievous irreverence for any serious principle it involved. She wrote to Cassandra of a ball at which she had danced with Tom Lefroy, with whom she facetiously represented herself to her sister as carrying on a shameless flirtation:

> Mr. Heathcote began with Elizabeth, and afterwards danced with her again. But *they* do not know how *to be particular*. I flatter myself, however, that they will profit by the three successive lessons which I have given them . . . in the way of dancing and sitting down together.   (*JAL* 1–2)

The hypocritical Isabella Thorpe appeals to the word to explain the fact that she does consent to dance with Captain Tilney, despite her avowed determination to abjure the activity entirely that evening as a sentimental tribute to the absent James Morland. She would much have preferred to sit the dances quietly out, she says, and when the artless Catherine asks her why she did not then do just that, she replies:

> "Oh! my dear! it would have looked so particular; and you know how I abhor doing that." (*NA* 134)

She means that a persistent refusal to dance would have looked singular, and so have merited the opprobrium incurred by *particularity* of conduct – to which she attributes to herself an aversion as strong, and about as convincing, as Mrs Norris claims for Maria's sensitivity to what is *proper*.

5 The Head

Abilities, powers, talents, understanding are all words which form in Jane Austen's prose part of a lexical set: that is, a group of terms referring to the same conceptual category – in this case, the quality today most commonly denoted by the word **intelligence**. *Talent(s)* could be used, as today, of special innate aptitude or flair in particular fields. But it was more often used to refer to mental endowments generally. Jane Austen's nephew explains his aunt's attachment to the much older Mrs Lefroy by alluding to the latter's excellence in all four of the major departments of character, using the word *talents* to signal her gifts of mind: her 'goodness, talents ... engaging manners ... enthusiastic eagerness' naturally endeared her to a 'clever and lively girl' such as Jane Austen herself (*Mem*. 310). The personae of the novels certainly divide themselves as clearly into the intelligent and the foolish as they do into those who are well or ill-natured and the blessed or otherwise with spirits and address. As a 'clever' woman, the authoress must herself have experienced the trials and problems, trivial or serious, of social communion with fools, and all her novels show themselves interested in assessing different kinds of sense and silliness, and in exploring the conjunction of the two within a community, within a family, within a marriage – even within one person.

Of those at Barton Park, only in Colonel Brandon, despite his want of the attractive *spirits* of Willoughby, does Elinor find anyone 'who could in any degree claim the respect of abilities, excite the interest of friendship, or give pleasure as a companion' (*SS* 55) – a carefully comprehensive analysis of the different kinds of qualifications (in intelligence, disposition and manners), one or more of which the Middletons and Mrs Jennings all lack, necessary for different kinds of positive response. In Edward, too, she has discerned "excellence of ... understanding", and assures the unbelieving Marianne that "His abilities in every respect improve as much upon acquaintance as his manners and person" (20). These *abilities* (a word for which 'mental endowments' is the gloss given by Crabb) are in each case supplemented by an acquaintance with literature and the arts and a "well-informed" mind (20, 51). "My idea of good company", Anne tells Mr Elliot (*P* 150), "is the company of clever, well-informed people, who have a great deal of conversation". Similarly, Elizabeth reproaches Darcy for his failure to make himself interesting company because, as a man of "sense and education" (*PP* 175), he should be able to do so.

Natural *abilities*, that is, must be supplemented by the acquired endowments of culture and education. This assumption found formal expression in those *accomplishments* which young ladies of good birth aimed at least to appear to possess – in music, drawing or the modern languages. Of Jane Austen's own heroines, Marianne, Jane Fairfax, Elizabeth Bennet and Anne Elliot all play the piano with a fair deal (Marianne and Jane with a great deal) of proficiency; Mary Crawford plays the harp – a particularly voguish accomplishment[1] suited to this sophisticated London-bred girl; Elinor and Emma draw well; Anne, Marianne and Fanny are all well-read and can discuss and quote from books, and Anne can speak Italian. Only Catherine Morland, for whom no claims of a strong head are made, appears to have no *accomplishments*; she reads, to be sure, but her taste in books has all the teenage garishness so often deplored in their offspring by cultivated parents – though regarded by the novel with amused tolerance and understanding.

Although Jane Austen can occasionally speak of those fashionable *accomplishments* with some dryness (*MP* 34), there is every sign that she took the underlying theory in its wider and deeper sense very seriously: minds need refining and 'finishing' (the word *accomplishment* is related to the word *completion*). That before-mentioned list of disqualifications for being *agreeable* (laboured under by all present at Mrs Ferrars's party) included 'Want of sense, either natural or improved' (*SS* 233). The reference in the word *improved* is to Lucy Steele, who is, we are repeatedly told, naturally a *clever* girl, 'but her powers had received no aid from education, she was ignorant and illiterate, and her want of information in the most common particulars, could not be concealed from Miss Dashwood . . . Elinor saw, and pitied her for, the neglect of abilities which education might have rendered so respectable' (127).

As to Marianne, it is made clear from the outset of the novel that her mistakes are not due to innate defect in her *abilities* (6), which are as good as her sister's. The two counts on which she *is* found guilty can only be accounted for by careful discrimination within the traditional categories of head and heart:

> Like half the rest of the world, if more than half there be that are clever and good, Marianne, with excellent abilities and an excellent disposition, was neither reasonable nor candid.
>
> (201–2)

Clever people ought logically to be able to use their *reason*, and good-hearted ones would seem likely to be 'not desirous to find faults' (*OED sv candid* 4). But the conventions of language flatten out distinctions, and in Marianne's case, as in that of 'half the rest of the world', the deduction would be false: there are different kinds of personal qualities misleadingly forced into some kind of uniformity because they fall by semantic convention amongst the possible referents of 'the head' on the one hand and 'the heart' on the other.

The novel's heroine, Elinor, makes much the same observations about Mr Palmer – an intelligent man who finds, like Mr Bennet of *Pride and Prejudice*, and 'like many others of his sex, that through some unaccountable bias in favour of beauty, he was the husband of a very silly woman' (112). He reacts by treating her and everybody else with an open sarcasm that does little justice to his understanding. Elinor thinks his original 'blunder . . . too common for any sensible man' to be permanently deranged by it (*ibid*), and finds herself marvelling at 'Mr. Palmer's acting so simply, with good abilities' (118). An intelligent man can choose foolishly and respond foolishly to the fact of that past error.

Nor is this the only novel in which innate intelligence fails to provide a guarantee against serious errors of judgement. Intelligence and folly, discernment and obtuseness, are very much at issue in *Pride and Prejudice*. There are those who rate their own *abilities* much higher than they deserve – such as Lady Catherine and Mary Bennet, who, conscious of having little else to recommend her, has decided to set up as accomplished, learned and profound; she succeeds only in being pedantic and sententious. She, apparently, 'rated [Mr. Collins's] abilities much higher than any of the others' (124) – which gives the real measure of her own; for Mr Collins, of course, though self-importantly unaware of his own absurdity, is a fool. Elizabeth herself, though she belongs with her father and Darcy to the trio readily recognizable as standing at the top of the novel's scale of *abilities*, at one point places herself in this same category of those who have shown a sad lack of the very discernment they pride themselves on. She impresses at once as acute and quick, and (half in jest, half in earnest) had at Netherfield Park professed herself a "studier of character" (42). Discovering how far she has been mistaken in her interpretation of Wickham and Darcy, she cries out in mortification: "How despicably have I acted! . . . I, who have prided myself on my discernment! – I, who have valued myself on my abilities!" She has not, she realizes, been objective in her assessment of the two men; but through a "vanity" flattered by the attentions of the one and "offended by the neglect of the other", has courted "prepossession and ignornace" (208).

Mr Bennet, a shrewd and reading man, can also make mistakes with far-reaching consequences. He has suffered Mr Palmer's fate of finding himself married to a woman of 'weak understanding' (236), and reacts as unwisely, if not as childishly, as the equally gifted Mr Palmer. He adopts the stance of ironically amused and detached observer of his wife's follies, and Elizabeth feels his error in this. Though 'respecting his abilities', she cannot but see the 'breach of conjugal obligation and decorum' that exposes his wife to the 'contempt of her own children', and deplores 'so ill-judged a direction of talents; talents which, rightly used, might at least have preserved the respectability of his daughters, even if incapable of enlarging the mind of his wife' (236–7).

Darcy himself is from the first presented as an exceptionally intelligent man – in fact the only eligible partner for Elizabeth in respect of a 'marriage of minds'. Of the two friends, Darcy is early declared to be 'In understanding . . . the superior' (16), though Bingley has qualities more calculated to recommend him. Elizabeth remains subconsciously aware of this even at her moments of deepest anger against him. Learning from Colonel Fitzwilliam of "very strong objections against the lady" Darcy had 'rescued' Bingley from, Elizabeth instantly interprets this (correctly) as

objections against Jane's family connections. But her angry de-
fensiveness in soliloquy to herself takes an interesting turn.
Though she eventually does persuade herself that Darcy's objections were based on mere pride and snobbery (thus allowing
herself the luxury of despising him for a quite irrational social
arrogance), her immediate instinct is to salvage what she cán of
her family's intelligence to throw against him in her imagination;
an intelligent girl herself, in looking at that family through his eyes
she instinctively knows that his distaste would have been more the
rational distaste of an intelligent and educated man for silliness
and ignorance rather than the silly distaste of a proud man for
relatively humble social status:

> "To Jane herself ... there could be no possibility of objec-
> tion . ... Her understanding excellent, her mind improved, and
> her manners captivating. Neither could any thing be urged
> against my father, who, though with some peculiarities, has
> abilities which Mr. Darcy himself need not disdain . ..." When
> she thought of her mother indeed, her confidence gave way a
> little, but she would not allow that any objection there had
> material weight with Mr. Darcy, whose pride, she was con-
> vinced, would receive a deeper wound from the want of
> importance in his friend's connections, than from their want of
> sense.   (186–7)

Intelligence in error also, of course, forms the basis of the plot in
Emma. Emma is perfectly aware that she ranks higher than those
around her in intelligence as in social position. Her deeply
offended reactions to Mr Elton's proposal derive from this perfect
knowledge of her own full worth:

> Perhaps it was not fair to expect him to feel how very much he
> was her inferior in talent, and all the elegancies of mind. The
> very want of such equality might prevent his perception of it; but
> he must know that in fortune and consequence she was greatly
> his superior.   (136)

Though 'elegance of mind' is not itself an unusual formulation (it is
a quality also attributed to Anne Elliot: *P* 5, 41), context creates
an implied contrast with the more external forms of **refinement** (in

manners and life-style) to which the term *elegance* was often
applied; the effect is to make *elegancies* function as something of a
transferred 'class' term (hinting at the sort of *elegancies* Mr
Elton's more superficial mind *could* understand) – transferred
from such contexts as that in which Mrs Elton snobbily refers to
families "moving in a certain circle . . . able to command the
elegancies of life" (301). The transference helps to make the point
that the class difference is to Emma only a symptom of a deeper
distinction that it takes more refined *talents* to perceive, and which
could not therefore be evident to his grosser faculties. Her even
angrier response to Mrs Elton's attempts to strike up a friendship
with her (and thus associate herself with the most distinguished
female in the neighbourbood) is based on the same dual pride. Mrs
Elton is a phoney and a fool, and her vulgar snobbery and affectation display the kind of ignorant conceit that Emma, with all her
disposition 'to think a little too well of herself' (5), is certainly
not guilty of. And if it was a little painful to witness Emma, with all
her real *talents*, making a close companion of the childlike Harriet,
it is far more repugnant to observe the mismatch of *talents* and
stupidity constituted by Mrs Elton's adoption of Jane Fairfax. Her
condescension toward a much more intelligent woman is insuffer-
able; and her patronizing, conceited and officious commendation
of Jane's *talents* to Emma gets the cool response it deserves (282).
With respect to *abilities*, unequal friendships are as unsatisfactory
as unequal marriages. Jane would have been a much more suitable
companion than Harriet for Emma herself, as Emma realizes:

> Birth, abilities, and education, had been equally marking one as
> an associate for her, to be received with gratitude; and the other
> – what was she?   (421)

Equality of *abilities* is at this point (as at others) interinvolved with
compatibility in social position. But the latter is ultimately sub-
ordinated to the former. Emma's mistake with regard to Harriet is
not, in the logic of the novel, her plan to marry the girl 'above her
station'. The story begins with an unequal marriage between a
governess and a wealthy local landowner, an event paralleled in
the marriage of Jane Fairfax to Frank Churchill. But Mrs Weston
and Jane are intelligent, cultivated women – as Harriet is not.
Emma's mistake is rather her interference in the natural direction
of Harriet's affections (the girl is already sweet on Robert Martin)

and *abilities*, which are both leading her to a position on the social scale no higher than that which her birth would also naturally dictate. Emma herself, choosing to ignore in her plans for Harriet the inequalities 'whether of mind or situation' (414) she is so strongly sensible of on her own account (in her response to Mr Elton's proposal), reacts more in character when contemplating a match between Mr Knightley and Harriet. Quite apart from her own personal disappointment, she is genuinely horrified at the disparagement such a marriage would constitute, a disparagement that develops as she reflects on it from social to intellectual:

> Such an elevation on her side! Such a debasement on his! It was horrible to Emma ... it was impossible. And yet ... Was it a new circumstance for a man of first-rate abilities to be captivated by very inferior powers?   (413)

Talent(s), aptitude (in general, or, as today, in specific directions), are something to which, for various reasons, *Mansfield Park* puts up a determined and sometimes painful resistance. Maria and Julia are by no means silly, and have enough aptitude to pick up the usual array of *accomplishments* without much difficulty (34) and to prove quick in the schoolroom. Indeed, they rather despise what they see as Fanny's slowness in learning; she apparently shows small taste for "music or drawing", the two most common channels for genteel female *accomplishment* – though she turns out later to have a real taste for a subject less fitted to social display: literature. It is, however, pointed out that, though their formal education is going so well, what is really operating to 'form [their] minds' is the flattery of Mrs Norris, so that it was 'not very wonderful that with all their promising talents and early information, they should be entirely deficient in the less common acquirements of self-knowledge, generosity, and humility' (19; cf. 463). Henry and Mary Crawford are also both naturally bright, Mary's *talents* being especially for 'the light and lively' (81). The novel appears for a time to hold out the possibility of some kind of satisfying marriage, literally and figuratively, between two sorts of gifts of the head: the serious wisdom of Fanny and Edmund and the quickness and wit of the Crawfords. Edmund sees possibilities in this direction, and looks forward to the meeting of Sir Thomas and Mary, on the grounds that, "He would enjoy her liveliness – and she has talents to value his powers" (199). Each is intelligent enough to appreciate the rather different intelligence of the other – though it is interesting that Sir Thomas's more austere brand of mental superiority requires the slightly weightier word *powers*. He resembles Lady Russell in being 'rather of sound than of quick abilities' (*P* 11) – the word *talent(s)* is used of neither of them: there is a deliberative rigour in their mental operations that makes the word (suggesting as it does something of the instinctive exercise of innate 'gifts') inappropriate.

Fanny herself is intelligent enough to value *talent*. It is not only deficiencies in heart and refinement of manners she discovers in Portsmouth: her mother has 'no talent, no conversation' as well as 'no affection towards herself' (390). As to Henry, the narrator herself tells us that Fanny was not so impervious to 'all that talent, manner, attention, and flattery can do' (231) as to have been able long to resist his suit – had she not been already in love with another man. It is not only Henry's specific gift for reading poetry aloud well – "no every-day talent" (338), as Edmund (rightly) observes – that certainly affects Fanny, but also the more general *talent* from which that gift derives – an innate awareness and perception that teaches him to find by instinct the right language and the right tone and expression: the natural intelligence that makes Fanny despite herself acknowledge that he spoke well of his love for her, 'and in the language, tone, and spirit of a man of talent, too' (328). *Talent* is an innate aptitude that, among other things, instructs to an innate apt*ness* of speech and behaviour. Neither of these marriages, of course, actually occurs, despite this sympathy in *abilities* which lends its weight to other attractions; each is aborted – even as is the ill-fated play – that arena for the enjoyable exercise for young *talent(s)* (123, 126, 134, 135) – which never does take place under the roof of Mansfield Park.

Intelligence is also frequently referred to by the term *sense*.[2] The special collocation *good sense*, however, often carries a moral weight the phrase does not have today and implies the possession of **sound values and priorities**. Take the following forbidding piece of wisdom, for instance:

> She loved amusement as the *amusement* of an imperfect existence, though her good sense, and still better principles, taught her to reject it as the *business* of an immortal being.
>
> (*Mar.* 292; cf. 82; *BLJ* 9.16)

In *Sanditon*, Clara Brereton, the protégée of Lady Denham, is said to have endeared herself to both her patroness and the whole neighbourhood by the 'good sence & merit' (*MW* 378, 379) evident in her conduct. The collocation with *merit* (as with *principles*) is significant. The whole description of Clara makes it clear that what recommends her is the probity and decorum of her behaviour – not her common sense. And Mr Parker also declares Lady Denham's choice of the niece Clara (rather than any of the daughters of the house of impoverished relatives she had decided to assist by domiciling one of the young ladies with herself) to be a tribute to the better part of that lady's nature, which shows a strange 'union of Littleness with Kindness with Good Sense with even Liberality' (378). Lady Denham's choice, that is, evinces moral discernment, a discriminating sense of values, evident also in her protégée's behaviour.

The flavour of the phrase can perhaps best be savoured in one of the 'Opinions on *Mansfield Park*' Jane Austen collected from amongst her friends and acquaintances: "I think it excellent – & of its good sense & moral Tendency there can be no doubt" (*MW* 434). Here, *good sense* is associated with the evident "moral Tendency" of the novel: *Mansfield Park* shows a proper sense of values, of what is and what is not ultimately important. Sir Thomas himself, the patriarch of that house, has similar *good sense*: that is, he is a man of propriety and integrity. When Lady Bertram laments the imminent departure for London of her two daughters, 'A great deal of good sense followed on Sir Thomas's side, tending to reconcile his wife to the arrangement' (284). The modern understanding of the phrase might lead us to predict that Sir Thomas's arguments were drawn from reason and common sense: Julia would not be gone for ever, Lady Bertram would not be alone in the meantime, etc. But they are in fact drawn from what may be called the morality of parental affection: 'Everything that a considerate parent *ought* to feel was advanced for her use; and everything that an affectionate mother *must* feel in promoting her children's enjoyment, was attributed to her nature' (285). The phrase is applied also to a similar piece of moral philosophy directed by Mrs Morland to Catherine, 'tending to reconcile' *her* to any 'neglect or unkindness of slight acquaintance like the Tilneys', which should not be allowed to outweigh 'the happiness of having such steady well-wishers as Mr. and Mrs. Allen', who are amongst her 'earliest friends': a position to which the narrator attributes 'a great deal of good sense' (*NA* 239) – powerless though it naturally is to operate on a lovesick young girl.

Good sense thus implies a worthiness and correctness in the priorities of the person (or sentiments) to whom it is attributed. It enters into the contrast between Elinor Tilney and Isabella Thorpe, which is a contrast in head, heart and manners. Of the former it is noted at once that 'Her manners shewed good sense and good breeding' (*NA* 56; cf. 249): two qualities markedly wanting in Isabella, who is both vulgar and without that special kind of judgement implied by *good sense*. When Catherine's brother says of Isabella that "she has so much good sense, and is so thoroughly unaffected and amiable" (50), we are obviously meant to hear the voice of a judgement very thoroughly overset by the partiality of a lover. We have already seen enough of the hypocritical Isabella to know that he is quite radically wrong on all three counts – but the irony of his attributing *good sense* to her is not quite what a modern reader might at first take it to be. It does not lie in Isabella's actual folly – she is, in fact, a shrewd and scheming girl; but rather in the shallowness of values and the want of any sense of the socially and morally becoming so evident in her speech and behaviour.

The word contemporaries commonly suggested as the nearest synonym for *sense* was 'judgement'.[3] Crabb makes *sense* (when used of mental rather than physical perception) 'synonymous with judgment'. Thomas Reid similarly informs us that 'in common language sense always implies judgment. A man of sense is a man of judgment. Good sense is good judgment' (*Essays on the Intellectual Powers of Man*, 330). *Common sense* is 'that degree of judgment which is common to men with whom we can converse and transact business' (337).

Sense can thus be used to indicate all the variety of perceptions and determinations that **judgement** still can. Hence, though often used in a general way of **intelligence**, it can also occur (even without the prefixed *good*) in contexts in which it is moral **discernment and evaluation** that is at issue. Henry Crawford (to take an example from that same novel of *good sense*), when he decides to court Fanny, says of the absent Maria and Julia: "They will now see what sort of woman it is that can attach me, that can attach a man of sense" (297). The contempt, arrogance and complacency of the comment are not uncharacteristic of the speaker – but neither are the **taste** and **discernment** Henry credits himself with. His *talents* are quite good enough to ensure him a degree of just appreciation or *sense* of the true worth of Fanny. He has 'too much sense not to feel the worth of good principles in a wife' (294). Similarly, Mr Knightley concedes to Emma that, ill-judged though her matrimonial plans for Mr Elton were, she had actually chosen for him better than he chose for himself. Harriet, "an unpretending, single-minded, artless girl" had qualities "infinitely to be preferred by any man of sense and taste to such a woman as Mrs. Elton" (*E* 331). Harriet could not today be called a suitable mate for a man of sense: she is pretty silly; but a man with some moral sense ought to have known how to value her ingenuous innocence. Mrs Smith concedes that Mr Elliot "has sense to understand the value of such a woman" as Anne (*P* 196). Anne's one regret in marrying Frank is that she has 'no relations to bestow on him which a man of sense could value' (251). [Frederick]

Sense, therefore, is a word denoting not (as it often does today) common sense, but (a) intelligence and discernment, with a tendency to connote (b) values that are not superficial. On occasion, there seems to be some interplay between the (morally) neutral and commendatory senses of the word. Elinor, trying to reconcile herself to Edward's marriage with Lucy, for her own sake and that of Marianne – whom she is addressing, whom she would spare further distress, and to whom she is indirectly attempting to set an example of patience – comforts herself with the thought that Edward will have married a woman who is at least not lacking in *understanding*; he will eventually be happy, for "Lucy does not want sense, and that is the foundation on which everything good may be built" (*SS* 263). Elinor is probably trying to argue from meaning (a) to meaning (b) of the word: since Lucy does not lack intelligence and discernment, she must also have some sense of rightness and decency. That Elinor is involved in some manipulation of the word is suggested by the fact that Lucy (though often called *clever*) is not elsewhere credited with *sense* – except once by Elinor herself, in a passage that clearly indicates a wry consciousness on her part that it is not *sense* in its fullest sense: on first meeting the Steeles, she 'soon allowed them credit for *some kind of* sense, when she saw with what constant and judicious attentions they were making themselves agreeable to Lady Middleton' (120: my italics).

When Colonel Brandon generously confers the living of Delaford upon Edward, John Dashwood's reaction is typical of his obsessive meanness. The living was a valuable one, and he wonders at "a man of Colonel Brandon's sense" doing such an "improvident" thing (295). John's entirely worldly interpretation of *sense* here is probably being played off against the more serious meaning of the word: for Brandon's value for Edward and his honourable and generous action could, in other mouths than John's, be held to prove, not disprove, his *sense*, his right-mindedness. Henry Tilney is certainly using the word in a different sense from that implied by John when he says, apropos of his brother and Isabella, that "Frederick will not be the first man who has chosen a wife with less sense than his family expected" (*NA* 205); he does not mean Isabella is thoughtless in practical matters, but that she is superficial. And when Elizabeth thinks with mortification of her mother's want of *sense* (*PP* 187), it is likewise something more than cleverness that is at issue. It is the narrow-minded values revealed in her mother's talk and behaviour that makes Elizabeth wince with shame when she contemplates her in imagination through Darcy's eyes.

Sense is thus an elastic word, which, though it can be used in a fairly perfunctory way of intelligence, can also be found in more morally serious contexts than those in which it usually appears today. For instance, of Lady Russell's dilemma over Sir Walter's debts, we are told:

> She was of strict integrity herself, with a delicate sense of honour; but she was as desirous of saving Sir Walter's feelings, as solicitous for the credit of the family, as aristocratic in her ideas of what was due to them, as any body of sense and honesty could well be.　(*P* 11)

Lady Russell's *sense* is here ranged with an 'integrity', 'honesty' and 'sense of honour' to express that part of her instincts which in this instance conflicts with her 'aristocratic' notions of the style of life proper to a distinguished household; where the latter resist very radical retrenchment of Sir Walter's expenses, the former, representing the sounder **values** of *honesty* and *integrity*, make her aware that paying their debts is more profoundly relevant to the honour and dignity of the family than the number of servants and horses it keeps.

The normal term for literal unconsciousness (when the senses do not function) was at this period *insensibility*, and Jane Austen herself so uses the word (*P* 112). And *sensible*, when it took a qualifier (in such expressions as 'sensible of...', 'sensible that...'), had the meaning 'conscious' or 'aware' that it still retains in such contexts. Even without a qualifier, *sensible* could be equivalent to 'strongly felt' or 'capable of feeling' in such phrases as 'sensible concern' and 'a heart so sensible' (*SCG* II.322, III.226), where *sensible* does not mean 'intelligent' any more than it does in the statement in the same novel that 'The most *sensible* ... creature on earth, is certainly a woman in Love' (V.650) – where it means 'having keen and alert senses', as the following question reveals: 'What can escape her penetration?' It is to the meaning of *sensible* in such expressions as these that the adverb *sensibly* frequently refers. Lady Russell, when Anne is not included by her father and sister in the visit to London, is said to have been 'sensibly open to all the injustice and all the discredit of the selfish arrangements that shut her out' (*P* 16): that is, she was feelingly aware of those things.

As applied to persons, *sensible* differed from its modern counterpart in ways analogous to the related noun *sense*. Again, *sensible* did not for Jane Austen connote that hard-headed, cool, practical type of 'common sense' it usually suggests today. **Intelligent** is often the nearest modern equivalent. The altered semantics of the word are perhaps most apparent in its application to Marianne in *Sense and Sensibility*:

> She was sensible and clever; but eager in everything; her sorrows, her joys, could have no moderation. She was generous, amiable, interesting: she was everything but prudent.   (6)

The other adjectives in this description will also be discussed in due course. As far as the head goes, it is worth noticing that Jane Austen here distinguishes between three adjectives that all relate to *abilities: sensible, clever* and *prudent*. The girl described here and portrayed more fully in the novel as a whole – idealistic, emotional, impulsive, never allowing moderation to temper her ardours, etc – could never qualify as a *sensible* candidate in the modern understanding of the word. Not even her best friend could today call even the reformed Marianne of the end of the novel a 'sensible' girl.

The word had travelled less far from its metaphorical origins (in the five senses) and so signalled in a broader (and often more serious) way 'able to sense', 'aware', 'perceptive'. Like *sense*, it too could be applied to moral/social awareness, and be equivalent to **well-judging**. It is particularly prone to that connotation (as is *sense*) when used in statements that invoke 'a sensible man/ person' as a standard of reactions, feelings and judgements in given situations. In *Mansfield Park*, Fanny, admitting Dr Grant's deficiencies as a minister, yet argues that his profession must exercise some good influence on him:

> "A man – a sensible man like Dr. Grant, cannot be in the habit of teaching others their duty every week . . . without being the better for it himself."   (112)

Sensible here (the opposite of *insensible* rather than *un-sensible*) is being applied to a capacity for moral awareness, a 'sense' of what is right. When Emma tries to convince Mr Knightley that it would have been very difficult for Frank Churchill to announce to the Churchills an intention to flout their wishes and pay the visit to his father he should have paid as a "mark of respect" soon after the latter's wedding, Mr Knightley replies forthrightly: "Depend upon it, Emma, a sensible man would find no difficulty in it. He would feel himself in the right; and the declaration – made, of course, as a man of sense would make it, in a proper manner" could only raise his credit with his foster-parents (*E* 147). *Sensible* and *sense* here again refer to a sense of moral and social decorum which would instruct a *sensible* man (in Mr Knightley's own words (146), "A man who felt rightly") both as to what his duty was and as to how it might with least offence be announced.

In *Persuasion*, the word is a key one. Lady Russell had genuinely believed she was acting wisely in dissuading Anne from marrying Captain Wentworth; it was always an object with her to be 'sensible and well-judging' (249). The second adjective provides a gloss on the first in Lady Russell's own reflections on various *sensible* responses. Of the lower standards of living Sir Walter must adopt to extricate himself from debt, she says, "the true dignity of Sir Walter Elliot will be very far from lessened, in the eyes of sensible people, by his acting like a man of principle" (12). She finds nothing surprising in Mr Elliot's sudden desire to be reconciled with Sir Walter – a man with 'a head naturally clear' must have realized that it would 'very generally recommend him, among all sensible people, to be on good terms with the head of his family' (147). Lady Russell aims herself to be *sensible* in the sense in which she herself uses the word: that is, **right-minded**, 'well-judging'.[4]

If Anne is dissuaded from the right marriage by a woman of *sense*, she is likewise very nearly inveigled into the wrong one by the deceptive *sense* of a very unprincipled man. Mr Elliot proves that a sound *sense* and perception of right and wrong conduct does not guarantee integrity of life and actions. Of his *sense* Anne finds constant proof (and Lady Russell had always known (29) she could only be tempted by a 'man of talents'):

> There could be no doubt of his being a sensible man. Ten minutes were enough to certify that. His tone, his expressions, his choice of subject, his knowing where to stop – it was all the operation of a sensible, discerning mind.   (143)

A social/moral nicety of judgement is obviously implied by *sensible* here. Lady Russell hears and relays his praise of Anne herself, and Anne 'could not know herself to be so highly rated by a sensible man, without many of those agreeable sensations which her friend meant to create' (159) – discernment and sound judgement and values are again obviously at issue. But Anne has inexplicable (at this point) reservations. When she sums up her feelings about him, she confirms the impression he has created of being a *sensible* man, summarizes all she understands by that word, and yet senses that an *awareness* of right and wrong, a good judgement, may not in this case have exercised a decisive influence on his life and behaviour:

> That he was a sensible man, an agreeable man, – that he talked well, professed *good opinions*, seemed to *judge properly* and as a man of *principle*, – this was all clear enough. He certainly *knew what was right* . . . but yet she would have been afraid to answer for his conduct.   (160: my italics)[5]

Sensible could thus be used (though it was not invariably so used) to mean **right-minded**, 'possessing proper values' – which explains why *Mansfield Park* was judged to be a *sensible* novel (*MW* 433), which is a compliment to its ethics and values rather than its level-headedness. These connotations gave the word a rather sober and moralizing flavour of which Jane Austen shows herself facetiously aware in one of her early works (which are predominantly burlesque in tendency) entitled 'The female philosopher', in which different kinds of 'good head' are contrasted. Charlotte has wit and vivacity and abounds in 'humorous Sallies, Bonmots & repartees'; her sister Julia, however, is *sensible*, and 'uttered Sentiments of Morality worthy a heart like her own'; as these *sensible* sentiments are further particularized, one becomes aware that 'sententious' might today be the more proper adjective:

> Mr. Millar observed ... that many events had befallen each during that interval of time, which gave occasion to the lovely Julia for making most sensible reflections on the many changes in their situation which so long a period had occasioned, on the advantages of some, & the disadvantages of others. From this subject she made a short digression to the instability of human pleasures & the uncertainty of their duration, which led her to observe that all earthly Joys must be imperfect. She was proceeding to illustrate this doctrine by examples from the Lives of great Men when the Carriage came to the Door and the amiable Moralist with her Father & Sister was obliged to depart. (*MW* 171)

This is what happens when those whose heads are not especially good determine to be *sensible*. Jane Austen knew how to deflate the vacuity consequent upon the facile repetition of moral *sententiae* and *exempla* by subjecting them in full flow to a comic interruption.

Another kind of caricature of a pseudo-*sensible* woman is found in the "reputation of being remarkably sensible and clever" which the dictatorial Lady Catherine enjoys, but which Wickham thinks derives in part from her rank and wealth and "part from her authoritative manner" (*PP* 84). A useful gloss on a *sensible* character of this type is provided by Susan Ferrier's portrait of the eldest of the three Scottish maiden aunts in her novel *Marriage*,

where the right-mindedness connoted by the word manifests itself
in sheer I-know-best, interfering bossiness:

> Miss Jacky . . . was what is reckoned a very sensible woman –
> which generally means, a very disagreeable, obstinate, illiberal
> director of all men, women, and children . . . . She had attained
> this eminence . . . principally from her dictatorial manner, and
> the pompous, decisive tone, in which she delivered the most
> common-place truths . . . she was a sort of post-mistress general
> – a detector of all abuses and impositions . . . . From what has
> been said, it may easily be inferred, that Miss Jacky was in fact
> any thing but a sensible woman . . . . But there is a spurious
> sense, which passes equally well with the multitude: it is easily
> assumed, and still easier maintained, common truth and a grave
> dictatorial air being all that is necessary for its support.   (39–40)

Clever is morally neutral. It could be used in a variety of different
contexts, but it appears that two types of clever *women* sprang
especially readily to mind. *Marriage* provides a caricature similar
to that it gives for *sensible* of the popular misappropriation of this
adjective – in the evening of *clever* company Scottish Aunt Grizzy
rather bemusedly enjoys in England (409–25): dinner with Mrs
Pullens, whose life is spent devising and executing economies and
ingenuities of housewifery, and who typifies the 'active, managing,
economical' housekeeper (412); followed by tea with Mrs
Bluemits, whose cleverness is (as her name indicates) of the
bluestocking kind. These two clever horrors in fact represent the
two main classes into which *cleverness* fell:

1. (a) ingenuity in conceiving and contriving, born of (b) innate
shrewdness and quickness on the uptake. Such talents are not
always put to very edifying use. The scheming and artful Mrs Clay
in *Persuasion* and Lucy Steele in *Sense and Sensibility* are both
called *clever* women. Mrs Clay is "a clever, insinuating, handsome
woman, poor and plausible" (*P* 206; cf. 15, 34). Lucy, another artful
young lady on the make who knows how to ingratiate herself with her
social superiors, is similarly 'naturally clever', though she has no
'integrity of mind' (*SS* 127). Neither could thus be called *sensible*.

2. aptitude in the interpretation and use of words, which could
take various forms: (a) academic ability – quickness to learn (*E* 37);

(b) bookishness and a taste for literature. Here, *clever* could be virtually equivalent to what we would today call **intellectual**, and signal something distinctly superior to mere soundness up top. Frank Wentworth sees some disparity of "mind" in Captain Benwick's engagement to Louisa; for though Louisa is not "deficient in understanding", Benwick "is something more. He is a clever man, a reading man" (*P* 182). Similarly, when Bingley and Darcy (also a reading man, who keeps an excellent library: *PP* 38, 55) are compared, we are told that, 'In understanding Darcy was the superior. Bingley was by no means deficient, but Darcy was clever' (16). (c) aptitude for verbal games (such as charades: *E* 78) and speaking well – wisely, wittily or eloquently (*BLJ* 6.97; *Mar.* 439). Mary Crawford's physical 'cleverness as a horsewoman' (*MP* 69) is matched by her wit in finding 'something clever to be said at the close of every air' on her harp (64), which she governs with the same adroitness as she does her tongue and her horse.

Clever, though not in itself derogatory, withholds the moral approval of *sensible*. It is possible to be *sensible* without being *clever* and vice versa. It is probably significant that Mr Elliot, in the course of that inner review of him conducted by Anne, moves almost imperceptibly, as her suspicions concerning him grow, from the *sensible* man he appears to be to the merely *clever* man she fears may lie beneath the facade:

> That he was a sensible man, an agreeable man . . . this was all clear enough . . . but yet she would have been afraid to answer for his conduct . . . who could answer for the true sentiments of a clever, cautious man, grown old enough to appreciate a fair character?[6]   (*P* 160–61)

Conversely, Lady Russell is called *clever* only by the simple and artless Henrietta Musgrove, who says of her to Anne: "I am afraid of her . . . quite afraid of her, because she is so very clever; but I respect her amazingly" (103). Lady Russell, a 'sensible, deserving woman' (5) of 'known good sense', is 'rather of sound than quick abilities' (11), and, though her head may be stronger than Henrietta's, she is not in the narrative termed *clever*. Henrietta simply mistakes seriousness for cleverness.

The Bertram sisters commit a more obvious error in assuming that their adoptive sister is "stupid" (*MP* 18–19) because, when she arrives at Mansfield, she is less informed than her more privileged cousins. Edmund, of course, knows better. He 'knew her to be clever, to have a quick apprehension as well as good sense, and a fondness for reading, which, properly directed, must be an education in itself' (22). The 'quickness' here associated with *cleverness* is distinct from the *good sense* which Edmund has already deduced from Fanny's 'having an affectionate heart, and a strong desire to do right' (17). Mr Woodhouse, who does not like to leave his own hearth and table in the evenings, receives with pleasure Mr Knightley's invitation of a day-time visit to Donwell Abbey:

> He thought it very well done of Mr. Knightley to invite them – very kind and sensible – much cleverer than dining out. – He was not fond of dining out. (*E* 357)

Sensible here refers to the laudable rightness of Mr Knightley's avoiding that common but deplorable habit of arranging parties for the evenings, and *clever* to his ingenuity in devising an alternative. Mr Woodhouse (to whom his late wife, his daughter and Mr Perry are all perfect prodigies) has low standards of cleverness.

He is, paradoxically, the begetter of the most decidedly *clever* of Jane Austen's heroines – Emma. She is introduced as such in the opening sentence of the novel – and the adjective is amply justified by the subsequent action, despite Emma's mistakes. It recurs in connection with her speed on the uptake in the classroom as a girl (37), and with the verbal dexterity apparent in her facility with charades (78) – a dexterity also apparent in her wit, and her articulate speeches (which include the "clever replies . . . delicate negatives" (264) she envisages herself making to a proposal from Frank), which particularly impress Harriet, from whom Emma's fluency in urging the advantages of a match with Mr Elton draws an admiring comment (though there is some comedy in the way Emma's eloquence convinces Harriet not so much by its content as by its immediate association, on the part of the less clever girl, with the same verbal facility as that which can devise and interpret charades):

> "How nicely you talk . . . .. You and Mr. Elton are one as clever as the other. This charade! – If I had studied a twelvemonth, I could never have made anything like it." (76)

The inventive ingenuity (mostly deflected into those elaborate schemes for Harriet and mischievous speculations on the past of the irritatingly irreproachable Jane Fairfax) is also a sign of the *clever* girl. It is significant that she is introduced as such, rather than as *sensible* – for the effect is to reserve moral judgement. No person with *sense* would indulge in the indiscretion of attempting to engineer the affections of others, speak slightingly and damage the interests of the decent Robert Martin, permit herself scandalous reflections on the past of a respectable acquaintance or an impertinently hurtful witticism against an older and less privileged woman. Emma does not fundamentally lack *good sense* (150), but the plot turns on the exercise of her frustrated *cleverness* somewhat at the expense of that *sense*.

Marianne, in being both *sensible* and *clever*, is therefore someone whose *abilities* – 'in many respects' as good as Elinor's – must rank high. It is only as the description continues that the slight qualification explains itself – through the introduction of yet a further discrimination within the general category: '. . . she was every thing but prudent' (*SS* 6). Jane Austen's *prudent* is actually rather closer to the modern 'sensible' than is her *sensible*. The word, related to 'provident', derives ultimately from the Latin verb *providere* ('to see or look ahead'). Thus *imprudence* was commonly predicated of actions which consult only the agent's immediate pleasure or desires with no eye to his or her longer-term interests.[7] The word had strong associations with disregard for one's own health or wealth.

1.   The prudent do not risk damage to their health by exposing it to unnecessary risks – especially those insidiously present in the outside air. In the early novel *Catherine*, the heroine is able to halt an awkward conversation in the arbour with her aunt by reminding her that it is growing late. The anxious Mrs Percival reacts as expected, her apprehensions for her health enlarging, with comic rapidity, from a chill, through prolonged illness, to certain death:

> "I am astonished at my own imprudence . . . . How could I be so forgetful as to sit down out of doors at such a time of night . . . I must have caught a dreadful cold by this time. I am sure of being lain up all the winter after it . . . who knows *now*, but what I may

never recover . . . It is unknown how many people have died in consequence of catching Cold!"   (*MW* 233; cf. *JAL* 434)

Mary Crawford uses the same argument, with her usual *lively* non-seriousness, when a conversation in the Parsonage shrubbery between herself and Fanny is interrupted by Edmund:

> "Well . . . and do not you scold us for our imprudence? What do you think we have been sitting down for but to be talked to about it, and entreated and supplicated never to do so again?"   (*MP* 211)

The hypochondriac Mr Woodhouse predictably takes *prudence* in such matters more seriously; and his concern makes him as vulnerable to manipulation by an astute member of the more careless younger generation as was Mrs Percival by her niece. Frank, endeavouring to persuade him of strong reasons for preferring the Crown to Randalls as the site of the projected ball, remarks shrewdly that at the former there will be "no occasion to open the windows at all", at which Mr Woodhouse exclaims in horror: "Open the windows! . . . Nobody could be so imprudent!" (*E* 251–2). The young and healthy in fact tend to appeal to such *prudence* only tactically (cf. *E* 110). The word is used more seriously of Louisa's fall in *Persuasion*, which is referred to as the consequence of *imprudence* (124, 126), in this rather specific sense of courting dangers to one's health or physical safety.

2.   Money is as important as health to a state of 'well-being' (which is what the word 'wealth' etymologically means). Here, too, it is necessary to exercise foresight in ensuring one's long-term interests are not damaged by heedless expenditure on immediate pleasures. Hence the word *prudent* also frequently occurs in financial contexts, where it is virtually equivalent to the modern 'provident'. *Imprudence* is often collocated with, and can be a euphemism for, *extravagance* – as in the case of the spendthrift habits of Wickham in *Pride and Prejudice* (96, 291; cf. 348). In the unfinished *Sanditon*, Sir Edward Denham, who fancies himself as a kind of Sir Jasper, contemplates abducting Clara to some dramatically remote neighbourhood ('Tombuctoo', for instance), but comically realizes that 'the Expense alas! of Measures in that masterly style was ill-suited to his Purse, and Prudence obliged

him to prefer the quietest sort of ruin & disgrace for the object of his Affections, to the more renowned' (*MW* 406). It is the mean John Dashwood who, significantly, provides us with a virtual definition of this sub-sense of *prudence*, in remarking of Mrs Jennings that "it is not to be imagined that she lives up to her income. Few people of common prudence will do *that*" (*SS* 227). John certainly makes sure that he stays well within his own means in executing his promise to his father to provide for his sisters.

As she often treats *prudence* about health with a touch of comedy, Jane Austen shows herself aware of the ambivalent value of the *prudence* that is providence. It can shade into downright stinginess and meanness, as with Mrs Norris, in whose case 'what was begun as a matter of prudence' (*MP* 8) has developed into an obsessive parsimony. In fact, *prudence* can be a euphemism for tight-fistedness – as in the early comic story 'The Three Sisters', where the two younger persuade themselves that the eldest will not be ill-advised to accept the proposal of a frightful Mr Watts, who will devolve upon one of them if she refuses him; they therefore rephrase all his vices, including his penny-pinching, as virtues: "They say he is stingy; We'll call that Prudence" (*MW* 62).

3.   (a) A special extension of this economic application of the word concerns marriage. *Prudence* in such contexts was a euphemism for which Byron, with a facetious brutalness typical of him, could provide a ready translation:

> I mean to marry, prudently if possible – that is wealthily, I can't afford anything to Love.   (*BLJ* 2.84)

The hard-headed and hard-hearted Isabella Thorpe, when she learns Catherine does not intend to marry her brother John, declares:

> "I confess, as soon as I read his letter, I thought it a very foolish, imprudent business . . . for what were you both to live upon, supposing you came together? You have both of you something to be sure, but it is not a trifle that will support a family now-a-days; and after all that romancers may say, there is no doing without money."   (*NA* 145–6; cf. *P* 201; *MW* 196, 352)

The frequency with which monetary considerations are brought to bear upon marriage in the literature of the time is not a sign merely of mercenariness. For a man without means to marry for love a woman he could not, on his own unsupplemented income, support in a decent manner, or for a woman who brought no money with her to burden a man of restricted means with the extra expense of a wife and family, was considered the very reverse of disinterested high-mindedness.[8] And Jane Austen would certainly have endorsed Isabella's closing statement as to the silly romanticism of marrying without *any* consideration of what the two of you were to live on. In one of her early comic works, a sister questions the "imprudent connection" her brother has made, and suggests he will have to apply to his father to be able to support his wife:

> "Support! What support will Laura want which she can receive from him?"
> "Only those very insignificant ones of Victuals and Drink."
> "Victuals and Drink! . . . and dost thou then imagine that there is no other support for an exalted Mind . . . than . . . Eating and Drinking?"
> "None that I know, so efficacious."
> "And . . . Does it appear impossible to your vile and corrupted Palate, to exist on Love?" (*MW* 83)

No-one can "exist on Love", of course – let alone two, and the indefinitely many more mouths they may produce. Fanny Price's mother marries with similar grand heedlessness (*MP* 3). The upshot of this 'very imprudent marriage' (4) is that she finds herself with insufficient means to bring up the nine children with which the marriage is blessed – or cursed. In this predicament she gets precious little sympathy from the authoress, who plainly feels that it is one Miss Frances should have had the 'prevision' or *prudence* to foresee.

On the other hand, her approval of this sort of *prudence* seems to be as qualified as it is of the other manifestations of this dubious virtue. To marry only if there is money enough between the two of you for decent comfort is one thing; to marry *for* money, or to refuse to sacrifice a few luxuries one may be (or wish to become) used to, is another. These novels suggest that *prudence* could be rather disingenuously invoked to justify the two latter proceedings. In the above passage from *Northanger Abbey*, the casuistry of Isabella Thorpe (who is preparing a justification for her own jilting of Catherine's (not rich) brother) is clear: "You have both of you something to be sure" implies that Catherine and John, though not wealthy, have *enough* to make a marriage between them feasible – with a little subsequent prudence. When Colonel Fitzwilliam, in *Pride and Prejudice*, hints to Elizabeth that she might be his choice, were he not one of those "younger sons" who cannot afford to consult only their own wishes in such matters, Elizabeth has no difficulty in exposing just how much sympathy on these grounds "the younger son of an Earl" can deserve (183). But the line between *prudence* and unscrupulous self-interest in this matter emerges as a fine one in this novel, and this is not the only occasion on which Elizabeth is confronted with the problem: to Mrs Gardiner's suspicions about Wickham's motives in his attentions to Miss King, she responds with semi-serious exasperation:

> "Pray, my dear aunt, what is the difference in matrimonial affairs, between the mercenary and the prudent motive? Where does discretion end, and avarice begin?" (153)

Perhaps the nicest case is that of Charlotte Lucas. Elizabeth is appalled at what she sees as the calculated cynicism of her friend's acceptance of Mr Collins, for Charlotte cannot possibly like or respect the man. Jane, predictably, defends her action as consistent with her "prudent, steady character" (135), and Elizabeth herself later concedes to Darcy, with expressive reserve, that "in a prudential light, it is certainly a very good match for her" (178). But to Jane she forthrightly rejects the applicability of the term to Charlotte's behaviour, and declares with emphasis:

> "You shall not, for the sake of one individual, change the meaning of principle and integrity, nor endeavour to persuade yourself or me, that selfishness is prudence, and insensibility of danger, security for happiness." (135–6)

It is difficult to know how unreservedly the novel supports Elizabeth's verdict. She, after all, can afford to be high-minded: she is young and pretty, and can be fairly sure, despite her want of fortune, of securing a partner not too offensive to her tastes. Charlotte is plain, poor and, at 27, an old maid. Mr Collins represents her only alternative to a dull and mortifying dependency in the parental home. Elizabeth's forebodings as to her happiness do not seem to be borne out. Charlotte finds occupation and diversion enough in her household activities, and fends off the irksome company of her husband by various shrewd diplomacies. A conjugal content procured by minimizing contact with one's spouse is not exactly an enviable one, but Charlotte does not seem to regret her decision. So it may be that the novel does not intend the *prudential* view to be entirely refuted by Elizabeth: the view, that is, that plain girls, no longer young and with no independent means, are perhaps best advised to cut their losses, and settle for the modest and unromantic kind of happiness Charlotte secures for herself.

But, provided there is enough to live on, this kind of *prudence* is not in general allowed any further proper role in selecting a partner. There is little sympathy in *Emma* for the yuppy Mr Elton's determination not to "make an imprudent match" (66) and a great deal for what is calmly labelled the *imprudence* (401: from Frank's point of view) of the match between Frank and Jane – which nobody but the odious Mrs Churchill is displeased by. Emma, it is true, affects to be shocked by "the imprudence of such a match" as one between Mr Knightley and Jane (224); but it is plain that the charge is merely a pretext for opposing a marriage Emma does not yet realize she has much more personal reasons for not being enthusiastic about. Certainly, in the last complete novel, *Persuasion*, the *prudence* partly responsible for Anne's withdrawal from her engagement with Frank Wentworth is productive of nothing but pain, resentment and misunderstanding. She has come to distrust that *prudence* (30), which had been exercised on Frank's behalf rather than on her own: 'The belief of being prudent, and self-denying principally for *his* advantage, was her chief consolation, under the misery of a parting' (28). When they do at last marry, any charge of *imprudence* is impatiently dismissed by a reference to the 'one independent fortune between them' (248). The role of *prudence* should, it appears, go no further than ensuring a *solvent* marriage.

(b) There can be slightly more respectable grounds for the exercise of marital *prudence*. One's long term happiness with the partner suggested by immediate desire may be adversely affected in foreseeable ways other than financial (*E* 64). And *imprudence* may result from inattention to the future effects on oneself of the *temper* of the beloved (*MP* 471; *PP* 236). Mrs Gardiner writes with playful innuendo to Elizabeth that Darcy "wants nothing but a little more liveliness, and that, if he marry *prudently*, his wife may teach him" (*PP* 325). The emphasis indicated for the word *prudently* here suggests Mrs Gardiner intends it to be noticed (as a kind of joke) that she is using the word of a prospective marriage in its more general, rather than its common financial, sense – which latter, of course, could never be applicable to Darcy's choice of Elizabeth.

4.   Apart from these specific applications, the word can be used generally of any kind of sagacious foresight, and can be equivalent to 'politic, cautious, circumspect, discreet'; as *imprudent* can be to 'heedless, impolitic, indiscreet'. *Prudence* can also be used of a carefully deliberate assessment of someone else's best interests as well as one's own (*SS* 173–4; *PP* 227). But even outside the specific contexts of health and finance, where it can imply a rather undesirable degree of self-protectiveness, *prudence* remains a somewhat suspect virtue; and the word is liable to be used in a disparaging and ironic way of the worldly-wise who do not consult much else apart from policy and self-interest. Henry Tilney, for instance, has "too good an opinion of Miss Thorpe's prudence, to suppose that she would part with one gentleman before the other was secured" (*NA* 206).

5.   Relevant to Marianne is an occasional connection of *im-prudence* with affections that are openly and unguardedly displayed (e.g. *E* 373). Edmund concedes that his sisters might have shown their interest in Henry "more unguardedly than was perfectly prudent" (*MP* 350). But, in such contexts, the term can be intended as only the mildest of condemnations of a fault stemming from nothing more serious, it is implied, than a pardonable openness and spontaneity. Edmund is intending to palliate the behaviour of all three parties, and obviously does not intend to choose a word very derogatory of their conduct. In fact, *imprudent* can be used in tactical rhetoric in this way by those who accuse themselves of an *imprudence* they intend to be interpreted as arising from a fundamentally laudable warmth and strength of feeling that is above being guarded or discreet. Lady Susan, anxious to withdraw from a relationship that it no longer suits her to maintain, writes:

> We have been hurried on by our feelings to a degree of
> Precipitance which ill accords with the claims of our Friends or
> the opinion of the World ... but we must not complete the
> imprudence by ratifying it.   (*MW* 300)

The idea of Lady Susan being 'hurried on' by her feelings to act in
defiance of worldly prudence is as laughably implausible as the
reasons Lucy Steele gives for entering into a secret engagement
with Edward: "I was too young and loved him too well to be so
prudent as I ought to have been" (*SS* 130). *Imprudent* can, in such
contexts, be a veiled compliment to youthful guilelessness and
ardour ('the impetuosity of youth' is particularly associated by
Crabb with *imprudent* conduct). Jane Austen used it in precisely
this way in her burlesque 'History of England', which retails all the
usual schoolroom prejudices and clichés, including the characterization of Mary Queen of Scots as a romantic victim entirely
innocent of all crimes, 'having never been guilty of anything more
than Imprudencies into which she was betrayed by the openness of
her Heart, her Youth, & her Education' (*MW* 146).

Prudence and *imprudence* are thus words whose moral balance
is somewhat precarious, indicating a virtue you might be the better
for lacking and a vice it might be to your credit to possess. So in
the description of Marianne it is not quite clear at that stage of the
novel how much of a reservation is intended in the commendation
of an otherwise excellent head and heart:

> Marianne's abilities were, in many respects, quite equal to
> Elinor's. She was sensible and clever . . .. She was generous,
> amiable, interesting: she was everything but prudent.   (*SS* 6)

Given the connotations of *prudent*, this might imply, 'She was only
too warm-hearted and impulsive for her own good' – which does
not sound like serious disapproval. Nor am I at all sure that the
rest of the novel does not as much emphasize how small a vice is
her want of *prudence* as how great a one it is (her behaviour causes
a great deal of pain both to herself and to those to whom she is
dear).

Given that Marianne is represented as a *romantic* girl, and that
romance was one of the antonyms of *prudence*,[9] it is not surprising
that *prudence* is neglected by her practically on principle. Her

imprudence manifests itself (and is duly labelled as such) in her want of foresight in money matters and in a general want of 'caution' (senses 2 and 4 above: *SS* 58, 48–9); though it is mainly, of course, the most mitigated *crime passionnelle* brand of the offence (sense 5) that is at issue: the unreserved warmth and openness of her relations with Willoughby (188, 345). Interinvolved with this is her failure in the area of *prudence* sense 1 (due caution with regard to health), which forms a crucial element in the plot. Her near fatal illness is brought on by the unguarded indulgence of another feature of her *romantic* tastes: her delight in solitary rambles, especially at dusk and especially where a little 'wildness' might be found. It is two such walks in the damp evening air, taken predictably 'where the trees were oldest, and the grass was the longest and wettest', which, 'assisted by the still greater imprudence of sitting in her wet shoes and stockings', cause her serious illness (306). This, presumably, is meant to stand as a kind of semi-symbolic analogue to the way in which her imprudent indulgence of a sensibility by no means discreditable in itself comes near to destroying her in a wider sense.

The contrasting *prudence* of Elinor figures in the provident and wisely circumspect versions of the virtue (senses 2 and 4 above: 14, 24, 156, 173–4, 317), and in the greater self-restraint under her amorous complications which acquits her of *imprudence* 5 (263). On the other hand, the horribly provident meanness of John Dashwood, and the self-interested caution that prompts the *prudent* marriages of Lucy and Willoughby (357, 376, 323), do not do much to recommend the virtue. Marianne deserves to be contrasted with these people to her advantage as well as with her sister to her disadvantage. As to the sense 5 in which her *imprudence* chiefly manifests itself, Edward Ferrars is also accused of this in the conduct of his romantic entanglements; remaining in a situation which could only increase the mutual regard between himself and Elinor was an *imprudence* (140) which is in fact treated as excusingly as it often was, and as a technical fault only: Elinor can offer 'a very earnest vindication of Edward from every charge but of imprudence' (261), though she later reprimands him for it – 'scolded him, harshly as ladies always scold the imprudence which compliments themselves' (368). This is scarcely a comment one would expect from a tale intent on instilling *prudence* as the primest virtue.

Nevertheless, the contrast between this first novel, setting

Elinor's *prudence* against Marianne's *romance*, and the last, in which the heroine displayed all the early caution in love Marianne so defies, remains remarkable. Anne is sick of *prudence*, and could have been eloquent in Marianne's defence:

> . . . how eloquent, at least, were her wishes on the side of early warm attachment, and a cheerful confidence in futurity, against that over-anxious caution which seems to insult exertion and distrust Providence! She had been forced into prudence in her youth, she learned romance as she grew older – the natural sequel of an unnatural beginning.   (*P* 30)

Witticism and jest may be represented by what is *pleasantly* spoken – often by *clever* characters indulging in those more alkaline forms of joking or facetiousness which are good-natured rather than hostile in intent, and which are occasionally resorted to by the intelligently diplomatic to pass off an awkward moment. An instance occurs when Admiral Croft declares in his downright way that Frederick would have to make up his mind quicker about which of the Musgrove girls he preferred if it were wartime; he then turns to his wife and asks her how long it was after their first meeting that they had their first meal together in their first lodgings:

> "We had better not talk about it, my dear," replied Mrs. Croft, pleasantly; "for if Miss Elliot were to hear how soon we came to an understanding, she would never be persuaded that we could be happy together."   (*P* 92)

Pleasantly here points to the mild jest that follows: if Anne knew on how short an acquaintance they had married, she would never believe that such incautiousness could have resulted in a happy marriage. The joke adds its own mite to the novel's Indian summer blessing upon marriages made in the warmth of unconsidering affection rather than the cool of *prudence*. It also intelligently lightens the tone to one in which the Admiral's blunt endorsement of brisk courtships need not be debated very seriously. Other intelligent persons who use *pleasant* means to make a correctively sensible point in a good-natured and inoffensive way include John

Knightley (*E* 95) and Frank Wentworth, who subjects the nautical ignorance of the Musgrove sisters to some *pleasant* ridicule (*P* 64; cf. *PP* 363, 388).

Henry Crawford's attempt to smooth over an awkwardness by the same means is less successful. He and Julia have enjoyed so many laughs together, he declares, that to see her play the part of Agatha would be "the ruin of all [his] solemnity" in his own role of Frederick. 'Pleasantly, courteously it was spoken; but the manner was lost in the matter to Julia's feelings' (*MP* 133).

The most inept use of the word (as it means **agreeably facetious**) occurs in the mouth of Mrs Palmer:

> "[Mr. Palmer] is so pleasant; and [he] is excessively pleased with you and your sisters I can tell you."   (*SS* 114)

Mr Palmer is neither *pleasant* nor 'pleased'. His sarcastic rudeness is even less *pleasant* than it is *droll* (113), since the former implies facetiousness designed to 'please'. The remark serves to epitomize with comic economy the absurd contrast between husband and wife, pointing at once to Mr Palmer's refusal to please or be pleased and at the same time to the totally opposite disposition of his wife. Charlotte is perhaps one of the rare instances of over-endowment with good *temper* – inanely amused and delighted by everything as she is (another possible candidate would be Charles Bingley, whose engaging compliancy and *sweetness* of temper become rather less engaging in Elizabeth's eyes when this 'easiness of temper' (*PP* 133) results in his being only too easily removed from Jane under the influence of his friend and sisters).

Rational was frequently used to distinguish what is serious or important from what is frivolous or vainglorious. One can thus find it stated that 'to a rational mind' religion is the only true consolation in affliction (*SCG* III.258). Harriet Byron contrasts the social whirl of *gaieties* with the more *rational* (serious and edifying) nature of her intercourse with the Grandisons (IV.408). With similar but more mock sententiousness, Henry Tilney contrasts the time Catherine must spend "much more rationally" in the country with that spent "in pursuit only of amusement all day long" (*NA* 79). The full import of the word may best be conveyed by the absurd misapplication of it by Dr Redgill, the gourmand in

Marriage, for whom any abatement of the gastronomic pleasures of dinner inevitably entails "an end of all rational happiness" (232).

When Emma hears that Frank has gone to London to get his hair cut, she judges this a piece of vanity and frivolity inconsistent with 'the rationality of plan' she had discerned in him the day before (205). The contrast between *rationality* and fashionable 'foppery and nonsense' (*ibid*) is once again in evidence. And the *rationality* Emma believes herself to have discerned in Frank must refer to what had chiefly struck her in his talk the day before: 'less of the spoiled child of fortune' than she had expected, he had shown, instead of worldly and frivolous preoccupations, an 'amiable inclination to settle early in life, and to marry, from worthy motives' (203–4).[10] The strictly moral **seriousness** the word could connote is at its most audible, predictably, in the speech of the relentlessly right-minded Mr Knightley, who (when Emma attempts to excuse to him Frank's delayed visit to his father) associates the acquisition of adult *rationality* with maturity of moral judgement: as he grew from child to man and "became rational", Frank ought to have found himself capable of "carrying through a resolution to do right" in defiance of his foster parents, and have acquired the habit of "following his duty" which would have made him oppose "the first attempt on their side to make him slight his father" (148). The possession of this kind of *rationality* by the charming Frank remains a rather problematic issue – a fact which contributes to the somewhat undeceived liking for him with which one emerges from the story. His attachment to Jane Fairfax speaks well for his *rationally* unworldly values, but the concealment and lack of moral courage involved in the secret engagement even he can find little excuse for (437), and Mr Knightley, on reading the relevant part of his letter, mercilessly declares as much:

> "He trifles here . . . as to the temptation. He knows he is wrong, and has nothing rational to urge. – Bad. – He ought not to have formed the engagement." (445)

These resonances of *rational* need to be remembered if one is to appreciate fully the sober implications, for instance, of that epigrammatic statement that Henry Crawford threw away his chances of gaining the one woman 'whom he had rationally, as well as passionately loved' (*MP* 469).

Lady Russell, a woman of 'strict integrity', was 'generally speaking, rational and consistent – but she had prejudices on the side of ancestry . . .' (*P* 11). The qualification implied by 'generally speaking' to the soundness of values suggested by *rational* is explained by what follows. Her prejudice in favour of what her judgement knows to be essentially not important (rank and consequence) 'blinded her a little to the faults' of the baronet. That is, her moral *consistency* could suffer lapses.

Consistent, though often used with much the same force as it has today, could also imply **constancy** or *per*sistence in a course of conduct that is right: 'not giving way, settled, persistent, durable' (cf. *OED consistent* A.2). Thus it can occur in moral contexts that raise the issue of adherence to or lapse from a course of conduct adopted on principle (cf. *SS* 295). The word figures frequently in its various senses in *Mansfield Park*, the story of a heroine constant to herself under almost unbearable pressures. In this, she is almost alone. Even Edmund has a major lapse of *consistency*. He has some misgivings about joining the theatricals he had disapproved, because (he says, with tactical emphasis) "No man can like being driven into the *appearance* of such inconsistency" (154); and torn 'between love and consistency' (163), he eventually surrenders – but is honest enough to admit to his father that he has more than *appeared* to be inconsistent, and that "Fanny is the only one who has judged rightly throughout, who has been consistent" (187). In these contexts, the *consistency* at issue is obviously not mere avoidance of contradiction in itself, but constancy and **perseverance** in principle.[11] Interestingly, Mrs Inchbald's play *Lovers' Vows* itself provides perhaps the best illustration of the moral resonance *consistent* could bear. When Baron Wildenhaim declares to Anhalt his intention to make his illegitimate son his heir, and to bestow the estate of Weldendorf on the boy's mother, Anhalt declares he must also marry Agatha. The Baron is startled, but Anhalt declares: "Baron Wildenhaim is a man who will not act inconsistently" (*MP* 533). He means, of course, that the Baron should make strict, not partial, reparation to Agatha: that he should not allow himself 'exceptions' in the course his conscience dictates.

When it is said of Lady Russell, then, that she is 'generally' *consistent*, the implication is that her 'prejudices on the side of ancestry' are the one area in which she can be seduced by worldly vanities from the more *rational* values to which she is usually **constant**.

Originally applied to the guardian spirit of a person or place, the word *genius* came, in its various extensions of meaning, to denote the quintessential nature or distinctive essence of a thing or person; characteristic disposition; innate aptitude (as with what Mr Knightley ironically refers to as Emma's "genius for foretelling and guessing": *E* 38); natural bent or inclination; or mental faculties in a general sense.[12] It can also occasionally be found in the modern sense, especially when it occurs as a personal noun ('a genius': cf. *NA* 27).

Beyond the above usages, however, there are some in Jane Austen's prose which imply some kind of 'natural capacity' that is less than that today suggested by the term, but apparently more or other than simply 'innate intelligence' (which is the gloss sometimes proposed[13]). The word is elsewhere (especially in the context of the arts) associated with invention and, therefore, originality:

> The first and leading quality of genius is *invention* . . . .
> (Gerard, 173; cf. 245)

> . . . a book worth much commendation, but of no genius; there is nothing original in the statement of the facts, or in the reflections they produce.   (*FBD* 215)

Crabb, who also stresses that *genius* is a quality of mind 'altogether individual in its character', further distinguishes it from other mental powers falling under the general heading of *intellect* by the fact that it respects specifically 'the operations of the imagination'. All this seems relevant to the fact that Jane Austen three times selects the word with reference to the improvements or transformations of property, where a specifically devising and inventing ability that we would today term **imagination** seems strongly implied. There are, for instance, General Tilney's improvements to his kitchen quarters, which he has had equipped with all mod cons, 'and, when the genius of others had failed, his own had often produced the perfection wanted' (*NA* 183). Catherine later sees 'a meadow, on which Henry's genius had begun to act' (214). And Mary Crawford declares that all had witnessed her brother's "genius take fire" in his survey of the possibilities at Sotherton (*MP* 244). The capacity to 'invent' is even more obviously present in some other usages in which the word is virtually equivalent to 'ingenuity':

> "And now, that your duty has brought you to this, even my genius is at a loss how to extricate you." (*Mar.* 448)

A natural capacity for music or drawing – which require some creative and imaginative ability – also elicits the term (*MP* 19); those gifted in this way were often termed *ingenious* (*FBD* 47, 77), and their *genius* is coupled by Crabb with *taste*, from which it is distinguished by the fact that it respects execution, while the latter refers merely to an instinctive responsive sympathy to whichever of the arts is in question. Marianne draws on the distinction when she expresses the hope that Edward's *taste* (his aesthetic appreciation) in art may be so far influenced by the performance skills of Elinor's *genius* as to prompt him to similar attempts at execution – for she naturally assumes that the development of Edward's sensibility in this respect must be of the utmost importance to her sister:

> "Edward will have greater opportunity of improving that natural taste for your favourite pursuit which must be so indispensibly necessary to your future felicity. – Oh! if he should be so far influenced by your genius as to learn to draw himself, how delightful it would be!" (*SS* 22)

Poor Mary Bennet's performance at the piano, despite her hard work at it, shows 'neither genius nor taste' (*PP* 25).

'Executive' talents in music, drawing or writing, then, testify to *genius*. So do the coruscations of wit and humour, which make for company that animates by furnishing conversation that is 'inventive', original and distinctive, as opposed to dully predictable. In *Catherine*, 'a something like humour' in Miss Stanley raises Kitty's hopes 'that she might at least have a natural genius, tho' not an improved one', but 'these Sparklings of Wit' turn out to be pretty accidental, and Camilla is after all found to be fairly ordinary (*MW* 201).[14] Those incipient 'Sparklings' in *Camilla* are a suitably reduced version of the *brilliance* and *fire* with which *genius* elsewhere collocates (cf. Crabb *sv fire*): such as the 'Genius, Fire & Feeling' (*MW* 404) that captivates Sir Edward in the 'Spirit' and 'Sagacity' with which the villains in his favourite pulp romances pursue the women they have become obsessed by. *Genius* accompanies both *fire* and *wit* in the list of *abilities* Henry Tilney jestingly claims women may lack – "Perhaps they may want observation, discernment, judgment, fire, genius, and wit" (*NA* 112) – where *genius* falls distinctly beyond the mid-point that clearly marks the transition from rational to imaginative virtues of mind. Lady Susan says of her daughter that she lacks "any of that Brilliancy of Intellect, that Genius, or Vigour of Mind . . ." (*MW* 288). *Brilliancy*[15] had associations with wit, with scintillating talk and with qualities which 'strike the imagination'. Such *brilliancy* is also associated by Marianne with the *genius* she feels Colonel Brandon lacks. While not denying Elinor's claims for him on the score of a sound head, she dismisses his *abilities* as being of the dully solid kind, since he has "neither genius, taste, nor spirit", for "his understanding has no brilliancy, his feelings no ardour, and his voice no expression" (*SS* 51). Here *genius* is again associated with *brilliancy*, and is plainly conceived of as appealing to the *romance* in Marianne. Since it is the novel's business to emphasize what she *under*values, Colonel Brandon's lack of *genius*, etc., does not prevent him from proving in the end what we are required to believe is a perfect husband for her. But in *Persuasion*, which reverses the emphasis of *Sense and Sensibility* in championing *romance* against *prudence*, the hero possesses all the *brilliancy* (*P* 26) and *genius* Marianne had so sadly missed in her husband-to-be. Anne has better luck, and is not required to do without what *Sense and Sensibility* rather implies are alluring but ultimately hollow virtues. Frank Wentworth had been as successful as his youthful confidence had prophesied, for 'His genius and ardour had seemed to foresee and to command his prosperous path' (29).

Frank's *genius*, which the structure of the sentence evidently couples with the verb 'foresee', appears here to be different only in degree and application from that **imagination** which enables General and Henry Tilney and Henry Crawford to conceive and plan the improvements they execute. Mary Crawford also contrasts with Colonel Brandon in being credited with the quantity he lacks. Edmund, despite his own disapproval of the projected amateur dramatics, is prompted by Mary's evident interest in the scheme to reflect that, after all, 'the charm of acting might well carry fascination to the mind of genius' (*MP* 129). Mary has no *genius* in the modern sense; and there might well be types of 'characteristic disposition' or 'natural aptitude' acting would not at all suit, so those senses of the word would produce poor logic even for a lover's reasonings. Edmund must in some way be referring to those qualities evident in her, such as wit and vivacity and *brilliant* talk, but which are not present in Colonel Brandon – for whom it is certainly hard to imagine that amateur acting could carry any fascination.

Genius, then, though it may be found in the other afore-mentioned specific senses, can also be used to denote a kind of innate capacity that carries a certain romantic charge: distinguishing the capacity for imagination, for originality, for creativeness and inventiveness from other powers of the mind, and associated with a forceful and/or attractive *fire* and *brilliance* of speech and conception. In fact, the originality and inventiveness essentially connoted by the word in the context of the creative arts seem to be indicated also, in a slightly more attenuated form, in some looser and less specialized usages, which often refer to minds that are imaginative, and 'original' at least in so far as being not dully conventional or ordinary.[16]

6 The Heart

The vocabulary of feeling is, in Jane Austen's prose, richer and denser than that falling under the other main heads of the scheme followed in this study, for all her novels bear testimony to the ultimate primacy she gave to it in assessing personal worth. This is true of *Sense and Sensibility* itself, even though the behaviour of the *eager* Marianne is in many ways contrasted unfavourably with that of her more restrained elder sister. And the novel may serve as the basis for an investigation into the vocabulary of *temper* – (good) nature,[1] disposition – and feeling, conceived of as they were as associated with the heart rather than the head.

The novel is an important one with regard to this subject, as it seems to be investigating, in the figure of Marianne, the whole nature of (and some of the dangers inherent in) the *romantic* ethos – an ethos emergent over the eighteenth century and later typified by those poets who have since become known as 'the Romantics' (Wordsworth, Coleridge, Shelley, Keats, Byron). The cultural developments of this period are commonly referred to as marking a transition from Augustan to Romantic values, a transition conceived of as consisting in a shift of emphasis from the social to the individual, from the head to the heart, as it were, and resulting in feeling and emotion acquiring that dominance of perceived value which had formerly belonged to judgement, reason and order. These labels, and the reasoning that underlies them, can be used to present a grossly over-simplified account of the cultural history of the period, one that gives the impression that no Augustan ever valued such things as sensibility and imagination, while Romantics were all rhapsodic introverts with no interest at all in rationality and order – a position so patently false as to make it absurd to give examples to refute it.

It nevertheless remains true that, although sensibility was not a phenomenon new to the period in question, the value for it did become in the course of it much more self-consciously held – as the history of the word itself testifies. Most of those instances of it cited by the *OED* which predate the mid-eighteenth century show it being used in a semi-scientific sense; or of human feelings in a general way; or of sensibility with regard to specific subjects or circumstances. A special entry is required for what the *OED* labels as a usage found in the eighteenth and early nineteenth centuries (the illustrations all post-date 1756) and which is rare thereafter: 'Capacity for refined emotion; delicate sensitiveness of taste . . . readiness to feel compassion for suffering, and to be moved by the pathetic in literature or art' (*sv Sensibility* 6). This shows the word being used in a new evaluative and discriminatory way. Such *sensibility* could, however, be 'regarded with approval (as a sort of fineness) or with disapproval (as excess)'.[2]

The word in the title of the novel thus refers to a whole ethos, of which Marianne bears many of the recognizable hallmarks. But it is important to realize that it does not merely mean that she is 'very emotional'. Her sensibility, as the novel portrays it, manifests itself in three distinct yet interconnected dimensions of a sensitivity (or what is called a *refinement* of mind) that is at once moral, emotional and aesthetic. The first two will be discussed together, since they are intimately related.

I

Marianne's *romance* itself should not be confused with the silliness and sentimentality often conveyed by the word today. *Romance* was used in various senses, but the one relevant to this novel was that in which it denoted a high-mindedness that refused to make concessions to worldly practicalities and realities. *Romance* is predicated of Marianne at the end of the first chapter (7), and the term is used on three other occasions of the attitudes of her or her mother (whom, we are told (6), Marianne strongly resembles). Fanny Dashwood, in her offensive haste to take over Norland, arrives on the premises almost immediately after Mr Dashwood's funeral. Such *un*feeling promptness would be offensive to anyone, Jane Austen remarks, adding, with reference to the reaction of Mrs Dashwood herself:

. . . but in *her* mind there was a sense of honour so keen, a generosity so romantic, that any offence of the kind, by whomsoever given or received, was to her a source of immoveable disgust.   (6)

The second occasion relates specifically to Marianne's views on 'second attachments'. Colonel Brandon remarks to Elinor that he understands Marianne does not approve of them:

"No," replied Elinor, "her opinions are all romantic . . . A few years however will settle her opinions on the reasonable basis of common sense and observation . . . ."

"This," said he, "cannot hold; but a change, a total change of sentiments – No, no, do not desire it, – for when the romantic refinements of a young mind are obliged to give way, how frequently are they succeeded by such opinions as are but too common, and too dangerous! I speak from experience . . . ."
                                                          (56–7)

The third instance occurs again in connection with Mrs Dashwood. Elinor urges her mother to ascertain from Marianne the exact nature of her relationship with Willoughby. Mrs Dashwood indignantly exclaims against any attempt to "force the confidence of any one", prompting the following reflections in Elinor:

Elinor thought this generosity overstrained, considering her sister's youth, and urged the matter farther, but in vain; common sense, common care, common prudence, were all sunk in Mrs Dashwood's romantic delicacy.   (85)

Romantic relates, in the above instances, to a moral sensitivity carried to extremes. It is the keen 'sense of honour' and the 'generosity' of Mrs Dashwood which is so offended by Fanny's selfish lack of consideration for the feelings of others; and it is her *generosity* and *delicacy* that makes her abhor the notion of pressing from anyone information about their private affairs which they do not choose voluntarily to confide. Marianne's distaste for 'second attachments' is similarly seen as evidence of a *refinement* of mind: it arises from a proper value for singleness and fidelity in love, and a distaste for all that may cheapen such constancy, which, when carried to the extreme of a blanket abhorrence of all 'second attachments', earns from Elinor and Colonel Brandon the epithet *romantic*. The word thus refers to a kind of idealism, arising from feelings and principles entirely proper and creditable in themselves, carried to unrealistic extremes. The definition that best suits the above instances is that given at *Romantic A. adj.* (3) by the *OED*: 'extravagant, quixotic; going beyond what is customary or practical'. *Quixotic* is well illustrated by one of the examples (from the year 1800) that follow: "It is his intention equally to share his future inheritance with his brother. A most romantic idea."[3]

The *romance* and quick feelings of Mrs Dashwood and Marianne, then, have a moral dimension. Their sensibility is not just something emotionally self-involved, but endows them also with a highly *refined* sense of what is right – what is *honourable* and *generous*. The discussion of 'second attachments' is designed to alert the reader to do justice to the *refinement* of mind that produces the *romantic* extremes that 'common sense' must condemn in Marianne – especially since the whole issue of second attachments is one that serves to focus some of the most important concerns of the novel. The attitudes of Elinor and Colonel Brandon toward this *romanticism* of hers importantly qualify each other. Elinor voices the common-sense view that there is something of immaturity in Marianne's feelings on this subject, and that she will probably grow out of them. Colonel Brandon agrees, but adds that a complete reversal of such "romantic refinements" of mind is undesirable. So the *romantic* extremeness of Marianne's views is, in this conversation, tempered by the intelligent rationality of Elinor; but the word is also used to characterize the underlying refinement of mind to which the promiscuous transfer of affections is offensive – a species of *romance* endorsed by the experience of Colonel Brandon, who has seen it exchanged for something worse. The novel as a whole in many ways reflects this qualified verdict on Marianne's *romance*. Though some of its unusually many second attachments are wise and happy ones, the utterly self-interested inconstancies of Lucy and Willoughby endorse Colonel Brandon's view that "a total change" of Marianne's romantically high-minded views is not desirable.

The *romantic* notions and ways of Marianne and her mother are, in the passages cited, consistently associated with other words that alert one to the moral dimension of their sensibility: 'sense of honour', *generosity, delicacy* and a quickness to feel *disgust* (**distaste, offence**); and these words, together with *amiable* and *interesting*, all deserve close attention if the Marianne described at the end of Chapter I – in a passage that is assumed to imply *romance* (7) – is to be properly understood:

> ... she was sensible and clever; but eager in every thing; her sorrows, her joys, could have no moderation. She was generous, amiable, interesting: she was every thing but prudent.   (6)

The disregard of 'common sense' which, in the second and third of the passages quoted, is associated with *romantic* is borne out by the fact that *romance* and *romantic* are often found as antonyms of *prudence* and *prudent*, which is obviously relevant here. In such contexts the former words imply a sentimental idealism (usually based on an absolute value for such things as disinterested love and generosity) that refuses to be compromised by realities and practicalities.[4] Isabella Thorpe (*NA* 146) contrasts a *prudent* concern with what one is to live on with the *romantic* notions that would regard such considerations as basely irrelevant. Her *prudent* marriage Charlotte Lucas explains to her horrified friend by pointing out, "I am not romantic you know" (*PP* 125). Anne Elliot, having been forced when a girl into that *prudence* which is not a virtue naturally incident to the young,[5] finds herself, as 'the natural sequel of an unnatural beginning' (*P* 30), learning *romance* as she grows older – in a passage which, equally unusually, implicitly forces *romance* into the positive pole in the antonymy with *prudence*.

Generous was rather wider in sense and application than it is today, as will be clear from its occurrence in connection with Mrs Dashwood in the passages quoted, where it is used of that in her which (a) makes her incapable of such inconsiderate inattention to the feelings of others as Fanny shows; and (b) prevents her from 'forcing a confidence' from anyone. *Generous* referred to all that was the opposite of *interested* (in its sense of 'self-interested'), to a heart exalted and enlarged enough to respond to considerations other than those of narrow self-interest. *Generosity* thus embraced not only compassion, forbearance, justice, charity (especially toward rivals or enemies), but also such emotions and actions as shame, self-accusation, confession of error (*SCG* III.44; IV.353; V.612), and the capacity for disinterested commitment to ideals and principles. This last is especially evident in Shelley's writing, which in spirit and usage epitomizes that highest kind of generosity. He can thus refer to the 'generous and enlarged' interest in the common good; to the pursuit of perfection as 'generous enthusiasm'; to the 'thirst for excellence' as a 'generous impulse'; and to the *generous* instincts that responded sympathetically to the aspirations underlying the French Revolution (255, 256, 316). 'Magnanimity' would be the nearest modern equivalent to all that *generosity* connoted. The former word means, literally, 'greatmindedness'; and *generosity* retained some of its etymological associations with what is 'great' and 'noble'. Johnson gives as the primary sense of the word 'Not of mean birth; of good extraction [i.e., coming of a good stock or *genus*]';[6] and he includes among its secondary or derivative senses 'noble of mind; magnanimous; open of heart', as well as 'liberal; munificent'. *Generous* could collocate with such words as *noble*, and is associated by Shelley with the more enlarged and refined views ideally found in aristocrats and gentlemen (245, 342). This is yet a further illustration of how frequently incentives to liberal and humane and *generous* thinking and doing issued from the standards ideally associated with the *gentleman* and with *gentle* status.[7] *Ungenerous* behaviour was characterized by terms that constituted comparable disincentives: *low, paltry, little, mean* (which originally meant 'low in rank or birth'). The *un*generous conduct and attitudes consistently referred to as *littlenesses* or *meannesses* include: spite and malice (*SS* 366; *E* 330); the mixture of pride and stubbornness that will not allow one to shift one's position, own to error or do anything that might offend one's *amour propre* (*MP* 258; *BLJ* 4.184, 3.103); what is called *triumph*, exultation at the defeat of an opponent, 'crowing' (*PP* 312); servility or obsequiousness to the rich or powerful (*MW* 402; *SS* 372); a concern with worldly or financial self-interest that goes beyond what is decent (*MW* 402; *BLJ* 4.207); envy; suspiciousness; resentment (*PP* 370; *BLJ* 4.87, 5.175), especially vindictiveness; and, most especially of all, any kind of disingenuity, trickery, scheming, concealment, duplicity – *littlenesses* which an upright mind should disdain to stoop or descend to (*MP* 238; *PP* 192, 199; *E* 397, 437). From the ignoble worldliness, artfulness, obsequiousness and mercenary motivation of a Lucy Steele the *generous* Marianne is thus quite free; for the word connotes high-mindedness as well as warmth, and thus emphasizes again the moral dimension of the *romantically* ready sensibility of Marianne and her mother.

This moral dimension of sensibility is best exemplified in the word *delicacy*, an important one in Jane Austen's vocabulary. As applied to persons, it is the *OED's delicate* (12) that is relevant: 'Finely sensitive to what is becoming, proper, or modest, or to the feelings of others'. *Delicacy* is thus the manifestation of sensibility in social behaviour – the *refinement* or sensitivity of conscience. The word is twice collocated with *conscience* in this novel. Marianne says of, and in front of, Edward that he has "the most delicate conscience in the world; the most scrupulous in performing every engagement however minute, and however it may make against his interest or pleasure. He is the most fearful of giving pain, of wounding expectation, and the most incapable of being selfish, of any body I ever saw" (243–4). Her words are both less and more true than she knows. Context (she is responding to Edward's excuse that an 'engagement' prevented him from attending the party at his mother's in Harley Street) imparts to the compliment a superbly painful comedy – agonizing to hear as it must be for Edward, who had presumably absented himself so as to avoid the embarrassment of an evening spent in the company of the woman he loves (Elinor) and the woman to whom he regards himself as engaged (Lucy). It is not surprising that this warmth, prompted by a lie from him and expressed in ignorance of matters he is not being open about, proves to appear 'very unexhilarating' to him (*ibid*). The scrupulousness, however, evident in his readiness to see through that *engagement* with Lucy, despite the fact that it makes most hugely against his "interest [= self-interest] and pleasure", his refusal to "wound the expectations" he has aroused in her by a "selfish" indulgence of his own (altered) preference – these facts imbue Marianne's words with profounder pertinence than she knows. The irony (in the sense of an application of his or her words the speaker is unconscious of) is, of course, released most especially by the interplay between the general sense *engagement* intended by Marianne and the more specific application of the word to a formal or (at this period) informal betrothal.

Marianne is well aware of the connection between the two,[8] and of the commitment, pledge or gage both involve, for the emotion with which she speaks indicates that there is an unspoken contrast in her mind with the way Willoughby has treated her.

She is therefore in a state of mind to deliver herself of a most feeling and comprehensive definition of that *delicacy* the want of which has caused so much pain to her, and the one she gives appears almost designed as an illustration to the *OED's delicate* (12). Edward's *delicacy* is a scrupulous integrity. Interestingly, those most emphatically found to want *delicacy* are, in this novel, those who breach *engagements* (in the narrower or more general sense). For delicacy of conscience is also attributed, ironically, to John Dashwood, when he issues to his sisters an invitation to stay with him – 'an attention, which the delicacy of his conscience pointed out to be requisite to its complete enfranchisement from his promise to his father' (253). The point of the irony lies in the inapplicability of the word *delicacy* to John's selfish disregard of the undertaking he had given his father (to provide generously for his sisters): he is the very reverse of scrupulously conscientious in fulfilling *that* engagement.

Delicacy exerts a largely negative influence on conduct, for it is that sensitivity that makes one recoil from and scruple to do what is ignoble, ungenerous, offensive or inattentive to the feelings of others. When Fanny Dashwood arrives at Norland, immediately after Mr Dashwood's funeral, without notice, and complete with child and servants, 'the indelicacy of her conduct' (6) is pointed out – its insensitive inattention to the feelings of Mrs Dashwood senior, its want of the *delicacy* that should have made her scruple to claim the house so promptly, and to flaunt her own good fortune so flagrantly before her less happily circumstanced mother-in-law. The latter is especially offended by it, since she herself possesses *delicacy* to such a *romantic* or **quixotic** degree that she scruples to press her own teenage daughter for information it much concerns her, as a mother, to know (85) – *delicacy* referring, again, to a scrupulousness quick to recoil from what might be distasteful in one's conduct or evince *in*sensibility to the feelings of others.

Such *delicacy* is one aspect of Marianne's sensibility. Her impatience with Mrs Jennings is the result of 'the irritable refinement of her own mind, and the too great importance placed by her on the delicacies of a strong sensibility, and the graces of a

polished manner' (201). Marianne is certainly criticized for judg-
ing the good-hearted Mrs Jennings over-harshly, but it is important that the *delicacy* she finds so wanting in her should be
interpreted correctly. The word is not much used with real
seriousness today, and might connect itself with a 'refinement' of
the type suggested by the mock mispronunciation 'refeened'.[9] But
that would be to confound Marianne's fastidiousness with that of
Lady Middleton. For the delicacy of the former is distinct from the
mere sense of propriety of the latter, and contemporaries were
conscious of the difference. Wagner, for instance, said of his wife
Minna that 'she had no inherent sense of delicacy (*Zartsinn*); in its
place she evinced only a sense of what is proper (*Schicklichkeits-
gefühl*), by which she meant 'doing the right thing', without being
able to see that that accomplishes nothing if delicacy is violated'
(129).[10]

Lucy and Willoughby, like John Dashwood, also break *engagements* or **commitments** (to Edward and Marianne) when it serves
their self-interest so to do. Elinor early notices the 'thorough want
of delicacy, of rectitude, and integrity of mind, which [Lucy's]
attentions, her assiduities, her flatteries at the Park betrayed' (127;
cf. 140); and the collocation of *delicacy* with *rectitude* and *integrity*
is significant. Lucy's conscience is not sensitive; she is *un*scrupulous in the pursuit of her 'own interest and pleasure'. And that
appallingly cruel letter from Willoughby to Marianne, which forms
the climax of the novel, especially strikes Elinor with its gross
violation of 'every honourable and delicate feeling' (184) – the
collocation with *honourable* supporting that with *integrity* and
conscience. The *OED* definition of *delicacy* as sensitivity both to
what is right and to the feelings of others is entirely apt in context.
It is, Elinor feels, a shamelessly (*impudently*) cruel letter; and that
he should not have scrupled to send it suggests a lack of *delicacy* in
him that really shocks her. We later learn that he sent it at his
fiancée's command, and at her dictation; and he is himself not so
without *delicacy* as to be *in*sensitive to its horribly indelicate
nature. For he remarks, ironically, of it, having revealed to Elinor
that Miss Grey was responsible for its wording, "delicate – tender
– truly feminine – was it not?" (328). Miss Grey's hand in the letter
mitigates Willoughby's guilt somewhat, but not totally. If her
delicacy should have made her recoil from composing it, his should
have prevented him from obliging her in writing and dispatching it

– and from betraying Marianne for the amiable Sophia's money. The most reprehensible conduct in the novel is not that caused by a want of *prudence* (of which Lucy, Willoughby and Fanny – who all ultimately put money first – have only too much), but by a want of a certain kind of sensibility.

Those to whom want of *delicacy* is chiefly attributed are discovered also to be not *amiable*, and there is a connection between the two defects. *Amiable* was a word central to the vocabulary of the heart, and the one most commonly used to put a tick in the category of *temper* or disposition – so commonly that it became a kind of cant word, with much the same meaning and no-meaning of the modern 'nice'. Its use became equally automatic and predictable in 'novel-ese', where, in expressions like 'the amiable *x*', it figured as a kind of fixed epithet – a usage Jane Austen burlesques in her early works by applying the word to persons to whom it is ridiculously inappropriate, such as 'the [drunk] amiable Alice' and 'the [fraudulent] amiable Youth' (*MW* 23,108; cf. 6–7). The word is also parodied by Byron in his account of the battle of Ismail in *Don Juan*, where it is applied in mock elegy to objects totally incapable of good nature and actually constructed specifically for the furtherance of very opposite emotions:

> Three fireships lost their amiable existence
> Before they reached a spot to take effect.   (VII.28)

The word could, however, be used with deliberateness and seriousness, and is usually so used by Jane Austen in her six full-length novels – where it is a term in a much more serious register, indicating **good nature** and **warmth of heart** in a far more positive manner, than is or does its modern counterpart. It is today a patronizing word, often collocating (revealingly) with 'old fellow': 'he's an amiable old fellow' implies a sort of placid geniality, and strikes an apologetic note, suggesting some compensation in a good heart for a weak head. In the early nineteenth century, the root of the word (Latin *amor*=love) evidently still exercised much influence over the way in which it was used – with subjective and objective implications apparently entering into the *-able* suffix:[11] it indicated a warm-hearted and feeling subject who was an appropriate object of warmth and regard. To pronounce someone *unamiable* was, therefore, to pass a very damning verdict on their *temper* or disposition, since it implied a cold and selfish *heart*. Take the following passage from *Northanger Abbey*:

> The morning had passed away so charmingly as to banish all her friendship and natural affection; for no thought of Isabella or James had crossed her during their walk. When the Tilneys were gone, she became amiable again . . . .   (114)

The tone is non-serious; but the word *amiable* signals the return of Catherine's 'friendship and natural affection' – all the concern for her friend and her brother instinctive to a **warm-hearted, good-natured** girl.

Mr Knightley, predictably, is more solemnly emphatic on the implications of *amiable* – for when a word had any moral resonance, this character is depressingly certain to insist on it[12] (he is speaking of Frank Churchill):

> "No, Emma, your amiable young man can be amiable only in French, not in English. He may be very 'aimable', have very good manners, and be very agreeable; but he can have no English delicacy towards the feelings of other people: nothing really amiable about him."   (*E* 149)

Mr Knightley's polemical tactics lead him to give a definition of *amiable* which might better apply to *delicate*; but consideration for others was certainly generally regarded as natural to the *amiable* – to those whose *heart* was in the right place.

The heroes and villains of *Sense and Sensibility* are primarily distinguished from each other on the grounds of *amiability*. Marianne, pre-eminently, *is* amiable: 'She was generous, amiable, interesting' (6). Colonel Brandon is also discovered to be *amiable*. Elinor, defending him to Marianne and Willoughby, pronounces him to be "a sensible man, well-bred, well-informed, of gentle address, and I believe possessing an amiable heart" (51). Colonel Brandon's soundness of head and manners are readily obvious. Though his gravity might suggest somewhat of hardness and sternness, and though he is not a demonstrative man, Elinor is inclined to believe that his heart is equally sound: he is, she opines, also *amiable* – a feeling man.

Conversely, all the people ultimately condemned by the novel are the *unamiable*, not those who are foolish, vulgar or wanting in spirits. It is certainly not a work that upholds *sense* against *sensibility*. Fanny Dashwood (probably the nastiest of the *dramatis personae*) is the first person to incur this condemnation. Had John Dashwood married 'a more amiable woman ... he might have even been made amiable himself .... But Mrs John Dashwood was a strong caricature of himself; – more narrow-minded and selfish' (5; cf. 16). *Narrow-minded* means 'self-centred'. The word is used also of Mr Collins (*PP* 135) and General Tilney (*NA* 247; cf. *JAL* 118), and indicates one who acts and thinks on no principles wider or higher than consultation of their own 'narrow' (often financial) interests. [13] John Dashwood has married a woman who merely encourages what is defined as *un*amiable in him by being even more 'narrow-minded and selfish' than he is.

Miss Grey, the heiress Willoughby ditches Marianne for, is also discovered to be *unamiable*. Elinor, on first hearing of her, asks Mrs Jennings: "Do you know what kind of a girl Miss Grey is? Is she said to be amiable?" (194). This is a question about her *temper* or disposition: is she 'nice'? Mrs Jennings does not know the answer, but it later becomes clear that Miss Grey is, in fact, rather an *ill*-natured and spiteful girl. And by the end of the novel, Elinor knows the answer to her question. Miss Grey is *not* amiable, and she can refer to that fact as an established certainty when she subsequently considers Willoughby's position, married as he then is to "a woman of a less amiable temper" than Marianne (351): that is, a woman whose heart and temperament lack the warmth and generosity of Marianne's.

Elinor's lover nearly meets the same fate as Marianne's. Edward assumes that he will have to honour his engagement to Lucy Steele, who is emphatically not *amiable*. She is selfish, hard and calculating, and it is this lack of *amiability* in her that particularly distresses Elinor on Edward's behalf. The *insolent* treatment she receives from Edward's mother provides Elinor with an opportunity to look on the bright side of the apparent impossibility of any union between him and herself: 'Or at least, if she did not bring herself quite to rejoice in Edward's being fettered to Lucy, she determined, that had Lucy been more amiable, she *ought* to have rejoiced' (238). Lucy, like Fanny and Miss Grey, is deficient in that natural feeling that would prompt her to act honourably and generously by others; she is thus *unamiable*. She does not lack one kind of *sense*: it is constantly said of her that she is naturally *clever*. She shows what *sense* is without the *sensibility* that renders one *amiable*: her intelligence cannot rise above a mere shrewd, self-interested cunning.

Willoughby's treatment of Marianne is also interpreted within the novel as proving him to be, ultimately, not *amiable*. Mrs Dashwood manages to convince herself, if not Elinor or the reader, that, "had Willoughby turned out as really amiable, as he has proved the contrary" (338), Marianne would nevertheless not have been as happy with him as she will be with Colonel Brandon. Willoughby is not actually an unfeeling man, and did not do what he did in callous indifference to the suffering he was causing Marianne. But moral feelings are not distinguished from humane ones in the semantic scope of *amiable*: Willoughby should not have had the *heart* to act so cruelly and dishonourably, conduct against which his better *feelings*, though they did protest, did not protest loudly enough.

Of the four categories of character, the *heart* (the temper) is thus of paramount importance. For what we would term 'morality' or 'integrity' turns out to be not a separate department of character, but a function of the *heart*. Unprincipled conduct is interpreted as a defect of *disposition* (*MP* 463); and the converse is also true:

> Like half the rest of the world, if more than half there be that are clever and *good*, Marianne, with excellent abilities and an excellent *disposition* . . . . (201: my italics)

The same assumption is evident elsewhere. Guilt is commonly viewed as attaching properly only to misdeeds that arise from '*offences* of the heart' rather than '*errors* of the understanding' (WS 202 (my italics); cf. 253). *The Young Man's Companion* bids farewell to its student with the following golden rule:

> . . . the destruction of your virtue is the destruction of your peace. Keep thy heart with all diligence, govern it with the greatest care, for out of it are the issues of life. (88)

with which may be compared:

> A feeling heart is a blessing that no one, who has it, would be
> without; and it is a moral security of innocence; since the heart
> that is able to partake of the distress of another, cannot wilfully
> give it.   (*SCG* III.258)

The assignment of moral scrupulosity to the larger category of
the *heart*, *temper* or *disposition* is likewise everywhere implicit in
Jane Austen – but occasionally becomes explicit enough to be less
indirectly demonstrable. Elizabeth declares of Charlotte's engagement to Mr Collins:

> "... were I persuaded that Charlotte had any regard for him, I
> should only think worse of her understanding, than I now do of
> her heart."   (*PP* 135)

The analysis sounds a little curious to modern ears, which are not
attuned to any regular contextual reference to 'moral feelings' in
the term *heart*. We might well assign effects and causes the other
way round: on the grounds that the heart that could feel affection
for such a man must be over-impressionable, and the judgement
that could choose him for any other reason disordered. Elizabeth,
however, would think the worse of Charlotte's *head* could she
believe her to have any regard for such a pompous fool. She
condemns her *heart* only because she knows that this is not the
case: knows that Charlotte is marrying for what she clearly sees as
the wrong reasons, and regards wrong-doing as self-evidently
symptomatic of a lack of 'proper feeling', a faulty *heart*. Similarly,
Willoughby can attribute his dishonourable decision to jilt Marianne
for Miss Grey's money to "the stupid, rascally folly of [his] own
heart" (325). Although in one sense his *heart* had always inclined
him *toward* Marianne, there was another dimension of 'feeling' to
which it had been obtusely insensible (*stupid*).

Furthermore, quite apart from the expression 'better feeling(s)'
itself (*MP* 418; *P* 30; *PP* 125), which bears the same moral
connotations as it does today, there are numerous other occasions
on which the words *feel*, *feelings*, *unfeeling*, etc., are associated
with moral perceptions and/or conduct (e.g. *E* 146–7).[14] Such
usages are especially frequent in *Mansfield Park*, where the

acuteness of Fanny's moral sensitivity is constantly associated with her capacity to feel, though the word is similarly used by and of other characters as well (101, 125, 185, 219, 386, 452). The potential moral connotations of the word lend poignance to Edmund's account of his horror at Mary's insensibility to anything but the 'folly' of Henry and Maria:

> "I could not answer, but I believe my looks spoke. She felt reproved. Sometimes how quick to feel!"   (454)

The negative implication of "sometimes" refers to feelings Mary's reaction shows her to lack, to what he goes on to call "her total ignorance, unsuspiciousness of their being such feelings" as he then had (456).

Paradoxically, it is *Mansfield Park* that comes nearest to creating a separate category for morals by its emphasis on what it terms *principle(s)*, which it sometimes treats as a quantity not really reducible to *temper* – let alone intelligence, manners or spirits. This is, in a sense, forced by the evidence of the story that the sort of "feelings" Edmund refers to can be absent in persons not basically ill-natured, whose *tempers* are not intrinsically vicious. When asked by her uncle if she has any reason to think ill of Mr Crawford's temper, Fanny replies in the negative, 'but longed to add, "but of his principles I have"' (317). Edmund, in his final post-mortem on Mary Crawford's character, likewise determines that, "Her's are not faults of temper. She would not voluntarily give unnecessary pain to anyone . . .. Her's are faults of principle, Fanny, of blunted delicacy and a corrupted, vitiated mind" (456).

Sir Thomas, however, sees the education of his daughters as having been defective in concentrating on the 'understanding and manners, not the disposition' (cf. 19: 'In every thing but disposition, they were admirably taught'); what had been wanting was 'principle, active principle', equated with a learned 'sense of duty' by which their 'inclinations and tempers' should have been governed (463). Unless the three passages are contradictory, a distinction between *disposition* and *temper* seems to be implied. Lack of principle(s) may argue a defective **(pre-)disposition** to obey certain rules, but not necessarily a defective **temperament** (ill-nature). *Disposition* is distinguished from *temper* by Crabb in his *English Synonymes* thus: the former word 'refers to the whole frame and texture of the mind', the latter only to the 'bias or tone of the feelings'. He adds that 'it is possible and not unfrequent to have a good *disposition* with a bad *temper*, and [the case in *Mansfield Park*] *vice versa*. A good *disposition* makes a man a useful member of society, but not always a good companion; a good *temper* renders him acceptable to all and peaceable with all', but does not guarantee that 'usefulness' (integrity and duty in social relations); 'a good *disposition* will go far towards correcting the errors of *temper* (cf. *MP* 463 *supra*); but where there is a bad *disposition*, there is no hope of amendment'.

Even in *Mansfield Park*, it is assumed that moral *delicacy* should properly issue from the *heart*. Since there are very evidently (in this novel) hearts not in such good order as infallibly to supply this, it must be *acquired* through a learned set of priorities or *principles*, which can influence the *disposition*, and, like an artificial limb, reinforce – or if necessary replace – what nature should provide in the form of the *heart*. So when Henry persists in his suit despite her distress, Fanny sees this as 'a want of delicacy' typical of him, and reflects:

> How evidently was there a gross want of feeling and humanity where his own pleasure was concerned – And, alas! how always known no principle to supply as a duty what the heart was deficient in. (329)[15]

Interesting differs importantly from its modern counterpart. Jane Austen uses it not as the opposite of 'boring', as we do, but to refer to that which evokes the opposite of the disinterest that is impartiality or neutrality. Modern usage, therefore, suggests rather more detached and intellectual engagement with the *interesting* phenomenon than Jane Austen means to suggest by the word. When she calls something or someone *interesting*, she means that it or they are such as to prevent a disinterested response, calculated to engage the feelings, not merely the attention. The word occurs, for instance, with reference to Mrs Dashwood's response to Willoughby's gallantry in carrying Marianne home after her fall. Mrs Dashwood would have been grateful even had he been old, ugly and vulgar, we are told; but, in this case, 'the influence of youth, beauty, and elegance, gave an interest to the action which came home to her feelings' (*SS* 42). A person or subject found *interesting* is one that 'comes home to the feelings', that precludes disinterestedness. It is, significantly, a word much used with reference to Willoughby (three times in the initial description of him: 42–3), whom it thus marks as a romantic and attractive figure.

In Colonel Brandon alone, 'of all her new acquaintance, did Elinor find a person who could . . . excite the interest of friendship' (55). Elinor 'felt really interested in the welfare of Colonel Brandon' (71): she did not, in short, view it as a disinterested party; since he has excited 'the interest of friendship' in her, it is a subject on which she has anxieties and hopes. This is one of the more dangerous words in the novels, as the modern meaning usually makes sense enough in context to be quite feasibile, but can be misleading with regard to tone. It might lead to the detection of a kind of irony not intended, for instance, when Jane Austen calls people 'interested' in matters extremely important to them – which could sound like ironic understatement: as when Elinor is said to find Edward an 'interesting' subject for her thoughts (105). The reference in such cases is to what interests, not by virtue of being objectively 'intriguing',[16] but by virtue of being something as to which one is **concerned**, in either or both senses of that word. The following exchange between Edmund and Mary in *Mansfield Park* may illustrate further the misconceptions as to implication that could arise from misinterpretation of the word:

> "How happy Mr. Rushworth looks! He is thinking of Novem-ber."
> Edmund . . . had nothing to say.
> "Your father's return will be an interesting event."
> "It will, indeed, after such an absence; an absence not only long, but including so many dangers."
> "It will be the fore-runner also of other interesting events: your sister's marriage, and your taking orders."
> "Yes." (108)

Mary's wit suffers under the modern meaning of *interesting*, which actually gives a rather unsubtle turn to her indirections. Sir Thomas's return will be *interesting* in that it must be one relevant to the concerns and feelings of his family – the word artfully leaves it open as to *what* feelings the event will evoke (especially in herself and Maria), though Edmund, of course, affects to take her in the most innocent and natural sense (his family will be glad to see him safe home after a long absence during which his health and safety had been at some risk). A marriage and an ordination would normally *interest*, involve the feelings of, friends and relatives in a fairly pleasurable way; but Edmund cannot even pretend to assume that Maria's marriage to Mr Rushworth will arouse much joy in her or himself, or that his own ordination will much gratify the most *interesting* of his own friends – Mary herself; he therefore simply assents shortly to the strict sense of the word *interesting* – yes, they are events by which none of them will be unmoved.

A couple of still current expressions seem to preserve the older sense of the word. The 'interesting condition' that sometimes acts as a coy euphemism for pregnancy assumes, one trusts, the humanity rather than the prurient curiosity of the populace at large: it is news by which people will not be unaffected, but will respond with goodwill and friendly concern. The type of female beauty called 'pale and interesting' is that which is **appealing** in its suggestion of fragility.[17]

With the word as it is applied to Marianne – 'generous, amiable, interesting' (6) – may be compared Elinor's ruminations about what might be Edward's present feelings toward Lucy, now that 'time, spent on her side in inferior society and more frivolous pursuits, had perhaps robbed her of that simplicity, which might once have given an interesting character to her beauty' (140). The reference is to beauty that appeals to and attaches the feelings, that has an affecting quality. When Marianne is called *interesting*, therefore, the word refers to her capacity to attach the feelings, the good will, of those who meet her. She is, in short, **prepossessing**; **engaging** might be the nearest gloss for the word as it is here applied to Marianne and later to the former character of Lucy's good looks. At any rate, what Jane Austen means to convey about the girl she is describing is, not that she is out of the ordinary, but that – in her warm-hearted fervour and lack of *prudent* self-interest – she is an **endearing** one.

Her imprudence is not the deficiency in Marianne which the novel, as it proceeds, chooses much to reprehend, nor is it one to which Marianne, in her own subsequent self-castigation, gives any stress. It is a lack of what Jane Austen calls *candour* that comes much nearer to being seen as a positive vice in her.

Candid had, generally, a meaning quite other than that which it carries today. From a basic sense of 'fair, just' there had developed one that implied a magnanimity that went rather beyond impartial fairness: 'liberal or generous in judgment of others, disinclined to think ill and desirous to think well of them, and ready to admit error in oneself'. Marianne has a ready scorn for those with minds less *refined* than her own, a scorn which is related to her unwillingness to *exert* herself on their behalf. Her adverse judgements are often too harsh and too hasty – a fault defined by the novel as a lack of *candour*.[18] This charge is first brought by Elinor, against Marianne and Willoughby jointly, after they have been ridiculing Colonel Brandon. When they make sarcastic rejoinders to Elinor's claim that he is an "informed" man, to the effect that he is probably capable of boring everyone with observations on the East Indies, Elinor pointedly replies:

> "I may venture to say that *his* observations have stretched much
> farther than *your* candour."   (51)

Willoughby and Marianne have, of course, been only too *candid* in the modern sense: 'unreserved in the expression of their feelings'. They have been the very reverse of that earlier *candid* which implied 'wishing to do justice to, unwilling to think or speak ill'. Elinor intends a rebuke at their illiberal sneering at Colonel Brandon – which is certainly very unfair, but they are very young. *Candour* is not a virtue for which the young are remarkable, and if Marianne's want of it extended no farther than her sharing with most seventeen-year-olds, however *amiable*, a tendency to find her elders and betters boring and ridiculous, one would not take it very seriously.

But she has rather a special tendency to do less than justice to her acquaintance. Elinor particularly notices this with regard to her behaviour towards the very vulgar but essentially good-hearted Mrs Jennings. The former quality offends Marianne to such a degree that she refuses to acknowledge the latter, and remarks at one point that the older woman's kindness to her in her distress is not genuine, and is motivated purely by Mrs Jennings's avidity (real enough) for food for gossip:

> Elinor had not needed this to be assured of the injustice to
> which her sister was often led in her opinions of others, by the

irritable refinement of her own mind ... Marianne, with excellent abilities and an excellent disposition, was neither reasonable nor candid.   (201–2)

One of the most important dangers attendant on Marianne's
genuinely *refined* sensibility is that in its very *irritability* (quickness
to be offended) it may lead her to condemn too readily. Marianne
accuses herself of such a failure of *candour* in her long confession
towards the end of the novel, in which she admits to having
misjudged nearly everyone; to having treated Mrs Jennings with
"ungrateful contempt"; and, as regards the Middletons, Palmers
and Steeles, to having been "insolent and unjust; with an heart
hardened against their merits, and a temper irritated by their very
attentions" (346). She feels, in short, that she has been ungener-
ously unjust to all. Marianne's new *candour* has all the *eager* lack
of *moderation* in all things initially ascribed to her; for she is surely
being too *candid* by the Steeles in including *them* in her list of
those wronged by her *insolence* (arrogance, scorn), since it is
difficult to conceive of a degree of contempt so strong as to be
unjust to *their* merits. That this is not the authoress herself losing
all sense of proportion in her own eagerness to make the moral
point is indicated by a later detail, which sounds like a smile at the
characteristic whole-heartedness with which Marianne has under-
taken a reform nevertheless meant to be taken seriously. Edward
is persuaded to seek a reconciliation with his mother through his
sister and brother-in-law:

> "And if they *do* interest themselves," said Marianne, in her
> new character of candour, "in bringing about a reconciliation, I
> shall think that even John and Fanny are not entirely without
> merit."   (372)

This, for Marianne, is a heroic effort of *candour*; one is not sorry
to see, however, that she has not lost *all* her 'irritable refinement'.

II

An important aspect of Marianne's sensitivity, as the novel
represents it, is her responsiveness to poetry, music and the

aesthetic qualities of nature and landscape. Responsiveness of this kind was called *taste*. There is no suggestion that Marianne's taste is either feigned or undiscerning. In literature she enjoys Thomson, Scott and Cowper (all favourites with the authoress herself), though she has suitably *romantic* reservations about the Augustan Pope (18, 47, 92); and, according to Willoughby, she detests literary clichés of the "thunderbolts" and "dagger to my heart" variety (325).

Then as now *taste* was a word applied primarily to aesthetic response, implying appreciation and discernment. Whereas the latter element probably predominates in modern usage, it is quite often the former that is at issue in these novels: the ability to appreciate, relish or savour.[19] It was also a more loaded word than it is today: the attribution or denial of it in a particular case implied an evaluative judgement. There was a whole cult of *taste*, of **feeling for** the arts and nature. It was also a socially significant word: refined people were expected to have corresponding refinement of aesthetic palate; and *taste* was important evidence of *sensibility*. Altogether, want of taste would suggest a lack of social, moral and emotional refinement which would make it rather a damaging criticism.[20]

The social implications of taste – the assumption that it was a virtue proper to the genteel, evidence of innately refined and cultivated minds – is apparent in two passages in *Sense and Sensibility*. When John Dashwood wants to suck up to Colonel Brandon, he finds, amongst other things, an opportunity to attribute taste to him. Brandon is fairly wealthy, and John is anxious to cultivate him because he believes him (mistakenly) to be interested in his sister, Elinor. He hands to Brandon a pair of screens painted by her:

> "These are done by my eldest sister," said he; "and you, as a man of taste, will, I dare say, be pleased with them."   (234)

John (who, like most snobs, is also obsequious) has not actually known Brandon long enough to have any knowledge at all of his taste; but what he is in effect saying is, "You are a cultivated man and a gentleman, and therefore must be a man with aesthetic taste".

When Elinor and Marianne accompany Fanny and John to a

small private concert, the account of the occasion includes the wry comment that

> The party [persons assembled], like other musical parties, comprehended a great many people who had real taste for the performance, and a great many more who had none at all.

Elinor, however, was 'neither musical, nor affecting to be so' (250). The implication of these remarks is that such occasions were often hosted and attended by persons without any taste for music, because they felt themselves under some pressure to believe or to pretend they had.

There has been a previous reference in the novel to the affectation of musical taste. One evening at Barton Park, Marianne (who is a very proficient pianist) is called on to sing and play, and Sir John and Lady Middleton profess themselves delighted, though it is quite clear that neither of them has the slightest interest in the performance:

> Marianne's performance was highly applauded. Sir John was loud in his admiration at the end of every song, and as loud in his conversation with the others while every song lasted. Lady Middleton frequently called him to order, wondered how any one's attention could be diverted from music for a moment, and asked Marianne to sing a particular song which Marianne had just finished. (35)

Colonel Brandon alone listens 'without being in raptures', and alone listens with any 'attention'. His pleasure does not amount to the 'extatic delight' which Marianne would require in order to see in him a kindred spirit, but it does, to her mind, contrast favourably with the 'shameless want of taste' and 'horrible insensibility' of everyone else (*ibid*). Her own *taste* or feeling for music is one manifestation of her *sensibility*, as the *want* of it is one kind of *insensibility*.

Though Jane Austen is clearly amused by the popular affectation of taste, and obviously does not regard it as much to the detriment of her heroine that she is neither musical nor as rapturous in her responses to nature and landscape as Marianne, there are indications that even this excellently level-headed young lady and her creatrix would regard a total want of taste, a lack of any aesthetic response, as constituting serious evidence of a deficient sensibility. Elinor herself has some real talent for drawing that is obviously meant to provide a toned-down counterpart to Marianne's passion for poetry, music and natural scenery. Her response to Marianne, when the latter impugns Edward's taste for drawing, is significant:

> "What a pity it is, Elinor," said Marianne, "that Edward should have no taste for drawing."
>
> "No taste for drawing," replied Elinor; "why should you think so? He does not draw himself, indeed, but he has great pleasure in seeing the performances of other people, and I assure you he is by no means deficient in natural taste ... he is always unwilling to give his opinion on any picture; but he has an innate propriety and simplicity of taste, which in general direct him perfectly right." (19)

Elinor's reaction to Marianne's comment is perhaps a little surprising, since the way the novel is going leads one to expect a response something along the lines of "What does that matter? He has other more sterling qualities". But Elinor obviously does not think Marianne's an insignificant charge. She earnestly defends Edward's taste; and it is clear that, in whatever other ways it might not bother her too much that Edward is not quite her *sister's* ideal man, his being "deficient in natural taste" (having no innate feeling for art) is not one of them. Marianne, though endearingly unwilling to hurt Elinor's feelings by pressing her point, remains unconvinced: Edward's responses do not evince the 'rapturous delight, which, in her opinion, could alone be called taste' (*ibid*); but she is gauging powers of aesthetic relish or *taste* by rather questionable criteria. Similarly, when she later declares that Colonel Brandon lacks *taste*, because his feelings are not expressed with *ardor* (51), she is presumably remembering his attention to her piano-playing, which had wanted 'extatic delight' – though the incident should have brought it home to her that the raptures expressed by everyone else had merely disguised what she saw was in fact a 'shameless want of taste' (35).

Elinor is unwilling to let the subject drop (further evidence that she feels Marianne's charge to cast aspersions on Edward's sensibility that she is very anxious to gainsay), and continues, with a playfulness rather belied by the concern implied by her insistence:

> "I hope, Marianne ... you do not consider him as deficient in general taste. Indeed, I think I may say that you cannot, for your behaviour to him is perfectly cordial, and if that were your opinion, I am sure you could never be civil to him." (19)

The contrast intended between *cordial* and *civil* here may have lost much of its force to modern ears, for which news bulletins on *cordial* summit talks, etc., have probably deprived the word of much of its earlier force and warmth. It derives from the Latin for 'heart' (*cor, cordis*), and Johnson defines it (*adj.* 2) as, 'Sincere; hearty; proceeding from the heart'. It was a stronger word than today, and here indicates a **heartfelt** warmth which is importantly distinct from the mere politeness of common *civility* (which Jane Austen often represents as being perfectly consistent with absence of good will). *Cordial* is a word much associated with Marianne, whose words and actions are always heartfelt (cf. 87, 341). In this, as in so much else, she is most unlike Fanny, in whom Mrs Jennings sees 'nothing more than a little proud-looking woman of uncordial address, who met her husband's sisters without any affection, and almost without having any thing to say to them' (229).

Marianne sees Elinor's concern and, unable to pretend that she does not suspect Edward of a general want of *taste*, she tries, like the *amiable* girl she is, to underplay it, commending his heart and head, and classifying his "inclinations and tastes" as his "minuter propensities", which she has not had the opportunity of observing. Elinor, after smilingly implying that one can really ask no more than a good heart and head, returns with more seriousness to the defence of Edward's "minuter propensities" – which phrase she takes up with a certain amused pointedness that shows her fully aware that it was used by Marianne as a tactful attempt to suggest subsidiary importance. These she has observed, she says, and proceeds to commend them in a passage which gives some idea of what she feels has been indirectly called in question by the suggestion that Edward may want *taste*. What she describes is no less, really, than a general cultural awareness and responsiveness: "sentiments and ... opinions on subjects of literature and taste [i.e., the arts]", a mind that is "well-informed", the ability to enjoy books, imagination, observation, and a *taste* that is *delicate* (20).

Taste: the metaphor from one of the senses points the connection with *sensibility*. The capacity to be *sensible to* the power of such things as music and poetry had implications as to larger and more general powers of receptivity and responsiveness. In this novel it is Marianne (whose virtues are primarily those of the heart) who has the most developed aesthetic taste. Her own ardour of response is perfectly genuine, though she does seem to make the mistake of deducing lack of sensitivity in others from lack of *exstasy* and *rapture*. Even Elinor needs to believe that the man she loves does have taste. Though she concedes that his "solid worth" is something quite separate from this faculty, she plainly feels that he would less justify her regard for him without it.

Two persons specifically said in sober fact to lack *taste* are the Middletons. Sir John is a good-hearted but shallow man, and his wife is an *elegant* nonentity. Because of the poverty of their intellectual resources, constant company is essential to both. Jane Austen explains this partly by reference to their common lack of *taste*: though very dissimilar in other ways, 'they strongly resembled each other in that total want of talent and taste which confined their employments, unconnected with such as society produced, within a very narrow compass' (32). They have neither *talent* nor *taste* (abilities or interests) to occupy them, and therefore seek constant diversion in company. The capacity to savour such things as books, music, natural scenery, might have enabled them to be less reliant on others for diversion. Lacking *taste*, they both lack interests, and are, in consequence, rather uninteres*ting* – or *insipid*.

Lady Middleton is frequently said to be *insipid*: **boring**. This is a word drawn from the same metaphor of the palate as *taste*. Johnson defines *insipidness* as, 'Want of taste [i.e., flavourless]' and 'Want of life or spirit'. What is *insipid* has no distinctive *sapor* or flavour, like food that has no taste. Jane Austen applies the word repeatedly to Lady Middleton. In Elinor's view, 'the cold insipidity of Lady Middleton was so particularly repulsive, that in comparison of it the gravity of Colonel Brandon, and even the boisterous mirth of Sir John ... was interesting [attractive, engaging]' (34). An evening spent in her company later confirms these impressions of the *insipidity* which can produce nothing to involve or *interest* (143).

> She had nothing to say one day that she had not said the day before. Her insipidity was invariable, for even her spirits were always the same; and though she did not oppose the parties arranged by her husband ... she never appeared to receive more enjoyment from them, than she might have experienced in sitting at home. (55)

Lady Middleton has no tastes, no preferences, no interests of her own. She has no taste, and is therefore untasteable: she takes no relish, and imparts none. Her manner has *elegance*, but with a head and heart incapable of attaching the attention or the affection, she is the *insipid* opposite of the *interesting* Marianne. She gets on very well with Fanny, because the two women 'sympathized with each other [felt alike] in an insipid propriety of demeanour, and a general want of understanding' (229).[21]

One of the areas in which the period took most care to demonstrate *taste* was in the appreciation of landscape. In *Northanger Abbey* Catherine endearingly feels herself very uncultivated in the company of the Tilneys, because of the *taste* with which they discuss the scenery:

> They were viewing the country with the eyes of persons accustomed to drawing, and decided on its capability of being formed into pictures, with all the eagerness of real taste. Here Catherine was quite lost. She knew nothing of drawing – nothing of taste. (110)

However, she listens so earnestly and respectfully to Henry's explanations about the *picturesque* that he naturally becomes perfectly satisfied of her having 'a great deal of natural taste' (111) – that is, innate appreciation of what is beautiful.

Marianne predictably does have a palate sensitive to and able to relish natural scenery. Her self-consciously poetic farewell to the trees in Norland Park is a case in point:

> "And you, ye well-known trees! – but you will continue the same. No leaf will decay because we are removed, nor any

branch become motionless although we can observe you no longer . . . . But who will remain to enjoy you?"   (27)

Marianne's response to such things is real, though there is a note of self-congratulation on her own sensibility betrayed in that last question. There will henceforth be at Norland no-one with sufficient taste to relish the trees after she and her mother and sisters have gone: Fanny and John being unlikely to waste the few emotional energies they have on ecstasies over flora.

Sensitivity to landscape had become something of a cult. The period saw the publication of a whole series of accounts of tours – of the Wye or the Highlands, and so on – complete with aquatints, and mapping out where good picturesque prospects were to be found, and coming out under such titles as 'The Principles of the Picturesque'.[22] There arose a special species of 'picturesque tourist', who roamed the country looking for scenery (s)he could admire and thus demonstrate real or affected sensibility and *taste* – possession of a palate capable of registering natural effects.

The important place held by landscape appreciation in the whole romantic ethos is reflected in a special sense acquired by the word *romantic* as applied to scenery. Johnson has a special entry for this landscape sense of the word (*sv Romantick 3*): 'full of wild scenery'. A *romantic* spot or view implied the wild and rugged; and the romantic preference for 'shaggy grots' and such like stood in contrast with the value for order and harmony often seen as hallmarks of classical taste. One of the above-mentioned landscape writers, for instance, explains that scenery 'in which every object is wild, abrupt, and fantastic . . . . This sort of scenery we call *romantic*'. Another says of a particular prospect that 'All is wild, and romantic'.[23]

Another word with a specific meaning as applied to landscape was *picturesque*. This adjective was applied to qualities felt to be pleasingly irregular, uneven, rough, random. It is often found coupled with *romantic*. One of the published Tours gives a good idea of the sort of scenery that could deserve to be described by these terms: '. . . this variety of wood breaking forth from the craggy cliffs and chasms of these noble rocks. This intermixture of rocks and wood is truly romantic and picturesque'.[24] One may compare the cottage described in the opening pages of *Sanditon* as 'romantically situated among wood on a high Eminence' (*MW* 364).

As well as the Tours, there were a number of essays devoted to the *picturesque*, one of which offers a definition of it, stressing again the quality of irregularity:

> Roughness and sudden variation are its "most efficient cause". Thus, Gothic architecture is picturesque; Grecian beautiful; but Grecian in ruins, picturesque.
>
> (Manwaring [summarizing Uvedale Price], 198)

Another essayist provides an exemplary selection of truly *picturesque* objects or scenes: 'An old tower in the middle of a deep wood, a bridge flung across a chasm between rocks; a cottage on a precipice'.[25] The cult of the *picturesque* so defined was such that some expense was gone to in order to have estates laid out in accord with the taste for it, giving rise to a particular phenomenon called *picturesque gardening*, for which the *OED* has a special entry (*sv picturesque adj.* 1b): 'the romantic style of gardening, aiming at irregular and rugged beauty'.

All this gives us some idea of the sort of scenes Marianne is admiring when, on the journey to London with Mrs Jennings, 'She sat in silence almost all the way, except when any object of picturesque beauty within their view drew from her an exclamation of delight exclusively addressed to her sister' (160) – Mrs Jennings being assumed by her (probably rightly) to be without the *taste* to enter into her feelings. For this capacity to relish landscape was an important part of what the period understood by that word.

Interestingly enough, Marianne's type of beauty is itself in accord with the *romantic* canons of taste. She and her sister are contrasted thus:

> Miss Dashwood had a delicate complexion, regular features, and a remarkably pretty figure. Marianne was still handsomer. Her form, though not so correct as her sister's, in having the advantage of height, was more striking.   (46)

Elinor's form and face (regular and correct) conform to classical tastes for harmonious proportion; whereas Marianne's figure is arresting rather than neat and well-proportioned. Barton Cottage itself achieves a nice balance as between Elinor and Marianne, classical regularity and romantic wild grandeur. For it is described as *neat, compact* and *regular*, but is surrounded by a magnificent range of hills which have all the *picturesque* irregularity that Marianne's heart could desire (28).

The capacity to appreciate what was in this way *picturesquely* irregular, random, rugged, would show one kind of *taste*. It is therefore significant that the second time the question of Edward's *taste* comes up in the novel it is in the context of his response to these hilly environs of Barton Cottage.[26] On this second occasion, however, it is not only *his* taste that comes under Marianne's critical view, but also Marianne's that comes under his. For, perhaps feeling a trifle defensive, fearful lest his response should be scorned as lacking in the 'eagerness of real taste' (*NA* 110) by Marianne, who evidently sets great store by such matters, he disavows with some sarcasm all knowledge of the *picturesque*, and subjects to audible irony the popular *romantic* preference for the untidy and the irregular in nature. He likes the place, he says, but, when Marianne invites him to expand, he goes on:

> "You must not inquire too far, Marianne – remember I have no knowledge in the picturesque, and I shall offend you by my ignorance and want of taste if we come to particulars. I shall call hills steep, which ought to be bold; surfaces strange and uncouth, which ought to be irregular and rugged; and distant objects out of sight, which ought only to be indistinct through the soft medium of a hazy atmosphere. You must be satisfied with such admiration as I can honestly give. I call it a very fine country – the hills are steep, the woods seem full of fine timber, and the valley looks comfortable and snug – with rich meadows and several neat farm houses scattered here and there. It exactly answers my idea of a fine country, because it unites beauty with utility – and I dare say it is a picturesque one too, because you admire it; I can easily believe it to be full of rocks and promontories, grey moss and brush wood, but these are all lost on me. I know nothing of the picturesque." . . .

> "I suspect," said Elinor, "that to avoid one kind of affectation, Edward here falls into another. Because he believes many people pretend to more admiration of the beauties of nature than they really feel, and is disgusted with such pretensions, he affects greater indifference and less discrimination in viewing

them himself than he possesses. He is fastidious and will have an affectation of his own."

"It is very true," said Marianne, "that admiration of land-scape scenery is become a mere jargon. Every body pretends to feel and tries to describe with the taste and elegance of him who first defined what picturesque beauty was. I detest jargon of every kind, and sometimes I have kept my feelings to myself, because I could find no language to describe them in but what was worn and hackneyed out of all sense and meaning."

"I am convinced," said Edward, "that you really feel all the delight in a fine prospect which you profess to feel. But, in return, your sister must allow me to feel no more than I profess. I like a fine prospect, but not on picturesque principles. I do not like crooked, twisted, blasted trees. I admire them much more if they are tall, straight and flourishing. I do not like ruined, tattered cottages. I am not fond of nettles, or thistles, or heath blossoms. I have more pleasure in a snug farm-house than a watch-tower – and a troop of tidy, happy villagers please me better than the finest banditti in the world." (96–8)

Banditti were particularly associated with the *picturesque* – a word Edward repeats several times, always in association with the ruined or rugged, and always with a certain ironic emphasis. The landscapes of Salvator Rosa were considered to epitomize the *picturesque*, and the *romantic* scenes he specialized in were felt to be enhanced by his frequent inclusion of *banditti*. One tour-writer, for instance, remarks of a prospect that it typifies the brush of Salvator Rosa, who, however, he thought, would probably have added 'gibbets of Banditti on an eminence'.[27]

Edward, it is plain, is here expressing some ironic impatience at the *romantic* taste for the gnarled, blasted, rugged qualities comprised in the cult word *picturesque*. He deliberately dissociates his own favourable impression of the countryside from the *picturesque* criteria according to which he rightly belives Marianne herself would judge of it; and, fearing he might lay himself open to appearing taste-less in her eyes, he defiantly applies instead the more old-fashioned and common-sense ones of utility, comfort, tidiness and fertility.

It would be a mistake, however, to conclude that Marianne's more *romantic* reactions to scenery are being unreservedly undercut, through Edward, by Jane Austen herself. Elinor clearly sees that Edward is being disingenuous and is over-reacting to the popular cult of *taste*, the widespread affectation of 'feeling for' the evocative, dramatic aspects of nature. His utilitarian attitude, conceding no value to scenic atmosphere, is as much an exaggerated pose, as much an "affectation", as the one he is reacting against: he is affecting to have less *taste*, to be less sensitive to the appeal of gothic irregularity, as evidently as others affect to have more.

Nor is Marianne's own delight in the wilder aspects of nature here presented in such a way as to suggest that it is an affectation. Edward himself acknowledges that, in her case, all that she professes to feel she really does feel. He has evidently been softened by her own regretfully expressed awareness that "Every body pretends to feel and tries to describe with the taste and elegance of him who first defined what picturesque beauty was" – a sentence full of word with a particular period sense: everybody pretends to feel with the same *taste* (relish, appreciation) and describe with the same *elegance* (grace or distinction of style) as those who first voiced their appreciation for nature in her less ordered, irregular or *picturesque* aspects. Marianne genuinely has such a *taste* or feeling for those wild and wayward scenes as had become rather a cult. The passage therefore acknowledges the real sensibility to effects of this kind that must not be discounted simply because it had become something of an affectation.[28]

Edward, as Elinor sees, is *disgusted* by such affectation; that is, he is **offended** by it. She turns this **distaste** against him in light mockery, when she ends by claiming with playful irony that, "He is fastidious and will have an affectation of his own": Edward is particular about his affectations; he won't have the same one as the common herd (that of pretending to more feeling for nature than they have); he will have one of his own, and pretend to less than he really has; that at least will be distinctive.

The word *fastidious* gives more point to her irony than may be at once apparent. The word connoted more of scorn than it does today. Johnson defines it as 'Disdainful; squeamish; delicate to a vice; insolently nice'. *Nice* he is using in its older sense of 'particular, choosy, finely discriminating'. *Insolent*, it may be recalled, meant **arrogant** or **contemptuous**, and so reinforces the earlier 'disdainful'. *Fastidious* is regularly used by Jane Austen of social choosiness, of tastes apt to find others 'not good enough' for some reason (not usually rank): Marianne, Darcy, Emma are *fastidious* (*SS* 155; *PP* 11, 16; *E* 35; cf. *P* 150); Miss Bates is not (*E* 85). The *fastidious*, in being *insolently nice*, implicitly impute inferiority to that which their discrimination rejects.[29]

Elinor's choice of the word, therefore (in preference to, for instance, *nice*), to characterize Edward's attitude toward the popular affectation of "admiration of landscape scenery" indicates that she has detected a certain contempt in his disclaimer of any such sensibility for the *picturesque* (behind the mock humility with which he attributes it to "ignorance and want of taste"). There is some *insolence* in the disavowal: he is, in fact, demurring upon Marianne, implying that she has tastes he is above, not beneath. Modern readers of the novel should not make the same mistake.

NOTES

1 The Social Context: Time, Place and Manner

1. All references to Jane Austen's works are to the six-volume edition by Chapman. Those interested in Jane Austen's language are recommended to consult (besides the other studies cited in the notes to this and the following chapters) the glossary and grammar provided by Chapman in the form of an appendix (entitled 'Miss Austen's English') to his edition of *Sense and Sensibility* (388–421).

2. I use double quote-marks throughout to indicate quotations from direct speech.

3. The term *lunch* was once used of any **snack**. Johnson defines it as 'As much food as one's hand can hold'.

4. See, for instance, *Evel.* 83; 310–11; *SCG* I.81; III.53, 104; IV.308–9, 424; VII.380.

5. See, for instance, *Piers Plowman*, XX.3–4; *The Canterbury Tales*, V.263–7 (and see note at p. 893).

6. Cf. *Evel.*: 'the air seems stagnant, the heat is intense, the dust intolerable', '... the heat of the public places in summer, – the emptiness of the town...' (172, 209; cf. 168). Henry James makes superbly atmospheric use of a 'stale', 'deserted', 'drowsy' London in September as an appropriate setting for the dénouement of *The Golden Bowl* (515). The summer exodus of the fashionable world from *town* to *country* is described in detail in Canto XIII of *Don Juan*.

7. Pp. 263–7 of Lewis's chapter on the term *world* (214–68) are relevant here.

8. On the history of this locution, see Lewis, 306ff.

9. *Aye* is used primarily by the vulgar, the not very intelligent, or those whose spoken idiom is markedly downright, informal or unsophisticated: John Thorpe, Sir John Middleton, Mrs Jennings, Mrs Bennet, Lydia, Mr Price of *Mansfield Park*, Mrs Allen of *Northanger Abbey*, Admiral and Mrs Croft, Mrs Musgrove, Captain Harville, Lady Catherine, Lady Denham of *Sanditon*. The most frequent *ayers* are Mrs Jennings, Admiral Croft, John Thorpe and Mrs Bennet. See also Tucker, 158. On colloquialisms, slang and substandard usages, see also, *passim*, Tucker; Page; Phillipps (the indexes to all three books provide precise page references).

10. *Evel.* 279, 396; *Mar.* 6–7, 53, 95, 129, 130, 139, 140, 146, 152, 154.

11. On other linguistic vices ascribed to women, see Tucker, 78–80; on *horrid*, Tucker, 226.

12. For further information on the incidence and distribution of these words, see the *Concordance to the Works of Jane Austen*.

13. *Quiz* – as a verb (to mock) or as a noun (an object of mockery, something/one to be laughed at) – also belonged to fashionable cant, and is used in Jane Austen only by John and Isabella Thorpe and Tom Bertram. When the Princess Royal uses it in reporting words uttered to her by the Queen, Fanny Burney comments, 'The word *quiz*, you may depend, was never the Queen's' (*FBD* 335).

14. Cf. *Mar.* 125. Scott's Chrystal Croftangry uses the word when recollecting the attitudes of his own irresponsible and pleasure-loving youth, implicitly mimicking what would have been his own expression at the time: 'a famous piece of rough upland pasture for rearing young colts' (WS 50).

15. On *knowing*, see also Tucker, 139.

16. Cf. *BLJ* 8.218, 4.294. *You were* was only just coming to be accepted as the 'correct' form. In *SCG*, for instance, *you was* is the form regularly used by all speakers, including the ultra-refined hero and heroine: II.409, III.11, 146, IV.359, 413, 420, V.475, VI.68, 87, 88, 89, 134, 216, 217, VII.379; *you were* is reserved for the subjective: 'If you were ever concerned...' (III.110); '... in what you could do, were you not a man of the strictest honour' (VI.108; cf. III.152, VII.334, 335).

17. On Lucy's bad grammar, see further K. C. Phillipps, 'Lucy Steele's English'.

18. Letters between unmarried persons of different sexes could only properly be received where there was an engagement: cf. *SS* 80 and Chapman's appendix to *Emma* (512–13).

19. *Nice* (from Latin *nescius*=ignorant) originally meant 'foolish'; its meaning developed through 'foolishly over-particular/hard to please' to 'fastidious/discriminating' and 'done with great care and exactness', in which latter senses it was still used (as Henry indicates: 108) in Jane Austen's time; though it was evidently beginning to be used in conversation as it is today – as a vague and general term of approval.

2 Character: The Conceptual Context

1. *Art and Illusion*, passim.

2. On the serious sense of *manners* in this novel, see further Lodge, 99–100.

3. For comparable comments on 'powers of conversation', see WS 113; *BLJ* 3.238, 9.21 (besides the references *passim* to the man whose talents in that line had earned him the nickname of (Richard) Conversation Sharp); *FBD* 171.

4. Cf. Tucker, 155–6. On *temper*, see also Phillipps, 61, 96.

5. See pp. 85–9 *infra*.

6. *SCG* I.89; *Evel.* 280, 41, 305; *SCG* I.210; *Mar.* 338; *SCG* VII.353.

7. *Nervous* means, not 'timid' or 'apprehensive', but something like 'over-wrought', 'suffering from hyperactive emotional sensibility' (cf. *BLJ*

6.214). Mrs Bennet likes to fancy herself 'highly-strung'; for *nervous* is associated with 'fine ladies' (cf. *BLJ* 2.111) and 'fine sensibilities'. A character genuinely *nervous* is that personification of *sensibility*, Marianne Dashwood (*SS* 180, 227, 237).

8.   See 12, 90, 232, 239, 325, 369, 380.

9.   The term can also be used to refer to intelligence or 'rational powers'; see pp. 117–24 *infra*.

3   Spirits

1.   See also Tave's discussion of the word *lively* (158ff); he does not, however, isolate from other usages the specific sense I am concerned with here.

2.   Edmund means to refer to subjects of the ultimate *seriousness*; for *serious* in certain contexts was commonly used to allude to **religious** matters; see Lewis, 'A Note on Jane Austen', 362; cf. Phillipps, 57–8.

3.   Cf. Crabb's assertion that 'a *spirited* man enters into plans, makes great exertions, and disregards difficulties'.

4.   *Eager* today connotes rather more of impatience than it did for Jane Austen, for whom it was closer to our **passionate** (*in bono*) or **intemperate** (*in malo*). Crabb informs us that it is used of 'desires or passions', and adds that it is 'mostly faulty'.

5.   Cf., for instance, '... the lovely and lively Miss P—, the gentle Mlle Montmoulin ...' (*FBD* 159), 'Lively, yet Gentle' (*MW* 150).

6.   Cf.: 'The activity of the mind, and its sensations and feelings depend upon the course of the animal spirits that circulate in the nerves ...' (Gerard, 284: from his translation of De Montesquieu's 'Essay on Taste'). Conversely, Crabb can define *dullness*, one of the opposites of *spirit* (see pp. 70–74 *infra*), as a condition 'arising principally from the state of the animal spirits'.

7.   *The Canterbury Tales*, VII.4.

8.   Cf. 'Brilliant conversers' (*FBD* 197), 'the flow of his conversation, the brilliancy of his wit' (*Mar.* 361; cf. 317 and *BLJ* 5.86, 6.258).

9.   Quoted in *Life and Letters*, 49; cf. *Mem.* 282: 'with more brilliancy than accuracy'; 'Wit is oftentimes false, though it may appear brilliant' (quoted in *OED sv brilliant adj* 2a).

10.   Their jewels will enable Charles Grandison's sisters to 'make an appearance [that is] brilliant' (*SCG* IV.324).

11.   For *brilliant* in this sense of **distinguished, celebrated**, cf. *BLJ* 2.187, 215 and *Mar.* 76, 362, where 'brilliant society', 'brilliant descent' and 'brilliant connexions' can be found. The word could also be used in a similar but less superficial sense of 'the achievements of men' (Crabb).

12.   Cf. WS 108: 'she liked books – they amused her'. On the word *amusement*, see also Tucker, 209–10.

13.   See illustrations in *OED* under *Languor sb* 4 and *Languid adj* 1.

14.   *Courage* is found in this sense also at *E* 483; *MP* 336; *SS* 270, 342.

15.   When *work* is mentioned in connection with ladies (as opposed

to servants) the reference is always (as here) to needlework, not house-work.

16.   *Stupid* could in fact be used to mean 'stunned, stupefied': 'the blows followed each other so rapidly that I am yet stupid from the shock' (*BLJ* 2.77; cf. 5.101).

17.   *Mar.* 449, 275, 188, 79; *Evel.* 217, 30; *SCG* III.172, VII.443; *WS* 287; *SCG* VI.163; *Evel.* 289.

18.   For the opposition with pride, see p. 94–5 *infra*.

19.   *SCG* VI.225, 190, 201; *NA* 36, *P* 25.

4   Manners

1.   In short, "he is gentil that dooth gentil dedis" (*The Canterbury Tales*, III.1170).

2.   On *gentleman* and *genteel*, see also Tucker, 50–51 and 225. Crabb defines the latter as referring essentially to a certain rank in life and the outward signs of that rank provided by such things as mode of living, appurtenances and decent manners.

3.   I have discussed *smart* at greater length in '*Smart* Talk by Miss Austen' (*Medieval Literature and Antiquities*, 187–97).

4.   Johnson gives 'not coarse' *sv elegant* 2.

5.   Cf. Page, 64–6; Tave, 222–8.

6.   *Complaisance* should not be confused with *complacency*, which means 'pleasure, satisfaction, cheerfulness', and does not at all connote the smugness usually implied by the word today (e.g. *PP* 208; *MP* 52; *E* 358). On these words, see also Tucker, 28, 214.

7.   Cf. *Evel.* 135, 259, 260; *Mar.* 129, 230, 297.

8.   On Elinor and her *exertion*, see also Tave (98ff.), whose discussion of the word is more concerned with the full range of all its uses than with the special contextual sense I have isolated here.

9.   It is used seriously by comparable characters elsewhere: the vulgar Madame Duval (*Evel.* 180); a Highlander (*WS* 87); and the older and older-fashioned (*Mar.* 352).

10.   '. . . everybody, gentle and simple, adored her' (*SCG* I.173; cf. *DJ* XIII.110).

11.   See pp. 77–9 *supra*.

12.   *FBD* 85, 346, 347; *Evel.* 30, 72 (cf. *PP* 261); *SCG* VII.443.

13.   Cf. *PP* 248, 316; *MP* 34; *P* 143; *SCG* VI.138, 139, 232. On *ease*, see also Tave, 228–32.

14.   *Proper* originally meant 'one's own', and could still be used in this sense (*BLJ* 7.61, 75).

15.   *SCG* VI.108.

16.   On the trivial and snobby senses that existed alongside more serious ones in the use of these words, see Tave, 182ff. (on *propriety*); Page, 73 (on *respectable*). On the determined seriousness with which the words *improper* and *decorum* (amongst others) are used in *MP*, see Lodge, 100–13. On *decorum* and *respectable*, see also Tucker, 121, 229.

17. See further Page, 69–70.

18. Cf. *SCG* II.240, 296; *Evel.* 255.

19. See also Tucker, 215–6.

20. In a similar way, the word could refer to a **depiction**, **likeness** or **description** of a person (cf. Tucker, 18). See also Phillipps, 42.

21. Cf. WS 78; *SCG* V.513.

22. *Credit*, according to Crabb, 'redounds to the honour of the individual, and prompts him to noble exertions; it is beneficial in its results to all mankind, individually or collectively'.

23. See also Phillipps, 30–1.

5 The Head

1. Cf. *E* 301; *PP* 48; *MW* 421, 428; *DJ* XIII.107; *Mar.* 23. The piano played by the rich and socially prestigious Lady Adeline in *Don Juan* was later altered to a harp (XVI.38).

2. On *sense* (and *sensibility*), see further Lewis, 133ff.; Phillipps, 37–40; Empson, 250–69.

3. Cf. Tucker, 249–51; Tave (who also quotes Reid), 213.

4. Cf. *Mar.* 437: "a sensible, well principled woman".

5. It may be relevant to this passage that Crabb distinguishes *sensible* – which he says is characteristically applied to conversation and the communication of ideas in someone who can be an agreeable 'companion' – from *judicious*, which he claims more properly applies to conduct.

6. *Character* here means 'reputation'.

7. 'The prudent man is he who carefully consults for his own good' (*SP* 51).

8. The quite unmercenary Lord L, genuinely in love with Caroline Grandison, thus refuses to take her without a 'portion': "I am sure, Sir Thomas, that you would not think a man worthy of your daughter, who had no regard to anything, but the gratification of his own wishes; who could think, for the sake of that, of involving a young lady in difficulties, which she never knew in her father's house" (*SCG* II.325).

9. See p. 157 *infra*.

10. Byron similarly describes his plan to settle down, 'be a decent citizen and found a house and a family' in South America as providing a scenario in which he would be more *rationally* occupied than in his present life as *cavaliere servente* in Italy (*BLJ* 6.226).

11. Cf. *FBD* 90: '. . . the consistency, integrity, and faithfulness of the friendship . . .'

12. For examples, see *BLJ* 8.211; *SCG* III.9; *Mar.* 162, 384; *SCG* IV.306; *SCG* III.99, VI.246.

13. See Phillipps, 24 ('inherent ability, aptitude, and inclination for study and for developing the mind'); Page, 74 ('natural ability or capacity'). On *genius*, see also Williams, 143–4, and the detailed history and analysis of the word in Smith, 95–114; Tucker (220–21) stresses the looseness with which it was used as an evaluative term.

14.   Cf. *JAL* 142 ('wit or genius'); *Evel*. 36; *PP* 226 (". . . such a spur to one's genius, such an opening for wit . . .").

15.   See pp. 62–3 *supra*.

16.   It appears, in fact, that *genius* could at this period suggest all that *wit* could in an earlier one; for the latter word had enjoyed a similar range of meaning (mental capacity in general, imagination, originality, humour, etc); Lewis's discussion (86–110) of *wit*, and the use of it to translate Latin *ingenium*, is relevant here.

6   The Heart

1.   'Good nature' was itself a more serious and less patronizing phrase than it often is today; cf. Tucker, 145.

2.   Lewis, 159. On *sensibility*, see further Tave, 74ff.; Williams, 280–3; and Janet Todd, *Sensibility: An Introduction*.

3.   Cf. *VF* 148 (where the word is again associated with *generosity*), 271; *Evel*. 275, 369. On other senses of this word (which included – due to the extravagance commonly associated with that type of narrative called *romance* – **fantastic, colourfully improbable**) see Tucker, 148–9; Williams, 274–6; Smith, 66–87.

4.   See pp. 143–5 *supra*; cf. *FBD* 316–17.

5.   See pp. 143 *supra*.

6.   Cf. Tucker, 156.

7.   See pp. 82–3 and 110–13 *supra*.

8.   Lucy has already spitefully pointed it out, in any case: "Perhaps, Miss Marianne . . . you think young men never stand upon engagements . . . little as well as great" (243). Tave (94) has also commented on the play on the word in this passage, though his discussion of *SS* is throughout unsympathetic to Marianne.

9.   *Refinement* is grouped by Crabb's *Synonymes* with *polish* and *politeness*, and distinguished from them in being natural rather than acquired, and in being applicable to mind as well as to manners; it is thus the innate *delicacy* that is the counterpart of external *polish*: 'There are *delicacies* of behaviour which are learnt by good breeding, but which minds of a refined cast are naturally alive to'.

10.   *Delicacy* itself could be used seriously or superficially: cf. Tave, 220–2.

11.   Cf. *OED* sv amiable. On this word, see further Tave, 117 ff.; Phillipps, 25; Page, 68–9.

12.   Cf. pp. 130 and 147 *supra*.

13.   See Phillipps, 54. 'A *narrow* soul is hemmed in by a single selfish passion' (Crabb).

14.   On the semantic connections between 'feeling' and 'knowing', see Lewis's discussion of English *sense* and Latin *sentire*, 134ff.

15.   Earlier thinking had associated morality with the *wit* as opposed to the *will*, with *reason* rather than the *affections*. On the rise of what he calls the 'philosophy of sentiment' (for which much of the original impetus was

apparently provided by the Earl of Shaftesbury's *Characteristics of Men, Manners, Opinions, Times* (1711), and which reversed the former emphasis) and a bibliography on the subject, see Duckworth (106–7), who quotes Hume's assertion that morality is 'more properly felt than judged of'; he proceeds to argue that *SS* provides only qualified support for this position.

Principle is 'that idea which we form of things, so as to regulate our conduct' (Crabb); since that 'idea' in turn owes much to Christian moral teaching, the word can carry a semi-religious weight (cf. Tave 112).

16.   *Curious* was in fact the term often used at this period for what is conveyed by the modern sense of *interesting*.

17.   'We have an *interest* in whatever touches or comes near to our feelings or our external circumstances ... it consists of either profit, advantage, gain, or amusement; it binds us to an object, and makes us think of it' (Crabb). In the latter context ('external circumstances'), *interest* could thus be equivalent to the modern **interests** or **self-interest**, and both it and *interested* could indicate a suspect lack of disinterest. The noun *interest* is also found in a more formal sense of **connections**, **influence**: 'His nephew's introduction to Admiral Crawford might be of service. The Admiral he believed had interest' (*MP* 266). The verb in the reflexive – 'to interest oneself in' – meant **to concern or involve oneself with**. On these and other aspects and senses of the word, see Tucker, 210–11; Williams, 171–2; Phillipps, 96–7.

18.   Cf. Tucker (212–14), who quotes Charles Churchill: 'CANDOUR ... Still thinks the best, when e'er she thinks at all'. *Candour* also makes us 'acknowledge whatever may make against ourselves' (Crabb). See further Empson, 307–10; Phillipps, 26–7; Tave (who discusses the instances in *SS*), 87ff.

19.   Gerard's *Essay on Taste* several times equates *taste* with *relish* (78, 80, 89, 101, 192) and associates it with *sensibility* (200; cf. 227). Thomas Reid refers to *taste* as an 'agreeable relish or sensation' (deriving basically from a responsive 'sense' of such things as beauty, grandeur, novelty, etc., and productive of a distinctive kind of imaginative pleasure: *Lectures on the Fine Arts*, 35ff.) and as the faculty by which we are 'made to receive pleasure from the contemplation of what we conceive to be excellent in its kind, the pleasure being annexed to the judgment and regulated by it' (*Essays on the Intellectual Powers of Man*, 394); Crabb as 'the capacity to derive pleasure from an object'. Marianne thus equates it with 'extatic' and 'rapturous delight'. The word is discussed by Williams, 313–15.

20.   Given the assignment of moral delicacy to *sensibility*, the want of that kind of *sensibility* that is *taste* might lead to even more radically adverse assumptions about the *disposition*. Duckworth (124) refers to the 'Shaftesburian' (see n. 15 *supra*) view that 'an excellence of aesthetic taste denotes an excellence of moral character'. See also Hermione Lee, ' 'Taste' and 'Tenderness' as Moral Values in the Novels of Jane Austen'.

21.   Cf. 'the inspidity of elegance' (*Mar.* 89); *insipid* is the opposite of *interesting* at Gerard, 298; and occurs elsewhere in the sense of **dull, boring, tiresome** (*Evel.* 107; *BLJ* 2.103).

22.   On these essays and tours, see chapter VII, 'The Cult of the Picturesque', in Manwaring (167–200). The standard study of the *picturesque* is that by Hussey (see Bibliography). On the word, see also Tucker, 125–6.

23.   From Knight's *An Analytical Inquiry into the Principles of Taste* and Arthur Young's *Eastern Tours*, quoted by Manwaring, 199, 181.

24.   From Arthur Young's *Tour of the North*, quoted by Manwaring, 181.

25.   Alison, quoted by Manwaring, 198.

26.   The first occasion had some indirect connection with landscape, since the connection between painting and drawing and an eye for landscape, for the picture-esque, was strong; the Tilneys' *taste* for scenery was that of people 'accustomed to drawing' (*NA* 110).

On Jane Austen and the *picturesque*, see the survey of literature on this subject given by John Dixon Hunt, 'The Picturesque', in *The Jane Austen Handbook*, ed. J. David Grey (326–30); Manwaring, 221–3; Martin Price, 'The Picturesque Moment', in Hilles and Bloom, *From Sensibility to Romanticism*, 259–92. On her knowledge and use of one eighteenth-century essayist in particular (William Gilpin), see Bradbrook, chapter 3 (50–68).

27.   Thomas Watkins, quoted by Manwaring, 196; cf. 169, 174.

28.   This seems to be acknowledged by Rosemarie Bodenheimer, 'Looking at the Landscape in Jane Austen' (609), though her discussion of the satire on the 'picturesque cult' (605) in this passage is not broadly sympathetic to Marianne.

29.   Crabb also explains *fastidious* as 'proudly nice', and distinguishes it from *squeamish* on the grounds of what we might call the 'criticism' implied by the former word; he gives as an example of the context in which it might be selected, 'A female is *fastidious* when she criticizes the dress or manners of her rival'.

Bibliography

A. TEXTS

I: Jane Austen

The Novels of Jane Austen (5 vols), ed. R. W. Chapman, 3rd edn (Oxford University Press, 1933)

The Works of Jane Austen: Volume VI: Minor Works, ed. R. W. Chapman (Oxford University Press, 1954)

Jane Austen's Letters, ed. R. W. Chapman, 2nd edn (Oxford University Press, 1952)

Jane Austen: Her Life and Letters: A Family Record, W. and R. W. Austen-Leigh (London, 1913)

A Memoir of Jane Austen, J. E. Austen Leigh [printed in the Penguin Classics edition of *Persuasion*, ed. D. W. Harding (Harmondsworth, 1965), 265–391]

II: Other

Burney, Fanny: *The Diary of Fanny Burney*, ed. Lewis Gibbs (Everyman, London, 1940)

____ *Evelina*, ed. Edward A. Bloom (Oxford University Press, 1982)

Byron, Lord: *Byron's Letters and Journals* (11 vols), ed. Leslie A. Marchand (John Murray, London, 1973–81)

____ *Don Juan*, eds T. G. Steffan, E. Steffan and W. W. Pratt (Penguin Classics, Harmondsworth, 1986)

Chaucer, Geoffrey: *The Riverside Chaucer*, ed. Larry D. Benson (Houghton Mifflin, 1987)

Ferrier, Susan: *Marriage*, ed. Herbert Foltinek (Oxford University Press, 1986)

Fielding, Henry: *Tom Jones* (Signet Classics, London, 1963)

Gerard, Alexander: *An Essay on Taste: 1759* (Scolar Press, 1971)

James, Henry: *The Golden Bowl* (Penguin Modern Classics, Harmondsworth, 1966)

Langland, William: *The Vision of Piers Plowman*, ed. A. V. C. Schmidt (Everyman, London, 1978)

Reid, Thomas: *Lectures on the Fine Arts*, ed. Peter King (Martinus Nijhoff, The Hague, 1973)

____ *Essays on the Intellectual Powers of Man*, ed. and abridged A. D. Woozley (Macmillan, London, 1941)

Richardson, Samuel: *The History of Sir Charles Grandison*, ed. Jocelyn Harris (Oxford University Press, 1986)

Scott, Sir Walter: *The Two Drovers and Other Stories*, ed. Graham Tulloch (Oxford University Press, 1987)

Shelley, Percy Bysshe: *Shelley's Prose*, ed. David Lee Clark (Fourth Estate, London, 1988)

Thackeray, William Makepeace: *Vanity Fair*, ed. J. I. M. Stewart (Penguin Classics, Harmondsworth, 1968)

Turner, Edward: *The Young Man's Companion*, compiled 1866 (Hugh Evelyn, London, 1965)

Wagner, Richard: *My Life*, tr. Andrew Gray, ed. Mary Whittall (Cambridge University Press, 1983)

B. DICTIONARIES AND CONCORDANCES

A Concordance to the Works of Jane Austen (3 vols), eds Peter L. De Rose and S. W. McGuire (Garland Reference Library of the Humanities 357, 1982)

Crabb, George: *English Synonymes*, 3rd edn (London, 1824)

Johnson, Samuel: *A Dictionary of the English Language* (London, 1785)

The Oxford English Dictionary, ed. J. A. H. Murray, *et al.* (1884–1928)

C. STUDIES

Bradbrook, Frank W., *Jane Austen and her Predecessors* (Cambridge University Press, 1967)

Davies, R. T. and Beatty, B. G., eds, *Literature of the Romantic Period, 1750–1850* (Liverpool University Press, 1976)

Duckworth, Alistair M., *The Improvement of the Estate: A Study of Jane Austen's Novels* (The Johns Hopkins Press, Baltimore and London, 1971)

Empson, William, *The Structure of Complex Words* (Chatto & Windus, London, 1951)

Gombrich, E. H., *Art and Illusion* (Phaidon Press, London, 1960)

Grey, J. David, ed., *The Jane Austen Handbook* (The Athlone Press, London, 1986)

Hilles, Frederick W. and Bloom, Harold, eds, *From Sensibility to Romanticism: Essays Presented to Frederick A. Pottle* (Oxford University Press, 1965)

Hussey, Christopher, *The Picturesque: Studies in a Point of View* (1927: rpt. Cass and Co., London, 1967)

Lewis, C. S., *Studies in Words*, 2nd edn (Cambridge University Press, 1967)

Lodge, David, *Language of Fiction: Essays in Criticism and Verbal Analysis of the English Novel* (Routledge, London; Columbia University Press, New York, 1966)

Manwaring, Elizabeth Wheeler, *Italian Landscape in Eighteenth Century England: A Study Chiefly of the Influence of Claude Lorrain and Salvator Rosa on English Taste 1700–1800* (Oxford University Press, 1925)

Page, Norman, *The Language of Jane Austen* (Basil Blackwell, Oxford, 1972)

Phillipps, K. C., *Jane Austen's English* (André Deutsch, London, 1970)

Smith, Logan Pearsall, *Words and Idioms*, 5th edn (Constable & Co., London, 1943)

Stokes, Myra and Burton, T. L., eds, *Medieval Literature and Antiquities: Studies in Honour of Basil Cottle* (Boydell & Brewer, Woodbridge, 1987)

Tave, Stuart M., *Some Words of Jane Austen* (University of Chicago Press, Chicago and London, 1973)

Todd, Janet, *Sensibility: An Introduction* (Methuen, London and New York, 1986)

Tucker, Susie I., *Protean Shape: A Study in Eighteenth-Century Vocabulary and Usage* (The Athlone Press, London, 1967)

Williams, Raymond, *Keywords*, rev. edn (Flamingo, Fontana Paperbacks, London, 1983)

Essays and Articles

Bodenheimer, Rosemarie, 'Looking at the Landscape in Jane Austen', *Studies in English Literature* 21 (1981) 605–23

Hunt, John Dixon, 'The Picturesque', in J. David Grey, ed., *The Jane Austen Handbook (qv)*, 326–30

Lee, Hermione, ' 'Taste' and 'Tenderness' as Moral Values in the Novels of Jane Austen', in R. T. Davies and B. G. Beatty, eds, *Literature of the Romantic Period, 1750–1850 (qv)*, 82–96

Lewis, C. S., 'A Note on Jane Austen', *Essays in Criticism* 4 (1954) 359–71

Phillipps, K. C., 'Lucy Steele's English', *English Studies* 50 (1969) lv–lxi

Price, Martin, 'The Picturesque Moment', in Frederick W. Hilles and Harold Bloom, eds, *From Sensibility to Romanticism (qv)*, 259–92

Stokes, Myra, '*Smart* Talk by Miss Austen', in Myra Stokes and T. L. Burton, eds, *Medieval Literature and Antiquities (qv)*, 187–97

INDEX OF WORDS